The Course
of Tolerance

**Recent Titles in Contributions to the Study of Mass Media
and Communications**

The Course
of Tolerance

Freedom of the Press
in Nineteenth-Century America

DONNA LEE DICKERSON

Contributions to the Study of Mass Media
and Communications, Number 24
Bernard K. Johnpoll, *Series Editor*

Greenwood Press
New York • Westport, Connecticut • London

Library of Congress Cataloging-in-Publication Data

Dickerson, Donna Lee. 1948-
   The course of tolerance : freedom of the press in nineteenth-century
America/Donna Lee Dickerson.
     p. cm—(Contributions to the study of mass media and
communications, ISSN 0732-4456 ; no. 24)
   Includes bibliographical references and index.
   ISBN 0-313-27534-3 (lib. bdg. : alk. paper)
   1. Freedom of the press—United States—History.   2. Press and
politics—United States—History.   I. Title. II. Series.
KF4774.D53 1990
342.73'0853—dc20
[347.302853]   90-38525

British Library Cataloguing in Publication Data is available.

Library of Congress Catalog Card Number: 90–38525
ISBN: 0-313-27534-3
ISSN: 0732-4456

First published in 1990

Greenwood Press, 88 Post Road West, Westport, CT 06881
An imprint of Greenwood Publishing Group, Inc.

Printed in the United States of America

The paper used in this book complies with the
Permanent Paper Standard issued by the National
Information Standards Organization (Z39.48-1984).

10 9 8 7 6 5 4 3 2 1

For C. Richard King
  teacher, mentor and friend

Contents

Preface and Acknowledgments

This study examines the operation of the First Amendment, with emphasis on freedom of the press, in the years between the demise of the Alien and Sedition Acts in 1801 and the turn of the twentieth century, a period that tested the strength of post-Revolutionary Enlightenment rhetoric that produced the Bill of Rights. Specifically, this study looks at contemporary nineteenth-century ideas about freedom of press, set against the background of the political and social events that prompted debate about the roles and values of the First Amendment.

While this study tries to portray the nineteenth century as an important chapter in the study of the development of freedom of the press, its emphases are on the political uses of the press. There is no attempt here to deal with contempt, lottery information, obscenity, or the publication of material by advocates of birth control, free thought, and atheism. Those subjects are best dealt with in works that explore freedom of expression more broadly to include both freedom of speech and press.

Methodologically, this work has two significant elements that distinguish it from the few First Amendment histories that have included the nineteenth century. First, I have provided great detail about the events that sparked discussions about the First Amendment. Detail is given so the reader will understand the historical context for the events and the social factors that shaped the ensuing debates.

Second, I have emphasized primary sources so the reader can discern from contemporary writings, not secondary interpretations, what nineteenth-century Americans thought about the values and limits of the First Amendment. This work is based on hundreds of nineteenth-century writings from a wide variety of sources. Contemporary writings have been found in newspapers,

magazines, journals, books, diaries, autobiographies, letters, sermons, treatises, government reports and documents, case reports, privately published
case reports, speeches, pamphlets, and personal papers. The writers have
been presidents, politicians, editors, military officers, legal scholars, preachers, social and political activists, and average citizens.

While no single conclusion can be drawn about the meaning of freedom
of press in the nineteenth century, it is obvious from this breadth of writings
that the First Amendment was an issue for many nineteenth-century Americans. They had strong beliefs about the values of the First Amendment in
a democratic society, and many took great personal risk to assert that
freedom and test their neighbors' tolerance. They held strongly to their
Enlightenment heritage, modifying their own concepts of the function of
the First Amendment as time and events dictated.

Unlike Leonard Levy who stated in the preface to his *Emergence of a
Free Press* that he had not planned to write his original *Legacy of Suppression*, I did plan to write this book almost 10 years before work actually
began. The original idea came when I was a doctoral student at Southern
Illinois University writing my dissertation on libel and retraction statutes.
From the research into the development of just one aspect of libel law, I
realized that our legal system owed its fundamentals more to developments
in the nineteenth century than to the eighteenth or twentieth centuries. But
as I looked at the traditional texts in the history of communications law,
the last century was all but ignored with only passing reference to abolitionism, the Civil War, and labor unrest.

I finally got the opportunity to work on this project when I received the
1984 Baskette Moss Award for Faculty Development from the Association
for Education in Journalism and Mass Communications, which provided
seed money for travel to libraries. I also want to acknowledge support from
the College of Arts and Letters at the University of South Florida for providing travel support. Because almost all of the research materials were
primary sources, I depended heavily on the patience and professionalism of
the staff of the Inter-Library Loan Department at the University of South
Florida Library. My thanks also to the library staffs at the University of
Texas at Austin, University of Illinois, William and Mary College, University
of North Carolina, and Duke University.

And finally, I wish to thank four important people who as mentors and
professors contributed to the advancement of my scholarship in history and
law: C. Richard King, retired, University of Texas at Austin; Harry Sto-
necipher, retired, Southern Illinois University; Robert Trager, University of
Colorado; and Emery L. "Pete" Sasser, West Virginia University.

Introduction

Recent years have witnessed a proliferation of scholarship on the eighteenth century and the Founding Fathers' original intent for the First Amendment. However, there has been a shortage of works examining the nineteenth-century heritage of the First Amendment.

The neglect of the last century can be blamed in part on the definitions traditionally used by historians when dealing with First Amendment freedoms. When freedom of expression is defined narrowly as freedom *from* government coercion, the only events of significance were the Alien and Sedition Acts and the Civil War. This lack of significant government interference has failed to hold the attention of scholars.

Before one can place a value on the current interpretations of the First Amendment or even suggest new interpretations or policy shifts, one must first know what freedom of expression is and how it came to be. By restricting the definition of freedom of expression to freedom from government abridgement, historians have missed an entire century of discussion that has contributed to the meaning, roles, and values of freedom of expression.

In the introduction to Harry Kalven's *A Worthy Tradition*, his son describes how Professor Kalven "conceived of the American experience under the First Amendment as something more than a body of legal precedent; he saw it as a tradition of society."[1] Kalven noted that the First Amendment is actually composed of dual traditions. The most obvious tradition common to all legal areas is the building up of a body of law on precedent. In the First Amendment area that tradition is recent, with all of the building blocks having been cast during this century.

The second tradition is that of the social, cultural, and political history of freedom expression. In no other area of constitutional law-making have historical traditions played so great a part in the reasoning process. More often than not, Supreme Court decisions are informed by an exposition of the forces that shaped the history of freedom of expression. And in significant decisions, the historical understanding may even be a warrant for the argument's central claim. For example, in *New York Times v. Sullivan*, Justice William Brennan wrote that the law of libel allowing public officials to win without proving malice was tantamount to sedition.[2] Since, according to Brennan, the Alien and Sedition Acts of 1798 had been declared by history to be unconstitutional, the present law was also unconstitutional. And in his dissent in *Abrams v. U.S.*, Justice Oliver Wendell Holmes disagreed that the common law of sedition still existed. "I had conceived that the U.S. through many years had shown its repentance for the Sedition Act of July 14, 1798."[3]

Because the historical tradition was formed by the people, not the courts, its addition to the tradition of legal precedent leavens the law, making contemporary interpretations greater than the sum of their dual traditions. And what we learn is that it is a combination of eighteenth-century Enlightenment heritage, tested by the realities of the nineteenth century, that has provided the context for the Supreme Court to articulate a theory of the First Amendment for the early twentieth century.

Probably no stronger statement about the historical role of freedom of expression in America exists than Oliver Wendell Holmes's dissent in *Abrams v. U.S.* written in 1919. In defending the right of five Russians to distribute anti-war leaflets, Holmes wrote:

But when men have realized that time has upset many fighting faiths, they may come to believe even more than they believe the very foundations of their own conduct that the ultimate good desired is better reached by free trade in ideas,—that the best test of truth is the power of the thought to get itself accepted in the competition of the market and that truth is the only ground upon which their wishes safely can be carried out.[4]

Indeed, the nineteenth century witnessed the upset of many ideas and traditions. Ancient concepts of common law were defeated by the new logic of the social contract; fears that political factions would result in civil war were calmed once the nation witnessed the peaceful transfer of government from one party to another. Although it took a war to erase the notion of private property rights in slaves, the truth of individual freedom won out. In the vortex of these changes was the First Amendment, ensuring that matters of public concern were discussed without the mailed glove of government censorship.

While there may be lingering doubts about the libertarian spirit of those who wrote the Constitution and the Bill of Rights, there is little doubt that nineteenth-century America embraced a strong libertarian ideology that endorsed a press unrestrained *by government* even in the most trying times. However, the libertarian spirit did not prohibit suppression of expression by the community itself.

While this book is not informed by any single theory or interpretation, the works of Robert H. Wiebe prove valuable in explaining the social context of nineteenth-century America and provide some focus for why restraint of expression took the form of civilian, rather than government, coercion. In *The Segmented Society* and *The Opening of American Society*, Wiebe describes the role communities played in assigning and maintaining certain moral norms.[5] His works provide some focus as to why communities, with little or no remorse, condoned extraordinary measures—banishment, organized destruction of property, riot, and personal violence—against dissenters who were for the most part peacefully going about their dissent.

Freedom of expression issues, at least until the Civil War, were local problems that each community dealt with in its own way. People were used to operating within relatively isolated or closed communities where there was a heterogenous population with an unambiguous set of values. Outside interference was unwelcome. The community's leaders—the doctor, teacher, editor—forged the community's values from a sense of moral rightness. Problems could always be solved based on what was proper and right— not just on private interests or interests of outsiders. As long as the problems were manageable, interference from the federal government was unnecessary and unwelcome.

Witness the reaction to the Alien and Sedition Laws—a federal law that dictated what were to be proper political viewpoints. After the Alien and Sedition Acts, Americans were firmly committed to the doctrine that the federal government could not control freedom of expression. The Acts became a nineteenth-century metaphor for federal despotism.

- When patronage printing became an issue in the 1820s, lawmakers charged that withdrawing printing contracts destroyed liberty of the press in a manner that was more effective than even the Alien and Sedition Acts.
- When Virginians called for a boycott of any newspaper that continued to discuss slavery, the Richmond *Whig* accused such censors of embarking on the same course as the Sedition Acts.
- During the 1836 debates over the Postal Bill, the specter of the Alien and Sedition Acts was used to remind lawmakers that Congress could not control content or circulation.
- The Confederate Congress was warned that the reaction to wartime censorship would be the same as it had been to the Alien and Sedition Acts.

The sense of a community's self-sustaining abilities was also carried into the doctrine of states' rights. It was the federation of communities (states) that was the backbone of the nation. The federal government merely provided the glue that kept the states from flying apart. While the federal government was a symbol of the broad consensus for democratic principles, it was up to the states and communities to decide how those principles fit into their own consciousness. For example, when abolitionists sent materials into the South, the Postmaster General, Amos Kendall, fearful of federal interference, left it to individual postmasters to decide how the material should be disposed of. This was an acknowledgement that local officials knew their own community's values better than did an official in Washington. Kendall wrote: "We owe an obligation to the laws, but a higher one to the communities in which we live."[6]

It is not surprising that the debates over censorship of the mails in the 1830s focused on states' rights rather than on the First Amendment. The editor of the New York *Commercial Advertiser* typified the emphasis on community and the de-emphasis on union when he criticized the fanaticism of abolitionists who were "not content with having distracted the churches, destroyed the peace of families and communities, embarrassed the literary and religious institutions, menaced the property *and even* the existence of the union."[7]

However, the efforts to solve the issue of abolitionist material using typical community-oriented solutions failed. This was indeed a national issue that was unmanageable at the local level. Southerners called upon their Northern neighbors to pass state legislation prohibiting the mailing of incendiary materials. But, when President Jackson proposed federal legislation to prohibit certain materials from being mailed, the staunchest pro-slavery Southerners opposed any bill that would give the federal government an excuse to regulate their affairs. Slavery and freedom of press were issues that belonged to the states, not the federal government.

Through meetings, resolutions, threats, and even violence, the majority was able to contain unpopular views and impress on citizens the value of conformity. The Baltimore Riots of 1812, the mobbing of abolitionists, the destruction of presses in the North during the Civil War, and even the Haymarket Massacre in 1874 were all typical forms of managing local problems in order to promote the community's sense of what was proper. Some, like Elijah P. Lovejoy, risked their very lives to fight such coercion.

The political parties also managed the news by continuing the dependence of publishers and editors on party favor and support. Through the local party machinery and the party-supported newspaper, they contributed to the process of internalizing basic democratic values and discouraging aberrant political thought.

Wiebe's explanations of the importance of character and moral rectitude also provide some understanding of why the law of libel was so slow to accommodate democracy. The press waged a relentless war against the ancient relics of sedition and criminal libel. Case after case pointed out the fallacy of using English common law precepts to effect the proper balance among self-government, freedom, and licentiousness.

However, until the late 1840s, a community's sense of moral rightness played a significant role in how libel law was interpreted. James Sullivan defined the moral obligation of editors when he argued that it was improper to publish anything about the character or reputation of a government officer; it was not proper for a newspaper to inform the public if an officer took a bribe or was corrupt. To publish such charges would create discontent and disillusionment with the political process; it would create unnecessary jealousies and infringe on private matters. Proper deportment and an unambiguous sense of morality made it "a crime against the community to publish human weaknesses because no one is without failings."[8]

Justice James Kent warned that if the press were allowed the freedom to print whatever it wanted about an official, "the press would become a pest, and destroy the public morals."[9] There was information that was proper for public dissemination and information that was not, all in the name of propriety.

As the century came to a close, economic transformations resulted in shifting the emphasis from moral character to the economic person and from the autonomous and value-driven community to a loose economy-driven community. As values shifted, so did relationships within a community. Larger segments of the population who did not have those material interests would find themselves at odds with the majority notions of rightness. Farmers, faced with monopolistic practices of railroads and industry, organized into a strong but short-lived populist movement. Immigrants formed labor unions to protect against factory owners. These new groups of dissenters—those to whom economic rather than political or social issues mattered—did not always contain their dissent. It was no longer the community that met dissent with violence. Instead, violence or intimidation were now met with "legitimate" organized forces such as the National Guard, hired thugs, or the Pinkertons, who often came from without the community. Also, violence associated with economic dissent rarely spilled into the community. It remained contained at the factory, mine, or rail yard.

Despite the control that secondary forces had on dissenters, neither democracy nor the First Amendment was dead. Quite the contrary. There was a strong consensus that the First Amendment was a vital link to democracy.

Defenders of the First Amendment reiterated those same values of freedom of discussion and freedom of press that their eighteenth-century fathers and grandfathers had promoted. Neither the progress of time nor the inevitable spiral of events nor the increasing social problems brought about in the nineteenth century appeared to destroy or even weaken the basic notions about the role of liberty of expression.

John Taylor wrote in 1814 that free discussion is the "creator, the pre-

ceptor and the organ of publick opinion; the guardian of national sovereignty and of religious freedom; the seedsman of political knowledge and
the guarantee of moderate government."[10] Still angered by John Adams's
Sedition Law, Taylor wrote that the rights of conscience and of the press
prevent the government from using superstition and ignorance to enslave
men. He spoke also of the intrinsic value of freedom of expression—"Expression is the respiration of the mind. Wherever it can breath freely, [the] mind
seems to begin to live; swells, as if by enchantment, to a sublime magnitude;
and suddenly acquires wonderful powers."

Those values of freedom of expression—a bulwark against oppression, a
teacher of political skills and knowledge, an instrument of self-fulfillment—
were recited throughout the century. "Cincinnatus," speaking out against the
1836 Postal Bill, alluded to John Milton when he warned that instead of allowing truth and error freedom to do battle, those who would censor the
mails enchained both, abridging the freedom of all except those who hold the
chain. Joseph Medill of the Chicago *Tribune* referred to the press during wartime as "watchmen on the walls" looking for the approach of danger.

Paul Murphy in *The Meaning of Freedom of Speech* wrote that the First
Amendment was "treated as a dearly won prize, protected in a symbolic
trophy case, but not used from day to day."[11] In other words, there was
consensus about the broad values of the First Amendment, but there was
conflict about how those values would be preserved and how the First
Amendment could be made operational.

The only time the First Amendment escaped the trophy case was when
community force as well as direct government abridgement failed—when a
court decision, a riot, a threat, a resolution, or a military act produced a
martyr or popular outcry or both. Some, like William Ellery Channing, saw
the First Amendment as a tool for everyday use to protect minority views
from the rage of the community. When popular violence increased against
abolitionists in the 1830s, those few writers who defended minority rights
found themselves waging battle with the local code of moral standards. It
was not seemly or fitting to allow persons into a community who would
upset the established sense of right and wrong.

After James Birney's abolitionist newspaper was mobbed in Cincinnati in
1836, William Goodell of The *Emancipator* wrote that the First Amendment
was written to protect the rights of the minority. In fact, a constitutional guarantee that protected only the majority was a "nullity."[12] Seeing the First
Amendment as a positive obligation on the part of government and communities to protect diversity was a novel and uncomfortable idea.

When Nat Hentoff wrote in *The First Freedom* that nineteenth-century
Americans, bent on mob violence, rejected the essence of the First Amendment despite the lessons taught by the Alien and Sedition Acts, he committed the error of assigning twentieth-century values to the nineteenth
century.[13] Americans had indeed learned their lesson from the Alien and

Sedition Acts, but that lesson was that government, not the citizen, was stripped of the power to control expression. Most Americans believed, without apology, as did the *Western Reserve Chronicle*, that if the exercise of opinion was obnoxious, the will of the people should be obeyed.[14]

While the seed of the new positive doctrine of the First Amendment was sown during the violence of the early nineteenth century, it would not begin to germinate until the majority's sense of rightness no longer encompassed only notions of propriety and decency, but instead included protection of personal and material interests.

The nineteenth century was a breeding period not only for new ideas about the role of the First Amendment, but also for questions still asked today about the boundaries of the First Amendment. Although the issue of criminal libel became almost moot by the middle of the century, courts were still uncertain about the extent of protection offered private and public persons in civil libel suits. Military censorship remains a serious issue as world politics and the venues of war change and as the tactics of warfare have been modernized. Postal censorship, a major issue during the middle of the twentieth century, began in the 1830s. Although mail censorship has been decried by most, the government has seen it as an appropriate avenue for censorship of all types of materials from military information and political propaganda to obscenity.

NOTES

1. Harry Kalven, Jr., *A Worthy Tradition: Freedom of Speech in America* (New York: Harper & Row, Pubs., 1988), p. xviii.

2. 376 U.S. 254 (1964).

3. 250 U.S. 616, 630–31 (1919).

4. Ibid.

5. Robert H. Wiebe, *The Segmented Society* (New York: Oxford University Press, 1975); *The Opening of American Society* (New York: Alfred A. Knopf, 1984).

6. *Niles Weekly Register*, August 22, 1835.

7. New York *Commercial Advertiser*, October 12, 1835.

8. [James Sullivan], A Dissertation Upon the Constitutional Freedom of the Press in the United States of America by an Impartial Citizen (Boston: Joseph Nancrede, 1801), p. 21.

9. James Kent, *Commentaries on American Law* 2 vols., rev. ed. (Philadelphia: Blackstone Pub. Co., 1889) 2: 69.

10. John Taylor, *An Inquiry into the Principles and Policy of the Government of the United States*, Loren Baritz, ed., (New York: The Bobbs-Merrill Co., Inc, 1969).

11. Paul Murphy, *The Meaning of Freedom of Speech: First Amendment Freedoms from Wilson to FDR* (Westport, Conn.: Greenwood Pub. Co., 1972), p. 4.

12. *Emancipator*, August 30, 1836.

13. Nat Hentoff, *The First Freedom* (New York: Dell Pub. Co., 1981), p. 89.

14. Reprinted in *Emancipator*, August 30, 1836.

The Course
of Tolerance

Chapter 1

"A Tendency to Calumny": Defining New Boundaries for Libel

In his first inaugural address, Thomas Jefferson called America's infant government "the world's best hope," and he invited all people no matter what party lines they espoused to join him in a "wise and frugal government, which shall restrain men from injuring one another, shall leave them otherwise free to regulate their own pursuits of industry and improvement, and shall not take from the mouth of labor the bread it has earned."

To those who had predicted that a Jeffersonian presidency would bring an end to religious freedom and a union with Jacobin France, he issued an invitation: "We are all republicans—we are all federalists. If there be any among us who would wish to dissolve this union, or to change its republican form, let them stand undisturbed as monuments of the safety with which error of opinion may be tolerated where reason is left free to combat it."[1]

However, Jefferson was not ushering in a new day of libertarianism and democracy. Instead, the Jeffersonian era was merely the continuation of an era of transition begun during the Federalist administrations, when great hopes were raised, but few changes were made.[2]

Parties, still referred to as factions, were seen as onerous, and politics remained the concern of the elite. The Alien and Sedition Acts were put aside and labeled as a black mark on American democracy; yet, the scurrilousness of the Federalist press after 1801 brought about similar, if not as pernicious, countermeasures. The judiciary struggled to create an American common law out of English common law, but the attempt resulted in contradictions that had their true basis in politics rather than law.

Thus, the nineteenth century opened with its feet still firmly planted in the eighteenth century, but reaching toward a government whose strength and energy "is to be estimated more by the affections of the people than by the exterior means provided for its defense; and that individual liberty is more precious than all the apparatus of power."[3] Nowhere was this era of transition more apparent than in the ensuing debates over the meaning of freedom of press and of speech. During the first quarter of the century, most discussions and opinions about freedom of expression centered around criminal (seditious) libel.

Any study of constitutional history necessarily implicates the broader cultural developments of the society. Our American legal system, while steeped in centuries of English tradition, began taking on its own identity as a unique order immediately after the Revolution. These changes were, and continue to be, intrinsically linked to the prevailing religious, political, economic, and intellectual mood of the country.

So, while legal historians may study the substantive changes in the law of libel and the meaning of freedom of press, and attribute shifts to modifications within the legal system (relaxation of common law principles, adoption of a more democratic court system, decline of party patronage on the courts, etc.), the ultimate agent of change, remission, or even constancy was the contemporary society in which that system was operating.

During the early years of the republic, criminal libel suits by public officials were commonplace and accepted artillery in political conflict. The two-party system, seen as pernicious with no potential benefits to the democratic system, was considered illegitimate by both Republicans and Federalists. Members of both factions considered each other dangerous and even treasonous. Yet, both parties had outspoken presses which spread lies, deceptions, rubbish, terror, calumny, and despotism.

Toleration of such falsehoods, agreed most tractarians of the time, would lead to the downfall of the country and its constitution. Unless political libelers were haled before the courts to answer for their lying scribbling, the public (which was never given much credit for being rational) would continue to be deceived and consequently make the wrong decisions at the polls. The law of libel was seen as the most efficacious way of protecting the government and the true party.

And the true party at the end of the eighteenth century was the Federalist party—whether the moderate Federalists of John Adams or the radical Federalists of Alexander Hamilton. Although neither Republicans nor Federalists conceded the legitimacy of political opposition, the Federalists have gone down in history as being the most fearful of factionalism and democracy.

According to Federalist dogma, America should not be too democratic, but should seek a tripartite balance of monarchy, aristocracy, and commoners like its British cousins. An economically independent, educated, landed aristocracy should rule over the multitudes with a long-term executive overseeing a government that represented the wealthy in one house and the poor in the other. The executive was necessary to check the rich and the poor who were always fighting each other, resulting in popular tumult, sedition, corruption and revolution.

Hamilton believed that the safety of the people depended upon a strong government in the hands of a few. Individual rights were inseparable from the rights of government, and whatever was necessary to the security of government was necessary for the individual. He placed little confidence in the ability of the common man to govern—"They do not possess the discernment and stability necessary for systematic government."[4]

John Adams and other Federalists often voiced the fear that riot and sedition were the necessary results when all men believed they were equal. Daniel Leonard wrote that sedition was the result of an unstable social order where men refuse to concede to authority and the spirit of defiance is perptuated. Seeds of sedition are always being sown where common man is urged to believe in his equality.[5] When men are always ready to speak evil of dignities, sermonized Jonathan Boucher, sedition has penetrated far too deeply, tearing at the vitals of the social order.[6]

In a letter to his close friend Benjamin Rush, John Adams wrote that a hereditary monarchy and an artistocracy were the only institutions that could possibly preserve the laws and liberties of the people and protect "against discord, sedition and civil war."[7] And a year later he repeated his fear that intrigue, riot, and sedition were too often associated with popular elections.[8]

This paternalistic attitude was simply a manifestation of the deep felt belief that the gentry class or elites were chosen by God to lead this new experiment. In his *The Opening of American Society*, Robert H. Wiebe discussed the emphasis placed by eighteenth- and nineteenth-century Americans on a man's character and honor—or the gentleman's code.[9] So intense was the preoccupation with honor that every man lived with the fear that he could be challenged to a duel in order to redeem another's honor.

But at the core of concern over reputation and honor was the belief that a strong American government and a stable American society could only be built on a firm foundation of character and honor. And those with the best character and sense of moral values were, of course, the elites who claimed the country's leadership. Because politics was a dirty game and every politician's reputation a fair target, and because "character, the most precious commodity of the eighteenth century, always deserved a fiery defense," gentlemen were forced to find remedy and redress for their muddied reputations in forms less bloody than the duel code.[10] One of those was the libel suit

Therefore, it is not surprising that a Federalist Congress and administration should pass the Sedition Act of 1798, a federal libel law aimed not only at taming a "too democratic" Republican press, but also at containing those licentious and seditious scribblers who questioned their honor.[11]

Until 1798, neither the Republicans nor Federalists had questioned the legitimacy of criminal libel prosecutions. For most, the common law of libel as defined by William Blackstone in his 1769 *Commentaries on the Law of England* was satisfactory to meet the demands of the new democracy. All they asked in a modified American common law was protection from any previous restraints and the right to plead the truth in a criminal prosecution where the jury rather than the judge determined criminality. In fact, these substantive requirements were so well engrained in the minds of most, that they were incorporated into the Sedition Act of 1798, which allowed truth as a defense, required criminal intent, and gave the jury a greater role in deciding that intent. Nevertheless, the Acts drew torrents of disparagement from the opposition party which saw the law as an instrument for Federalist policy-making and the inevitable result of Federalist political thought.

There was no legal need for such a law because the federal courts were already free to prosecute criminal libel as a federal common law crime. Also, the states, all of whom had adopted the common law, were able to pursue such prosecutions in their own courts. Since there was no legal urgency for the Sedition Act, it was obviously a political statement that the opinions from the pens of Republicans would be considered licentious. To preserve the Union and its Federalist protectors, it was necessary to control public opinion and elections; and what better way to accomplish those goals than to pass legislation that would ensure enforcement against Republican scribblers.

To oust the Federalists from office and restore order under the true party of the people, it was necessary for Republicans to fashion a new theory about freedom of speech and press that would reject all sedition laws. Tunis Wortman, James Madison, and George Hay became the foremost leaders of this "New Libertarianism," as Leonard Levy calls it, and they advanced concepts based upon the intellectual value of opinions. They disavowed the Blackstonian definition of prior restraint and the substance of common law, renounced the doctrine of seditious libels, and advocated an absolute freedom of political discussion.[12] Thus, out of political necessity, the "Revolution of 1800" was begun and a new legal theory was born to throw old ideas out of office.

LIBERTARIAN APPROACHES TO LIBEL

The Sedition Act and its companion Alien Act had taught the nation hard-learned lessons about the role of the federal government, popular sovereignty, and civil rights. Madison believed the laws were repugnant to a system of government that required separation of powers and specifically prohibited interference of the federal government with rights of free speech and press. Madison's Virginia Resolutions railed against the laws, stating that whatever the limits of freedom of press were, the laws went beyond those boundaries because they "repressed that information and communication among the people, which is indispensable to the just exercise of their electoral rights."[13]

The eighteenth-century views of James Madison, George Hay, and Tunis Wortman were echoed during the first quarter of the nineteenth century by such men as the legal scholar St. George Tucker, college president Thomas Cooper, politician and philosopher John Tyler, political theorist Thomas Paine, and others. Yet, their minority views met resistance from the courts, from legislatures, from Federalists, and even from Republicans such as Jefferson and Judge Thomas McKean of Pennsylvania. But, as Levy writes, "That the Jeffersonians in power did not always adhere to their new principles does not diminish the enduring nobility and rightness of those principles. It proves only that the Jeffersonians set the highest standards of freedom for themselves and posterity."[14]

To understand the philosophical, political, and social forces that played upon the field of libel after 1800, it is instructive to examine the works, not only of those who built upon the earlier writings of the new libertarians, but also of those with opposing views. It is also important to look at the events and actual cases which came before courts to understand how the various theories were actually utilized.

Federalist heads were not turned by the new theories set abroad by Republicans. In fact, evidence indicates many became more entrenched in a strict Blackstonian definition of libel and freedom of press and continued to support federal prosecutions of the press even after the defeat of John Adams in 1800. For example, a House resolution directing a committee to report a bill continuing the effect of the Sedition Act passed by a narrow 49-48. When the bill favoring extension was reported out of committee less than two weeks before the Sedition Act would expire, it was defeated by a slim 53-49 margin.[15]

One of those who voted for continuation of the act was Representative Archibald Henry of North Carolina. In a letter to his constituents after the bill had been defeated, he explained his vote. He felt the law was constitutional because it did not place any previous restraints on the press. "The words freedom of press mean, in their technical import, an exemption from any control previous to publication.... Its meaning is as well ascertained as that of any word in our language."[16] A law which punishes only malicious falsehoods against the government or its officers is "as essential to its existence ... as it is to have the power of suppressing insurrection or repelling invasion."

To the argument that government cannot be injured if its acts are just and that if its acts are unjust, the people ought to be informed, he countered that the people are not always in a position to judge government and its officers. If the newspapers "teem with falsehood and malicious abuse, [the people] will be deceived; and instead of forming just opinions they will be constantly led astray.... I am convinced that no government can exist for any length of time, if it is continually abused by malicious slanderers, without having the power to punish them," concluded Henry.

Endorsing Henry's attitude was South Carolina Congressman Robert Goodloe Harper, a Federalist. A year before the law expired, Harper wrote that the Sedition Law is "proper at all times, and at all times necessary."[17] In February 1801, he told the people in his district the four basic reasons why he voted to continue the act: (1) truth was allowed as evidence; (2) the law limited fines and imprisonments; (3) courts had upheld its validity against charges of unconstitutionality; and (4) the law was necessary to protect the federal government.[18]

Determined to join the small majority that would defeat the bill to continue the Sedition Act, Tennessee Congressman William C. C. Claiborne wrote that "our code of laws will no longer be disgraced by an act so odious to a free people and so invasive of their rights."[19]

One of the Sedition Act's most articulate critics was John Thomson, a New York lawyer, who wrote an obscure essay in 1801, which mirrored much of the earlier writings of John Milton, John Locke, Cato, Hay, and Wortman.[20] Man is born with the power to think, said Thomson, and since he has no control over his thoughts, he has no power to delegate that control to government. "Consequently it must follow, that men should be allowed to express those thoughts, with the same freedom that they arise. In other words—speak, or publish, whatever you believe to be *truth*."

And since every man has a natural propensity to differ in opinion and every man believes his own opinions to be the best, logic requires that all of these opinions be discussed openly. It is through difference of opinion that discoveries are made; if it can work in such a way for science, why not in politics, asks Thomson. "Government then ought no more to interfere with the discussion of politics, than with that of any other art or science."

If government does interfere, it saps the foundations of government and produces either revolution or slavery. The Sedition Act, said Thomson, comes perilously close to abrogating those precious freedoms that are necessary for a sovereign people. "What is the amount of the late Sedition Law? It is this. 'You citizens of the United States, shall believe that all we do is right; if not, you shall be fined and imprisoned. Your understanding we despise; arguments we will not bestow upon you; coercion shall convince you.' This surely is the language of despotism."

Sedition laws, said Thomson, are less for the maintenance of peace than for the protection of certain public persons. "Nothing can be more pernicious, nothing more dangerous. What individual is of that vast importance to society, that he should have a particular clause in the criminal code of the country, for his particular safety." Such laws do nothing but shield government from public censure and allow public officers to lay claim to a questionable infallibility. "The flattering sycophant will always escape the censure of Government; while the honest man who boldly speaks disagreeable truths, will fall a victim to his sincerity, and patriotism."

Thomson contested the benefit of allowing truth as a defense in seditious libels. In sedition trials where a judge is of the same party as that in power, any opinion contrary to his beliefs will be seen as false; any opinion that coincides with his will be seen as true. However, said Thomson, opinions are neither true nor false, and therefore, should not be punished.

Thomson also added an unusual twist to the traditional argument that sedition laws abridge the First Amendment. He was the first American to suggest that the privileges accorded congressmen through the Speech and Debate Clause should be extended to the electorate as well.[21] If the representatives are at liberty to say what they please in Congress, why should they abridge this right of the people through the Sedition Laws? Why should the servants of the sovereign people have greater privileges?

Thomson's argument struck at the very heart of the difficulty encountered when English tradition failed to accommodate American democracy. The Speech and Debate Clause is a direct descendant of parliamentary privilege. By the mid–1700s, the Whig concept of a sovereign Parliament was well engrained in British constitutional theory. According to Blackstone, there must be a supreme absolute, indivisible, uncontrolled authority in which sovereignty resides. In England, that sovereignty was lodged in Parliament, whose actions "no power on earth can undo."

As a direct result of the Glorious Revolution, Parliament established broad rights of parliamentary privilege to protect itself from royal prerogatives and to protect those it governed. No longer could members be punished for what they said on the floor of debate. Nor could anyone, particularly dissidents, criticize the actions of Parliament without suffering severe penalties for breach of privilege. Because Parliament was absolute, it was the only body that could enjoy absolute privilege of expression. Therefore, absolute freedom of expression belonged to the sovereign; freedom of expression qualified by sedition law belonged to the people. The only way Parliament could be controlled was through limited suffrage.

The American constitution, steeped in the theories of popular sovereignty and social contract, adopted the substance of Parliamentary privilege in its Speech and Debate Clause, and Congress adopted the concept of breach of privilege through the Sedition Act. But the contradiction among the First Amendment, Speech and Debate Clause, and the Sedition Act obviously escaped the wisdom of the eighteenth-century leaders. If absolute privilege of speech belongs to the sovereign authority and that sovereign is the people, should not the people enjoy absolute privilege to criticize their government?

The underlying principle behind the Speech and Debate Clause, explained Thomson, was to allow the unrestrained airing of all opinions which occur in legislative debate. "If free discussion be advantageous to them, it must be equally so to the people." Absolute liberty of opinion on matters of government is inherent in a system where the people, not the governors, are sovereign.

But similar contradictions between parliamentary and constitutional traditions would continue to spring up in the face of Americans schooled in classical Whig orthodoxy, but struggling to live in the real world of a popular democracy. This was especially difficult for Federalists who tried to cling to British institutions that were clearly contradictory to the Declaration of Independence and the Constitution. Yet, again, the era of Federalist political thought was merely a transition period when America had yet to develop a concensual theory of constitutional government, and instead, relied on its British heritage.

Thomson refused to establish a line between liberty and licentiousness, saying that to do so only invited repression. "I have no hesitation in asserting—that the Licentiousness of the Press, is a term destitute of any meaning; or, if it ever exists, like anarchy it carries the seeds of its immediate destruction along with it." Limits on public discussion should occur only after the words lead to a breach of peace. Then, punishment is for actions and not opinions.

The best censor of pernicious ideas and malicious libels, according to Thomson, was public opinion and good taste. For example, "In all investigations of a public nature, personal invective ought, in justice to be avoided. ...If men differ in opinion, surely the common rules of politeness ought not therefore to be thrown aside. But even should this impropriety sometimes happen, it ought never to be adduced as proof of licentiousness of the Press; nor used as an argument for the necessity of infringing its Liberty."

But, where personal charges are leveled at individuals, Thomson was less a libertarian and more a Blackstone. He alluded to the correctness of criminal libel when he suggested that if a person were convicted of publishing a malicious falsehood, that person should be prohibited, by public pressure, from ever publishing again. "Let not Government interfere. The laws of society, as before observed, are fully sufficient to the purpose." Although Thomson makes no mention of civil libel, he probably held views similar to those of other libertarians, that the common law of libel as administered by a state's civil courts was sufficient to handle falsehoods against non-public persons.

Many of Thomson's extremist views are reflected in a work by one of the Sedition Act's more famous victims, Dr. Thomas Cooper. Cooper served six months in jail and was fined $400 for libels against President John Adams, whom he accused of improperly influencing a judge. In 1830, when Cooper was 84 years old and serving as president of Columbia College in South Carolina, he wrote a lengthy essay about sedition and the Sedition Acts.[22] The work repeats much of an earlier essay, *On the Property and Expediency of Unlimited Inquiry*, published in 1800.

"I hold that it is not necessary to pass any law prohibiting, controlling, or punishing the publication of any opinions or public discussion of any kind; because there can be no control over opinion," wrote Cooper. He was not referring merely to federal sedition laws and prosecutions, but also to state sedition laws. Such laws, said Cooper, were of illegitimate origins and served only to doom people "to voluntary ignorance, to imperfect knowledge, and place themselves, bound and blindfold, under the guidance of men who assume to govern them."

He attacked the laws from both an historical and a philosophical angle to conclude that "much good and no injury will ensue to the public interest, by permitting the unlimited and unrestrained, unpunished investigation of any and every question of a public character, and of whatever description. ... It is thus that the doubtful truths of one generation become the axioms of the next."

Historically, explained Cooper, the modern common law of libel was the bastard of Lord Coke's Star Chamber and had its origins in neither the common law nor statute prior to the infamous Star Chamber ruling in the case of *de Libellis Famosis*. That case defined libel as anything, true or false, which tended to a breach of peace and created a scandal of government. The decision also upheld a previous ruling that juries were restricted to determining only whether the defendant wrote or published the alleged libels; only the judges had the wisdom to determine whether the material was libelous.

"The whole therefore is completely extrajudicial, and amounts strictly and literally to a code of laws drawn up by Coke and enacted by the judges of the Star Chamber on their own authority." Regretably, the law of sedition did not expire with the Star Chamber in 1641; instead, judges built upon it, creating a system of judge-made law founded upon the leanings and inclinations of those who govern. It was this system, said Cooper, which was transplanted to the colonies, retained by states in their sedition prosecutions, and adopted in part by Congress in the Sedition Act. Although the legislation of 1798 improved on the English law by allowing truth to be given in evidence, that law was still unconstitutional, said Cooper. "It was so clearly and indisputably unconstitutional, that nothing could account for this usurpation of prohibited authority but the rancor of party politicians."

Cooper was concerned that since the law was never held unconstitutional and expired before being repealed, the law's provisions were still valid and could be exercised through a federal common law. It is uncertain why he continued to hold this concern in 1830, after the Supreme Court had already nullified the concept of a federal common law. However, it is certain that he not only feared, but knew that the substance of the law would also be upheld as valid in state courts.

The one concession of the Sedition Act which most concerned Cooper was the privilege of giving truth in evidence. This provision, which most defendants fought hard for in state courts as late as 1825, was, according to Cooper, "absolutely nugatory, considering the infinite trouble, the enormous expense, and time requisite to procure evidence of the plainest propositions."

Biased by the memories of his own case, he allowed that the proof of all the facts in his charges against Adams "would have been attended with an expense, a labor and a vexation, equal of themselves to no slight punishment." Cooper argued that only the truth of what is denied should be proven, not the truth of every statement. Also, public rumor and commonly held information should be accepted in defense and no person should be punished for relating opinion. As to intent and motive, Cooper supported the belief that truth with good motives and for justifiable ends should be the defense in all libel cases. The intent and tendency of the publication to do harm should be proven and not presumed, and the jury should judge intent.

On the philosophical front, Cooper attacked sedition with the same arguments used by John Milton and John Locke. Opinion, said Cooper, should never be punished because it is an involuntary act of the mind based upon evidence which is beyond the control of law and man. And every person has errors of opinion; that is part of human nature. If one feels an opinion is clearly false, then its own absurdity prevents it from doing any harm, and it will eventually be refuted by open discussion. If, on the other hand, the false opinion is plausible, it will only gain strength if permitted to work in secret.

Sedition laws, explained Cooper, are based upon the need to shut out all inquiry as to the character and conduct of men in public office, thus depriving the people "of the means of information as to the extent of their own rights and privileges and the infringements made upon them by the bad intentions, mistakes or misconduct of their public servants." While temporary inconveniences may occur when full discussion is allowed, they are only to be expected and tolerated until they cure themselves. It is improper, said Cooper, to argue against something based upon the "possibility" of its abuse. Everything has the potential of being abused; yet, when has more harm than good resulted from full discussion?

Although Cooper's views on sedition are considered generous for his time, the doctor was still an eighteenth-century philosopher who set limits on the freedoms he espoused. His discussion on freedom of press and speech related only to questions of a "general and public" nature where discussion is "expedient to elicit a truth proper for the public to know." This did not include private libels, "which are so seldom committed from public or praiseworthy motives" and are of so little moment to the public at large and so frequent and troublesome that "this tendency to calumny among neighbors ought to be repressed."

Nevertheless, Cooper stood on the extreme edge of First Amendment theory, advocating concepts that would not be adopted with any wholeheartedness until the middle of the twentieth century. His fear that the substance of the Sedition Laws of 1798 would linger beyond their expiration was realized over 100 years later with the passage of the Espionage Act of 1917.

George Hay, who had made significant contributions to early libertarian thought in his 1799 *An Essay on the Liberty of the Press*, continued his discussions on freedom of the press in an 1803 essay of the same name. But this latest essay dealt not with seditious libel but with injuries to private character.[23] The essay was written following a nasty little episode involving James Callender, a one time Jefferson scribbler who had since turned against Republicans. Callender, who had been convicted under the Sedition Act and later pardoned by Jefferson, was co-editor of the Richmond *Recorder*. Hay, a candidate for public office on the Republican ticket, became a target of Callender's anti-Republican attacks. In retaliation for the libels that Callender was printing, Hay beat the editor over the head with his walking stick. Fearing future attacks, Callender went to court to force Hay to provide security for his recognizance. Like a common thief, Hay would have to find at least two people who would put up money to insure his good behavior.[24]

Hay struck back in court where Callender was also forced to provide a personal recognizance bond and obtain securities against printing any further libels against Hay. Callender refused to obey the court's order claiming that he had made no physical attacks or threats against Hay and any security attached to what he would publish in the future was a denial of his freedom of press. Callender spent a week in jail awaiting his appeal. Finally he obtained a discharge from his recognizance. However, when Hay tried to obtain a discharge for his own securities, the court refused and the securities were retained for twelve months.[25]

Hay was criticized by Federalists and Republicans alike for persuing a remedy that restrained freedom of the press. He defended his actions in a series of newspaper articles that were later collected into the 1803 essay. In this essay, Hay reiterates much that he had said earlier about seditious libel and libel against public men.

He contended, as did most libertarians, that freedom of the press was never meant to apply equally to political libels and to personal libels. On matters of public concern every man may say what he pleases, "however absurd or immoral, whether religious, philosophical, moral, political or legal," but as to private character, he must speak the truth. The reason for this double standard, insisted Hay, was that the welfare of the nation does not depend on discussions relating to private questions."[26]

As for public candidates or officials, Hay would extend protection only over their public acts and not their private character, "which would be left open to every miscreant." False and malicious statements about an individual's private aspects are subject to criminal punishment. Hay's distinction between public act and private character reflected the gentry's claim that the character of public servants was unapproachable. In his words, public officers are "generally men who are advanced in age, who have been long in public service, and whose characters, whatever they may be, are well understood".

These understandings of libel law proceed from Andrew Hamilton's defense in John Peter Zenger's sedition trial in 1735 and other libertarian views of libel. Because some of the offensive statements made by Callender involved Hay's public character and fitness for office, Hay could not very well back out of these words and sue for libel. He had to find another remedy, one that many felt was more detrimental to Callender's freedom than a libel suit would have been. Punishment for libel comes after a court of law has found falsity and malice. But, the requirement of a security for not printing more libels, argued Callender's attorney, was a prior restraint on the editor before any judicial finding of fact and therefore unconstitutional.

While Hay was a libertarian when it came to public libels, he turned to his *Blackstone* to support restraints against private libels. Since a private libel has a tendency to create a breach of peace, then society requires that measures be set in motion to deter any further disturbance. Using precedent from English common law, Hay likened libellers to street brawlers, vandals, thieves, and drunkards.

If a printer can be punished for a false and malicious libel on a person's private character, then it follows that he has no right to publish that libel. And if he has no right to publish that libel, continued Hay, it also follows that a security to prevent the publication of future libels does not violate freedom of press rights. Using that argument, Hay might just as easily have argued that with foreknowledge that a libel is to be printed, an officer of the court could shut down the newspaper to prevent the publication of the libel and all subsequent libels.

Hay's arguments, like those of Cooper, are simply another example of the tug and pull that the early libertarians experienced as they tried to justify new theories while sustaining conventional standards of moral conduct and mannerly behavior. From a twentieth-century perspective, the result appears as a maze of unexplainable and illogical legal contradictions.

The man who had the best opportunity to spread libertarian thought through the legal community was St. George Tucker, a professor of law at the College of William and Mary and an eminent jurist. Tucker, like all American lawyers, had been nursed on *Blackstone's Commentaries* as the final word on English common law. But recognizing the inadequacy of the English classic, Tucker produced an annotated version of the *Commentaries*. Tucker's *Blackstone* contained a lengthy discussion of the American constitution, including his views on freedom of expression.

Above all, Tucker rejected Blackstone's narrow prior restraint doctrine.

Like Thomson, Tucker argued that America's constitution mandated that the people were sovereign and as long as they retained that sovereignty, the people must have an "absolute freedom of discussion."[27] The only manner in which citizens could retain those special privileges was to prohibit the federal government from restraining or prosecuting libels. Instead, that power should be left to the state governments to exercise as their constitutions and laws permitted. Like Cooper and Hay, he believed that libels against the reputation of private character were subject to redress in the state courts. He is vague on the issue of whether such redress could include criminal prosecution.

John Taylor of Virginia was an outspoken Republican on John Adams's administration, the Federalist reign of terror, and the Sedition Acts. As a leader of the minority Republicans or Tertium Quids, Taylor held a deep suspicion of the federal government and the Federalist leaders who had threatened American life. In 1814, Taylor published a venomous strike at the elitist form of government that Adams had proposed in a book written in 1788.[28] Taylor believed that the rights of conscience and of the press "constitute our most useful division of power." They are necessary in order to protect a great deal of political ground that would otherwise be lost by laws such as the Alien and Sedition Acts. To protect that "government of the people," said Taylor, the policy of the United States dictates an unlimited freedom of discussion, free from any regulation by law, judges, or juries.

For the nation to retain these powers of self government, the electorate must be composed of intelligent beings who can resist frauds and lash out against deviations from the national will. "Expression is the respiration of the mind," reminded Taylor. Free discussion will correct licentiousness and promote truth, knowledge, and liberty. No one can prescribe what another thinks, and if government pretends to, the result is sovereignty of government and not of the people.

Taylor echoed John Thomson when he surmised that the Federalists passed the Sedition Act out of fear and jealousy, the need for individual officials to fend off attacks upon themselves, and a desire to create reverence for their positions. "These murderers of discussion, knowledge and patriotism, engrave upon their tomb, 'that private citizens have neither the right nor capacity to canvass the measures of government.'"

"If our constitution," continued Taylor, "admit the sovereignty of the people; if the federal government is erected on that foundation; and if no species of sovereignty can exist without freedom of will and of discussion, it follows, that laws for restraining or regulating discussion are axes which cut up our policy at its root." Taylor's remarks on sedition are so sweeping it is difficult to guess where if at all he would have drawn the line on freedom of expression and press. However, he is consistent in his use of the word "opinion" when referring to the substance of expression he would protect.

One of the major faults of the Sedition Act, according to its many detractors, was that neither the law nor the courts differentiated between statements of fact and opinion.

"The only abuse pretended to be checked by sedition laws, is the promulgation of falsehood. Their efficacy for attaining this solitary end, is questionable." If sedition laws destroy falsehoods against individuals, said Taylor, they in turn create adulation of government, thus destroying a small evil in order to foster a greater one. "Thus also sedition laws create more falsehood than they destroy, and of a more pernicious nature."

That Taylor was chafing under the bit of the federal Sedition Law was also evidenced by his role in the Virginia Resolutions. Although written by Madison, Taylor introduced the resolutions into the legislature and carried much of the burden of debate. He was a strong states' rightist and was willing to go as far as submitting the nullification question to the people of Virginia. However, he was talked out of that move by Jefferson who explained the futility of its success.

While Thomson, Hay, Cooper, and Taylor represented liberal views about the First Amendment and libel, men like Jefferson, and James Sullivan of Massachusetts, reflected more moderate notions. While these moderates acknowledged that the federal government could pass no laws abridging freedom of the press, they were unwilling to go so far as to render all sedition unconstitutional and thereby leave governments and public officers helpless against libels.

James Sullivan, attorney general and future governor of Massachusetts, wrote in 1801 that the Sedition Act's major flaw was its failure to have been "drawn on the rules of prudence, or executed with that discretion which might procure the confidence, and merit the support of the people." The law, continued Sullivan, had its origin in "an apprehension that the president and Congress, or a majority of the latter, were in danger from their fellow-citizens . . . and was received . . . as a measure adopted to maintain party influence."[29]

Certain that a federal sedition law smacked too much of partisan politics, Sullivan felt that existing common law was sufficient to handle any real evils government might encounter. There was some dispute whether a federal common law existed, particularly in light of the separation of powers clause in the Constitution. In *United States v. Worrall*, Justice Samuel Chase had stated that there was no federal common law and Congress had only those powers specifically outlined in the Constitution.[30] Sullivan, a firm believer in the English common law, felt that denying a federal common law left the government without the powers of protecting itself.

If restraint of sedition is necessary to the preservation of the government, said Sullivan, and "there is no where, in the catalogue of powers given to Congress, any one in regard to sedition, then it must fall to the common law to protect government."[31] Suggesting that libels against men can always be remedied in state courts, Sullivan redefined sedition as it would be punishable by federal common law: "The writing or publishing of a libel with an intent to subvert the government of the United States, to bring it into hatred or contempt, or . . . with an intent to alarm the people or to cause them to withdraw their love and support from the government."

If such actions are a crime, they may be punished under the existing common law of sedition. Fines, imprisonments, and reasonable restraints may be employed according to existing understanding and may be administered without any act of Congress. If these punishments are not adequate, the legislature of the nation may increase the punishment. "There never was a necessity for Congress to do anything more than to provide for the punishment of sedition, without an attempt to define it by statute."

Thus, Sullivan would have legitimized sedition by shifting it back to its traditional place in common law. The issue was finally put to rest in 1812, when the U. S. Supreme Court decided in *U.S. v. Hudson and Godwin* that federal courts have no jurisdiction in common law crimes.[32]

Sullivan defined freedom of press as "an unrestrained use, and free improvement of the privilege of writing, and printing in the communication of sentiments and opinions, on matters of public concernment, governmental measures and political procedures." In other words, the official conduct of men and government may be investigated and no indictment for libel may be had as long as the publication is not made falsely, maliciously, or with intent to injure the government.[33]

As for the reputation and character of governmental officers, Sullivan subscribed to that elitist view that political leaders had not only a greater stake in their reputations than the average citizen, but also had better reputations. Therefore, there are certain charges which Sullivan considered improper for publication. The law was never intended to mean more than the license to publish "what had been in fact done by the government, or by its officers, in an official capacity, independent of any charge for gross immoralities, corruption or frauds, by them personally committed."

For example, if an officer acts treasonously, "there could be no necessity for gazette publications on this point, because a public prosecution for a crime of the first magnitude ought to be immediately commenced." Or, if an officer takes a bribe, it is not the proper subject for a newspaper, but a matter for an indictment or impeachment. However, if the officer takes action as a result of the bribe or refuses to do his duty as a public official, explained Sullivan, that information may be published without the danger of its being charged with a libel, unless the facts published are false. Thus gentlemen's reputations were to be spared too public an airing.

Most of Sullivan's criticism of the law of libel centered around Pennsylvania's libel statute, which allowed truth to be entered into evidence where material was proper for public information. Sullivan could not believe that the statute intended "that a tale of bribery and corruption of a public officer, may be made the subject of a gazette publication, and then be justified, upon proof of the facts charged, when there should be a prosecution." To publish what a public officer has officially done is one thing, continued Sullivan, but to charge him with a crime is another matter that should not be countenanced unless the publisher can prove all the facts of the crime.

"Productions addressed to the understanding of mankind, on the subject of civil government have never been deemed to be seditious; but essays made on false facts to influence the minds of the people, to create unnecessary jealousies, and to disaffect the people to the government, always have been, and no doubt always will be, held as highly criminal." Sullivan typified the hardline state attorney, who sought a politically expedient compromise between Blackstonian and Zengerian principles. Only by paying homage to both could he successfully enforce statutory or common law libel provisions.

Compromise and fence straddling certainly were not the trademarks of Thomas Paine. Although Paine was a strong supporter of the Republican party and had been prosecuted for sedition in England, he wrote a short article in 1807 criticizing the new interpretations of libel law that had surfaced in recent years. Prompted by an ongoing verbal battle with Federalists and recent dismissal of libel charges against Federalist editors, the seventy-year-old Paine accused newspapers of a certain arrogance by seeking more privileges than allowed others.[34]

Eschewing much of the recent discussions about freedom of press, Paine reminded readers that freedom of the press "refers to the fact of printing free from prior restraint." It meant nothing more nor less than the end of a licensing system. And those who argued that certain opinions were immune from persecution had their history mixed up. While he agreed with Jefferson that error of opinion should be tolerated when reason was allowed to refute it, Paine insisted there was a difference between error (of Republican papers) and licentiousness (of Federalist papers).

JEFFERSON AND THE LAW OF LIBEL

It is difficult to even guess how much of Zenger or Blackstone that Jefferson would have adopted in a definition of libel. The president was unfamiliar with the substance of common law libel and, except for some confusing questions to a lawyer, never discussed its details in any of his writings. Nevertheless, Jefferson had numerous occasions to air his opinions about libel and the First Amendment, and those opinions were far from being libertarian in the same sense as Cooper or Thomson.

Despite a lack of detailed knowledge about libel, Jefferson had no serious concerns about the legality of common law libel prosecutions. In fact, his antipathy toward the federal sedition law, as expressed in the Kentucky Resolutions, resulted less from any deep-seated certainties about prior restraint or libertarianism and more from his strong convictions about the

Constitution's separation of powers doctrine. The authority to punish seditious libel, said Jefferson, is reserved by the states, who "must retain to themselves the right of judging how far the licentiousness of speech and of the press, may be abridged without lessening their useful freedom."[35] While Jefferson vacillated on the usefulness or the need for sedition prosecutions, he never waivered from this state's rights stand.

Three years after the demise of the Sedition Laws, Jefferson wrote to Abigail Adams, explaining that he had released all those prosecuted under the law "because I considered and now consider that law to be a nullity as absolute and as palpable as if Congress had ordered us to fall down and worship a golden image." He defended his actions as "the obligations of an oath to protect the constitution, violated by an unauthorized act of Congress."[36] He explained, further:

The power to [restrain slander] is fully possessed by the several state legislatures. It was reserved to them, and was denied to the general government by the constitution according to our construction of it. While we deny that Congress has a right to control the freedom of the press, we have ever asserted the right of the states, and their exclusive right, to do so.[37]

Not convinced of the legality of Jefferson's actions in releasing victims of the law, Abigail Adams challenged him: "I have understood that the power which makes a Law, is alone competent to the repeal. If a Chief Majestrate [sic] can by his will annul a Law, where is the difference between a republican, and a despotic government?"[38] Her understanding was that only Congress or the courts could remit sentences. She questioned whether Jefferson in his ardent desire to rectify the mistakes and abuses of the Adams administration "had not led to measures still more fatal to the constitution and more derogatory to your honour, and independence of Character?"

Jefferson answered that as president he was bound to remit the sentences because that power was given to him by the constitution. And, while judges may hold beliefs about the constitutionality of a law, they have no right to foist their opinions upon the Congress or the executive. To allow judges to decide what is right and what is not, not only for themselves, but for the legislature and the executive, "would make the judiciary a despotic branch."[39] Jefferson never questioned the propriety of trying sedition cases in state courts. The power to punish the "overwhelming torrent of slander which is confounding all vice and virtue, all truth and falsehood in the U.S. [is] fully possessed by the several state legislatures. It was reserved to them, and denied to the general government, by the constitution according to our construction of it."[40]

The case of William Duane, editor of the Philadelphia *Aurora*, demonstrates Jefferson's posture on the sedition question. A man of strong Republican influence in Pennsylvania, Duane was typical of the newspaper editors who were hostile toward the Federalists. One of the many scrapes in which he became entangled involved an article he wrote about a Senate bill that set out the methods for deciding disputed elections. On February 19, 1800, he wrote that the Senate had passed the bill after a Senate committee had held secret meetings without the presence of the bill's author, South Carolina Republican Thomas Pinckney, and that such secret caucuses were common in the Senate.[41]

Incensed at the lies (the bill had not passed and Pinckney had indeed attended the secret caucus), the Senate brought breach of privilege charges against Duane. The charges, brought under the Sedition Act, sought punishment for writings which were "false, defamatory, scandalous, and malicious, tending to defame the Senate of the United States and to bring them into contempt and disrepute, and to excite against them the hatred of the good people of the United States."[42]

After Duane refused to appear on the charges, Vice President Jefferson signed a warrant for Duane's arrest on charges of contempt of Congress. The editor was jailed for a short period. When the Senate adjourned in May 1800, President Adams was requested to carry on the prosecution against Duane.[43] However, when Jefferson assumed the presidency, he found that the prosecution had not yet begun. Jefferson knew that to release Duane as he had other victims of the Sedition Acts would be politically unwise since the Senate remained predominantly Federalist. Yet, to make Duane an exception and continue the case would not only be repugnant to his beliefs about the law, but would also alienate Republicans.

Jefferson wrote to a lawyer, Robert R. Livingston, in May 1801, seeking advice on the Duane case. Claiming to be out of touch with the common law of libel, he asked whether or not England accepted the defense of truth in libels and contempts, and if it did not, did the U.S. Constitution require truth. If truth cannot be entered as a justification, was it not within the power of the president to pardon Duane?[44]

Determining that political expediency was the safest road in the case, he wrote to Duane that "out of respect for [the Senate] [I] should be obliged to refer to the attorney of the district to consider whether there was ground of prosecution in any court and under any law acknowledged of force."[45]

Prosecution was begun in Philadelphia, under Pennsylvania's common law of criminal libel. However, the grand jury returned a no bill and Duane was released from all charges. Jefferson was uncomfortable explaining to the Senate and the public what had transpired in the Duane case. In fact, he wrote to Secretary of State Edward Livingston: "You are sensible I must avoid committing myself in that channel of justification, and that were I to do it in this case I might be called on by other printers in other cases where it might be inexpedient to say anything." However, he considered it impolite to ignore the invitation to publicly comment on the situation and asked Livingston to deliver the explanation which he dictated:

The President is to have the laws executed. He may order an offence then to be prosecuted. If he sees a prosecution put into a train which is not lawful, he may order it to be discontinued and put into legal train....I therefore directed that prosecution to be discontinued and a new one to be commenced, founded on whatever other law might be in evidence against the offence. This was done and the grand jury finding no other law against it, declined doing anything under the bill. There appears to be no weak part in any of these actions or inferences.[46]

The president had no real love for libelers no matter what party they represented, as demonstrated in his handling of the case of Republican Duane and his silence during the prosecutions of Joseph Dennie, editor of the *Port Folio*, and of Harry Croswell, Federalist editor of *The Wasp* (Hudson, N.Y.).

In one of Jefferson's oft-quoted letters, he wrote to Pennsylvania Governor Thomas McKean that he had lost patience with Federalist scribblers who were "attacking freedom of press by pushing it's [sic] licentiousness and its lying to such a degree of prostitution as to deprive it of all credit." Believing that the credibility of the press could be restored only by the proper restraint of state law, he wrote: "I have therefore long thought that a few prosecutions of the most prominent offenders would have a wholesome effect in restoring the integrity of the presses. Not a general prosecution, for that would look like persecution; but a selected one." He enclosed a clip, probably from Dennie's *Port Folio*, "to make an example of."[47]

By the election of 1804, Federalist editors were demonstrating daily their outrage against the party's diminished power in Congress, against Jefferson's usurpation of the state's rights doctrine through the purchase of the Louisiana Territory, and against what they perceived as the failure of the democratic system. The president answered these noxious scribblers in his second inaugural address by calling on states to correct the malignancies of the press. "He who has time, renders a service to public morals and public tranquility, in reforming these abuses by the salutary coercions of the law."[48]

THE COURTS STRUGGLE TO DEFINE LIBEL

While essayists and philosophers were willing to relinquish some eighteenth-century libel doctrines, judges and prosecutors held tenaciously to their *Blackstones*. Unmoved by the spurious theories of libertarians, state courts continued even after the demise of the Sedition Act to prosecute in an attempt to muffle political criticism.

Much can be made of the all too obvious contradictions between what people wrote about freedom of expression in the early nineteenth century and how the courts defined it on a case-by-case basis. However, much of the disparity can be explained by an understanding of the traditions in legal education.[49]

American lawyers and judges were schooled in the ancient principles of British common law and all of its timeworn precedents, which supported a system that knew nothing of popular democracy. The American court did not have a body of American precedent built on the foundation of the American Constitution, nor did the system accommodate novel approaches based on the Great Experiment.

Most of the legal precedent cited by American lawyers and judges in the eighteenth and nineteenth centuries came from the British system where sovereignty rested with Parliament and not with the people. In Britain, only limited suffrage was granted to the governed, and unlimited freedoms were retained for the governors. For example, freedom of discussion was essential for Parliament if it was to retain its sovereignty: hence, the tradition of absolute privilege in debate. Likewise, the power to punish for sedition was also essential if Parliament was to govern the people for their own social good and to thwart any attempts to usurp that body's sovereignty.

This political and legal tradition was antithetical to the American constitutional system in which the people retained sovereignty through elections and maintained it with free discussion. John Taylor recognized the inconsistency between a sovereignty of the people and government's power to regulate the thoughts of that sovereignty. "The inconsistency is such as to render it impossible that both qualities can subsist in one government."[50]

Yet that very inconsistency was being practiced by American courts. The existence of a popular sovereignty was asserted everywhere—in the Declaration of Independence, in the Constitution, and in state constitutions. Yet the common law adopted by the American court system asserted a governmental sovereignty that recognized the governors' right to silence the governed. In those policy areas such as freedom of expression, where the inconsistency existed, either the people or the government would have to surrender its sovereignty. In the American experiment, it would be the traditions of governmental sovereignty that would succumb.

But the relinquishing of English common law by a profession so deeply steeped in English legal tradition would be painful, requiring several generations of lawyers and judges to build a body of American common law. The resulting body of American law would be the work of jurists who placed great faith in the checks and balances of a popular democracy.

Nevertheless, between 1801 and the early 1820s, political pressure inspired litigation and commentary urging that seditious libel was still legitimate despite the limitations put on those actions by new understandings of the First Amendment. Lawyers, judges, juries, and defendants continued to play an uncertain game of "What is Libel?" with no fixed rules, a poorly marked field, and numerous political fouls. The uncertainty was a creature of the Sedition Acts, which had introduced new concepts about libel (truth as a defense, proof of criminal intent, jury to judge the law as well as the facts) that contradicted accepted common law principles. Were these new ideas to be adopted into a revised American common law? Or were they to be ignored because they had been strictly statutory? Had not each state, upon passing its own constitution, stated that all laws existing in the colony and not touched by the Constitution continued in force as the common law of the state? Just what did the state constitutional provisions for freedom of the press mean?

These questions were addressed in more than a dozen libel cases reported in the first quarter of the nineteenth century. The answers emerging from the earliest cases are as varied as the geographical and political differences of the states in which the prosecutions were begun. But as party fervor died down and a more democratic common law was propounded, the contradictions among states dissolved into a surprising concensus on the definitions of libel and freedom of press.

Throughout those early years, the major legal question was what role if any truth should play in political libel cases. If it was to be allowed, arguments centered around the degree of proof necessary and the place of intent or motive. Another interesting question that surfaced early was what type of political libel would benefit from the defense of truth. Does a charge of criminal activity receive as much protection from libel laws as a charge of impropriety or dereliction of duty? As noted earlier, this is a distinction James Sullivan of Massachusetts would have made. Also, does an appointed public officer receive more protection from the courts than an elected one? And where is the line to be drawn between public libels and private libels?

For decades, the courts struggled with the common law of libel, trying to modify it to fit democratic systems of state governments. The major stumbling block, however, was the persistent belief, held even by the likes of George Hay, that it was necessary to punish dangerous expression in order to preserve the public peace. The publication of a libel was "an offence which must be adhered to so long as the restraint of all tendencies to the breach of publick peace, and to private animosity and revenge is salutary to the commonwealth."[51]

The fear of violence or revenge as the result of a published libel was not an unfounded fear in the early 1800s. Tumultuous crowds, riots, and mobs had long been accepted as a tolerable part of the political system. If the government was not performing as expected, it was often necessary for the people to resort to extra-institutional means to meet the needs of the community. As long as just enough force was used to rectify the injustice, pubic officials granted a temporary license to the mob.[52] It was not uncommon for riots and mobs to form at the behest of a local newspaper editorial calling on the public to act for their own good. Nor was it unheard of for a newspaper article attacking an individual to result in mob attacks on that person or on the newspaper itself.

Many used the breach of peace reasoning to argue that truth played no role in determining the outcome of a libel prosecution. If the purpose of criminal libel was to prevent a breach of peace and the offending article was found to have that tendency, then the truth or falsity of the article was not a necessary avenue of discovery. As Chief Justice Theophilus Parsons said in *Commonwealth v. Clapp*, "In the defense of a libel, as an offense against law, it is not considered whether publication be true or false; because a man may maliciously publish the truth against another, with the intent to defame his character, and if the publication be true, the tendency of it to inflame the passions, and to excite revenge, is not diminished, but may sometimes be strengthened."[53] The greater the truth, the greater the libel.

Those who argued that truth was a legitimate defense in a criminal libel case saw that the good that came from truthful discussions of public questions was much greater than any evil that might occur. As Thomas Cooper said, the temporary inconveniences resulting from truth are to be expected and will cure themselves. One cannot argue against something based upon possibility of abuse because everything has the possibility of abuse.[54]

Croswell v. N.Y., the most influential post-Sedition Act criminal libel case, reflected these two opposing views.[55] Harry Croswell, editor of an extremist Federalist paper in Hudson, New York, called the *Wasp*, unmindfully reprinted many of the scurrilities previously produced by James Callender. These libels, most of which were against Thomas Jefferson, accused the president of having a slave mistress, of seducing a friend's wife, of acting against the Constitution of the United States, and of having paid Callender to lie about Washington and Adams. It was the latter two accusations which resulted in an indictment for libel on two counts.

Before trial, Croswell's lawyers moved for a postponement of the trial in order that Callender could be brought from Virginia to New York to prove the truth of the accusations. The judge denied the motion because according to his reading of the common law, the truth was not a justification in a criminal libel case. After six months of legal scuffling, Croswell's case was removed to a district court where a state supreme court justice would be sitting.

At the trial before Chief Justice Morgan Lewis, a Republican, the lawyers once again were denied a postponement in order to get Callender. Lewis also denied a motion to convene a commission to examine Callender in Virginia. After arguments and testimony were presented, Justice Lewis instructed the jury that it was confined to finding the facts alone and that it was not within its province to inquire into the intent of the defendant or into the truth or falsity of the materials. The only questions for their consideration and decision were whether the defendant was the publisher of the piece and whether the *innuendoes* were true. If they were satisfied as to these two points, it was their duty to find Croswell guilty, which is just what the jury found.[56]

Croswell's lawyers moved for a new trial based on their claim that the judge had misdirected the jury by not allowing the defendant to prove the truth of the allegations. A hearing on the motion was granted by the New York Supreme Court. Croswell's Federalist friends had hired Alexander Hamilton to help the defense team of Richard Harrison and William P. Van Ness. The defense would be facing three Republican judges—Lewis, Brockholst Livingston and Smith Thompson—and one Federalist (and a staunch supporter of Hamilton's), James Kent. Ambrose Spencer, New York Attorney General who had led the prosecution of this case from the beginning, had since been appointed to the Supreme Court but abstained from hearing the case.

Justice Lewis' opinion in the case sums up the political significance of the whole controversy: "This cause has assumed an air of importance which I should be disposed to ascribe, in a great measure, to the spirit of the times, rather than to its intrinsic merits."[57] Yet, despite its political overtones and motivations, Croswell's dispute with the New York Republicans produced significant opinions that would be widely quoted during the next 25 years.

As was typical of courtroom oratory of that day, the attorneys spent hours finding support in dozens of English common law libel cases. However, it was Hamilton's lengthy defense that placed those cases in perspective and asked the court to examine the American experience. Hamilton's arguments were not too different from those proposed by another Hamilton (Andrew) 70 years earlier in the Zenger case. Both argued that truth should be allowed to be presented before the jury and that the jury should judge intent and criminality as well as the facts of publication.

The significant difference between the Zenger and Croswell arguments was that Alexander Hamilton was pleading for the use of truth, not as a defense, but as evidence to show Croswell's good motives and justifiable ends. "I contend for the liberty of publishing truth with good motives and for justifiable ends, even though it reflects on government, magistrates or private persons. I contend for it under the restraint of our tribunals—when this is exceeded let them interpose and punish."[58]

Hamilton drew a parallel between libel and other crimes where intent and motive were central to deciding guilt and innocence. Just as in other crimes, argued Hamilton, the intent is the essence of the crime. "If it have a good intent it ought not to be a libel, for it then is an innocent transaction, and it ought to have this intent against which the jury have in their discretion to pronounce."[59] And one means of showing the intent is to allow the introduction of evidence of truth, which would go toward proving the lack of malice. "It is inherent in the nature of things that the assertion of truth cannot be a crime. . . . Its being a truth is a reason to infer that there was no design to injure another."[60]

Public prosecutor George Caines repudiated Hamilton's arguments, retreating to Star Chamber cases where it was ruled that a libel was punishable not because it was false, but because of its evil tendency to a breach of peace. "A libel is correctly said to be more libelous for being true for it has an increased tendency to a breach of peace. In a moral view the malicious relating of either truth or falsehood for the purpose of creating misery is equally reprehensive."[61] According to Caine's reading of English cases, it was the tendency of the material to create harm, not the intent of the writer, which was the essence of the crime.

After several days of arguments, the court rendered a split decision on a new trial, leaving the guilty verdict intact. Justices Lewis and Livingston voted against a new trial and Justices Kent and Thomas voted for it. The case was eventually dropped and judgment never rendered against Crosswell, who later found a quieter calling as an Episcopal rector.

Lewis's written opinion, which was reported at a later date, indicates that he was not altogether heedless of Hamilton's arguments regarding truth and intent. Lewis wrote that the rule of libel was that the truth cannot be given in evidence as a justification in a criminal prosecution for a libel.[62] Even Hamilton agreed with this point for he only argued that it should be offered in evidence as it related to intent, and not as a defense or justification for the entire libel. "This is a distinction," said Lewis, "for the discovery of which we are indebted to the ingenuity of our own times; there is certainly nothing to be met with in the books to rob us of the honor of it."

He agreed that whenever a case "shall arise in which the intent shall be a fit subject of inquiry for a jury, and the truth shall be capable of opening an avenue to the heart, through which it may be discovered," he would not hesitate to admit truth as evidence. Where a criminal act does not carry intention on its face and the guilt or innocence depend on the surrounding circumstances, then it is necessary to inquire into the intent.

However, he did not consider the present case to fit those circumstances. He admitted that even a person uninfluenced by the strongest party prejudice would find it difficult to conclude that these charges against the president did not carry with them "conclusive evidence of a most malicious and seditious intention."

Justice Kent repeated much of Hamilton's argument and historical precedent in arriving at the same conclusions as the defense. "The true rule of law is, that the intent and tendency of the publication is, in every instance, to be the substantial inquiry on the trial, and that the truth is admissible in evidence, to explain that intent, and not in every instance to justify it."[63] To shut out an inquiry into the truth, said Kent, is to abridge the means of defending oneself against libel charges. "It is to weaken the arm of the defendant, and to convict him, by means of a presumption which he might easily destroy by proof that the charge was true." What can be a more important circumstance than truth, asked Kent, when the charge is against the competency or purity of a public official or a candidate?

Nevertheless, Kent had a warning for those who, like Madison or Cooper, would have done away with political libels altogether. "If this doctrine [of allowing even false and malicious writings to be free of prosecution] was

to prevail, the press would become a pest, and destroy the public morals.
. . . The founders of our government were too wise and too just ever to
have intended, by the freedom of the press, a right to circulate falsehood
as well as truth, or that the press should be the lawful vehicle of malicious
defamation."

Justice Lewis wrote that all he had done was pronounce the law as he
saw it, and he would leave any alteration of the law, when found necessary,
to the power of the legislature.[64] The next year, the New York legislature
did pass libel reforms that allowed truth to be given as evidence, as long as
the matter charged was published with good motives and for justifiable
ends. The law also limited fines to $5,000 and imprisonment to 18 months.

These were significant steps away from the common law rules of the
eighteenth century and indicated a greater appreciation for public discussion
of political matters. Pennsylvania's 1790 constitution provided that where
publications were proper for public information, truth could be entered into
evidence, but not as a defense in all prosecutions for criminal libel. Delaware
and Kentucky followed Pennsylvania's lead with similar provisions in 1792,
and Tennessee adopted similar provisions in 1796.

It was Pennsylvania's constitutional provisions which caused James Sullivan much concern. The Massachusetts Attorney General believed that
Pennsylvania's law had a "restrained meaning, and is not intended to be
taken altogether in its literal sense."[65] He was troubled that the law did not
provide an adequate balance between free press and security of reputation.
Truth, even when published with good motives, can harm reputation.

According to Sullivan, there never is a proper justification for publishing
that a public official has committed a crime or that the same person is guilty
of human failings. In the first instance, the person should be tried in a court;
and in the second, it is a crime against the community to publish human
weaknesses because no one is without failings. "What advantage can there
result from printing a charge, which, if true, can be inquired into by a court
of justice?"[66]

"It is hard to be believed that it is intended there that a tale of bribery
and corruption of a public officer, may be made the subject of a gazette
publication, and then be justified, upon proof of the facts charged, when
there should be a prosecution." To publish what an officer has done in his
official capacity is one thing, but if he should be charged with having abused
his office, the printer ought to be punished.[67]

There is no reason to believe, concluded Sullivan, "that Pennsylvania ever
intended anything more, than a mere license to publish what had been in
fact done by the government, or by its officers, in an official capacity,
independent of any charge for gross immoralities, corruption or frauds, by
them personally committed."[68]

There is no doubt that Pennsylvania's constitutional provisions protected
those who spoke out against government. This was well demonstrated in

the case of Joseph Dennie and his *Port Folio*. Dennie, an ardent Anglophile and critic of the Constitution, was one source of the "infamous and seditous libels, published almost daily in our newspapers," wrote Governor Thomas McKean to Jefferson. Jefferson was also disturbed by Dennie's scribbling, particularly since some of the libels were hitting too close to home. Dennie, like Croswell, was reprinting much of Callender's scurrilities about Jefferson's relationship with his slave Sally Hemmings.

Jefferson wrote McKean that the press was in a sad state and that "a few prosecutions of the most prominent offenders would have a wholesome effect in restoring the integrity of the presses." The newspaper he sent along with the letter was undoubtedly an issue of the *Port Folio*.[69]

Armed with his penchant for libel suits and Jefferson's nod of approval, McKean charged Dennie with libel of the government. The article that resulted in the arrest stated that democracy was a futile form of government that always led to civil wars and anarchy. "No wise man but discerns its imperfections; no good man but shudders at its miseries, no honest man but proclaims its fraud, and no brave man but draws his sword against its force."[70]

The indictment was entered at the mayor's court in Philadelphia, but was removed to the Pennsylvania Supreme Court where friendlier Republicans sat. Dennie was found not guilty after the jury listened to an inspiring set of instructions from Chief Justice Jasper Yeates. He asked the jury to divest itself of all political prejudices and to dispassionately study the passages under indictment.[71] In prosecutions for publications which investigate the conduct of government and its officer, said Yeates, truth may be given in evidence. However, if an editor uses truth to disturb the peace, the matter is not proper for publication: "The common weal is not interested in such communication except to suppress it."

However, the enlightened advocates of republican government pride themselves in the fact that the more deeply the government is examined, "the more fully will the judgments of honest men be satisfied that it is the most conducive to the safety and happiness of a free people." The jury had been instructed to find a verdict of not guilty if it found that the "production was honestly meant to inform the public mind and warn them against supposed dangers in society, though the subject may have been treated erroneously."[72] Dennie was found not guilty.

Dennie was but an obnoxious fly in McKean's delicate political empire. His real enemy was William Duane, editor of the *Aurora* and a former McKean supporter. After McKean's first election to governorship in 1799, Duane took a decided turn against the wealthy and aristocratic Republican moderates, or Quids, and became a leader of the Democratic Republicans. The Federalist party was on the outs in Philadelphia, and the new political struggles would be between these two factions of the Republican party. The Quids represented the wealthy commercial and professional class in the state and the Democrats received their strength from the working class and immigrants. The social distance represented by these two classes would obviously result in political in-fighting, and Duane took the lead. Yet, Duane's switch from the Quids to the Democrats was not altogether an altruistic move; it was motivated by several personal grudges against his former political champion, Governor McKean.

During the election of 1799, Duane was physically attacked by the candidate's oldest son after accusing the son of abandoning his father's political friends. Duane brought charges against the young man, and the case remained in the courts for several years before any resolution was had. Also, Duane was bitterly disappointed that his work for McKean during the campaign had not resulted in a patronage job. In fact, McKean had retained many Federalists in office, while ignoring Democrats.

All of Duane's disappointments with McKean manifested themselves in the columns of the *Aurora*. At first, McKean's attitude was to ignore Duane and attack the problem through legislative reform. In December of 1802, in an address to the Pennsylvania Assembly, he called on the legislature to do something about the "unparalleled licentiousness" of the press. However, he was speaking to deaf ears, since the senate was predominately Federalist and the Democrats had made inroads into the house.

During the election of 1805, McKean became entangled in an embarassing situation involving the Spanish Minister Don Carlos Martinez D'Yrujo who was also McKean's son-in-law. The faux pas committed by Yrujo and McKean unleashed the most vitriolic attacks by the *Aurora*.

The incident involved the cashing of two fradulent checks authorized by one of Yrujo's aides, Don Joseph Cabrera. Although Cabrera enjoyed diplomatic immunity and the state of Pennsylvania had no authority to arrest him, McKean bowed to Yrujo's demands for incarceration and had the aide arrested and jailed. After several days in jail, Cabrera waived his diplomatic immunity and agreed to be tried by a state court, where he was indicted and bail was set at $2,000. However, Cabrera did not have the bail, and he insisted on being tried in Spain. The indictment was dropped until the Spanish government decided what to do with the aide.

Meanwhile, at Yrujo's insistence, McKean kept Cabrera in jail. Finally, after months of negotiations among the Spanish government, Pennsylvania courts, and federal courts, Cabrera was tried in Pennsylvania and found guilty of forgery and sentenced to two years at hard labor and fined $2,000. Two weeks later, McKean granted him a partial pardon and ordered him released from the hard labor and from being clothed in jail garb. Finally, Cabrera paid back the bank and McKean granted him a full pardon.[73]

Duane denounced McKean's role in the incident, saying that the governor had committed illegal, unconstitutional, and impeachable offenses when he chose to accede to his son-in-law's wishes rather than to the law of nations. He accused McKean of creating a higher law than that of the Constitution:

"The United Kingdom belongs to George the Third, so does Pennsylvania belong to Thomas the First." Duane had opened an all-out war on McKean that eventually resulted in the editor calling for the governor's impeachment.[74]

After the sting of the Cabrera affair and a hard-fought campaign, McKean stood on unstable political ground. Rather than create an uproar with criminal libel prosecutions, he chose to play the role of private citizen and use the civil courts to make his point to those who had attacked him during the campaign. He brought libel suits totaling $200,000 against five men, including Duane.

The *Aurora's* editor was carefully laying the groundwork for an impeachment effort against McKean. Daily, he displayed articles accusing McKean of packing offices with relatives, of bribery, lying, and arrogance toward the law. In August 1806, following verbal attacks on his family and Yrujo, McKean instituted a criminal prosecution against Duane. Yrujo followed the next day with similar charges.

The governor then followed up this volley with an address to the Pennsylvania Assembly in December 1806, asking for major reforms in the laws of libel. "Libeling has become the crying sin of the nation and the times," he said. "It was the general prostitution of the liberty of the press, the overwhelming torrent of political dissention; the indiscriminate demolition of pubic characters; and the barbarous inroads upon the peace and happiness of the private individuals" that supported his call for reforms. As to the substance of these reforms, McKean asked that a bill be returned that would compel a publisher who printed libels to provide reply space to the victim. Also, printers and editors should be required to register at an appropriate county office so that at trial there would be no doubt as to who the publisher was. And finally, he would require a bond for good behavior to be posted against any editor who was indicted for libel, and the court would be allowed to suppress the publication for a short period of time.[75]

The house response to McKean's message was piercing. For the legislature to entertain the governor's reforms, stated the report, would be to place every member in defiance of the state's constitution. A month later, another report struck at the governor's remarks, comparing them to Star Chamber tactics and the "deadly nightshade of the common law on libels."

The report questioned why reforms in the criminal law were so important to a governor who had been so successful in the civil courts. "Whence, then, the necessity of any criminal law on this subject, when the common law is so fruitful in actions upon the case?" The report asked for a committee to consider a bill which would prohibit all criminal libels. To abolish the types of civil suits McKean had brought against non-publishers, the report called for a prohibition of all libels upon public character or public conduct except when published in a newspaper.[76]

Reforms in Pennsylvania's libel law were forthcoming and proved to be a radical shift from common law understanding. The new law, passed in March 1809, appeared on the books just in time for Duane's defense to feel its effects. The law read that no person could be charged with a criminal libel for publications which examined the legislature, any branch of government, or any official conduct of public officeholders. Section 2 provided that any prosecutions contrary to the intent of the law were null and void.[77]

Duane, who had been convicted of criminal libel before Justice Yeates, moved for an arrest of the judgment after the new law was passed. Duane's counsel argued that section 2 of the new law was retroactive over all prosecutions pending in the courts. The state attorney, however, argued that section 2 had no effect on prosecutions begun before passage of the law, and that the law was unconstitutional because it denied public officials a recourse to the courts when their reputation was injured.

Chief Justice William Tilghman, who had been appointed to the bench by McKean over the governor's own son, reviewed the provisons of the law and concluded that it did not deny due process because civil remedies were still available.[78] As to Section 2, Tilghman said, albeit hesitantly, that "if the legislature intended that the proceedings should be continued on indictments already commenced, they ought to have said so expressly." Therefore, the law was retroactive and the judgment against Duane was arrested. Tilghman was joined in the opinion by Justice Yeates.

If James Sullivan had qualms about Pennsylvania's 1790 constitutional provisions regarding libel, he certainly would have had problems with Pennsylvania's new law. The law, which did not result from changes in the judiciary, but was a manifestation of the political climate of Pennsylvania, had a direct effect on libel in that state by forcing public officials to find their redress in the civil courts. Such reforms were a long time in coming to other states, and political pressure on libel prosecutions continued to be common in many states.

While Jefferson played a behind-the-scenes role in the prosecution of Joseph Dennie, his participation in a series of federal libel cases in Connecticut was not as well disguised. The five libel indictments were brought in 1806 against a Federalist judge, a seminary student, a preacher, and three newspaper editors. All of the defendants were indicted by federal grand juries in Connecticut under a federal common law of sedition.

Although Jefferson denied, several years later, knowing of the prosecutions, correspondence shows he was made aware of the cases in December 1806, four months before trials were scheduled.[79] Also, Congressman Samuel Dana of Connecticut introduced the facts of the cases in Congress in January 1807, three months before the defendants were to go on trial.[80] And it is most certain that Jefferson knew the prosecutions were a vendetta by U.S. District Judge Pierpont Edwards against Connecticut Federalists. Edwards, in a charge to the New Haven grand jury that would be hearing the libel cases, said that "regardless of decency of truth, under the conduct of daring men, stimulated by a spirit of events and unchecked in its career," the press could eventually destroy the government.[81]

The grand jury handed down indictments against Connecticut Judge Tapping Reeve, seminary student Thaddeus Osgood, and *Litchfield Monitor* editor Thomas Collier. The charges against Reeve were later dropped, and the remainder of the cases postponed several times. During the next session the grand jury issued indictments against editors Hudson and Godwin of the *Connecticut Courant* and against Rev. Aza Backus. Backus, like Croswell and Dennie before him, allegedly had repeated accusations made public by James Callender to the effect that Jefferson had attempted to seduce Mrs. John Walker, the wife of a close friend. When Jefferson learned the content of the libel, he urged immediate dismissal.[82]

Connecticut was a Federalist stronghold. The Hartford *American Mercury* noted that in Connecticut, Republicans from the president on down could be called "knaves, liars, atheists ... adulterers and murderers" without ever finding vindication in the state courts.[83] Through presidential appointment, however, Republicans did manage to gain control of the federal courts and used that forum to strike back at Federalists who criticized the president.

Although Jefferson had criticized the use of federal courts to try sedition cases under the Alien and Sedition Laws, he apparently had no problem with the concept of a federal common law being used in these particular prosecutions. He wrote Thomas Seymour that such prosecutions, although arising out of a spirit of indignation and retaliation, "cannot lessen the usefullness of freedom of the press," as long as truth was not made to suffer. He hoped that through these prosecutions, "republican principles" would eventually prevail, and urged Connecticut's Republicans to continue their struggle against those who resorted to "falsehoods and artifices."[84]

To many, Jefferson's statements appear inconsistent not only because of his vocal defense of civil liberties, but also because the Republican party had often argued, as it did during the Sedition Act years, that federal courts had no jurisdiction in libel cases. Even Connecticut's Federalist representative Dana submitted a resolution to Congress calling for a committee to study whether prosecutions for libel against federal officers could be brought in federal courts. Jefferson's son-in-law, Representative John W. Eppes, supported the notion that English common law did not automatically become part of federal law unless so legislated and that federal prosecutions for libel were unconstitutional.[85]

Two years later, in 1809, Representative John Randolph of Virginia asked Congress to appoint a committee to investigate the Connecticut libel cases, but Representative Dana in an attempt to deflect any investigation reminded members that no one had actually suffered except by "inconvenience and expense." Nothing ever came of the committee.[86]

By April 1808, only *U.S. v. Hudson & Godwin* was left to test the issue of federal jurisdiction. Six years after the original indictments, the U.S. Supreme Court ruled that federal courts "possess no jurisdiction but what is given them by the power that creates them.... All exercise of criminal jurisdiction in common law cases ... is not within their implied powers."[87]

The decision closed the door to federal common law prosecutions for libel, and left the way open for continued common law prosecutions in state courts. The more typical approach to libel in most states was the "truth with good motives" argument first proposed by Alexander Hamilton in the Croswell case, or the "truth for public information" found in Pennsylvania's constitution.

Typifying these more conservative approaches was *Commonwealth v. Morris*, a Virginia case. Morris, a landowner, petitioned the Virginia General Assembly about a local sheriff who was abusing his office.[88] The petitioner claimed that the sheriff was promising landowners he would be lax in tax collection if they would sign a petition to have the justices court held on his property. Apparently, the sheriff would receive a sizable remuneration from the court for the use of his property.

The sheriff sued Morris for criminal libel. The Virginia Supreme Court stated the common law rule of defamation that truth is not a justification in libel suits. However, people do have a right to be informed of the conduct of public officials. The court solved the dilemma of definitions by ruling that when a publication's intent is to show that a person is unfit for public office, then truth can be entered.

It was very important in these early cases that truth not enter the decision process until intent was shown. In a Massachusetts case, William Clapp posted notices claiming that the public auctioneer was a "liar, a scoundrel, a cheat and a swindler."[89] The trial judge refused to allow evidence of truth, and Clapp was found guilty of criminal libel. On appeal, Massachusetts Chief Justice Theophilus Parsons ruled that it must be determined first whether the intent of the defendant was malicious. "In the defense of libel, as an offense against law, it is not considered whether publication be true or false; because a man may maliciously publish the truth against another, with the intent to defame his character, and if the publication be true, the tendency of it to inflame the passions, and to excite revenge, is not diminished, but may sometimes be strengthened."[90]

While truth cannot justify a libel, it may be introduced to prove that the publication was for justifiable purposes. It is not libel, concluded Parsons, if the publication of the truth about fitness, qualifications, and character of an elected official is made with the honest intention of informing the people. However, Parsons's words held little hope for Clapp because the auctioneer was not an elected official, but an appointed one. Clapp's conviction was upheld.

Eighteen years and dozens of libel prosecutions would pass before Massachusetts caught up with Pennsylvania by allowing truth as a defense in libels. The road to change began with a series of cases brought against Joseph T. Buckingham, editor of the Boston *Galaxy*, and ended with *Commonwealth v. Blanding.*

Buckingham's first encounter with libel was a prosecution on behalf of a Methodist minister, Rev. John N. Maffitt, who was making the New England circuit during 1822. There was some doubt as to whether Maffitt was indeed a preacher and Buckingham increased these doubts with a violent attack upon the preacher's morals. The *Galaxy* accused Maffitt of illicit sexual relations with men and women, plagiarizing sermons of English clergy, failing to keep confidences, denying the existence of God and "malicious tattling."[91]

Buckingham claimed that the accusations were "communicated as facts in a letter from Providence [Rhode Island]. The letter was anonymous; but it came under circumstances that admitted of no doubt as to the personal identity of the writer." Nevertheless, Buckingham was indicted in Boston's municipal court before Judge Josiah Quincy. Witnesses to support the accusations were allowed and two days later the trial ended in a verdict of not guilty.

Quincy's decision, which went counter to *Clapp*, noted that the basic dilemma in solving the libel riddle was coming to terms with the repugnancy between the liberty of the press and the common law doctrine that truth shall not be given as justification. If there is a repugnancy between these two, which is paramount—"Which shall be limited, the nature of the liberty by the principles of the doctrine, or the principles of the doctrine by the nature of the liberty?"[92]

He answered by selecting the latter and ruled that the right of giving the truth was inseparable from the motive or intent. Quoting Andrew Hamilton's defense of Zenger, Quincy concluded that truth with good motives and for justifiable ends was a defense in all cases of libel. "It is better for the public to take the risk of the evils, and for individuals to suffer the inconvenience resulting from a press without other restraints... than for the state to incur the dangers resulting from any uncertainty in the tenure of liberty."

Because Quincy's reasoning and holding were contrary to that of the common law and of Judge Parsons decision in *Clapp*, it was debated in pamphlets and letters by a number of lawyers in Boston.[93] Some saw danger in allowing the liberty of the press to spill over into licentiousness; others praised the decision as forward looking and as the proper balance between common law and constitutionally guaranteed liberties.

Within a year, the *Galaxy's* editor was again summoned to answer an indictment based on complaints of the Russian Consul, whom Buckingham referred to as "an autocrat of the fashionable world of Boston."[94] The newspaper published a lampoon on the Russian and in another article accused the "rugged Russian Bear" of being involved in a fight at a ball.

This time around, Josiah Quincy was one of Buckingham's lawyers and Judge Peter O. Thacher sat on the bench. Thacher ignored Quincy's earlier decision and returned to the *Clapp* ruling that required motive and intent to be shown before truth could be considered. Because articles appearing over a period of several years were the basis of the complaint, motive was found to be bad. Buckingham, who was not the writer of the articles, was found guilty on one of three counts and fined $100. On appeal to the Massachusetts Supreme Court, the indictment was withdrawn.

Meanwhile, one of the counts that had been thrown out earlier in municipal court was resurrected in a new indictment and the editor was found guilty and sentenced to 30 days in jail, which was affirmed on appeal. In his recollections, Buckingham admits that while the suits were vexatious and time-consuming, "I am not aware that they produced any change in my resolution to publish whatever I thought proper for publication, or in my determination to sustain the freedom and independence of the press at any hazard."[95]

Quincy's decision in the Maffit case stirred the legal community to consider changes in libel law, but the course toward change was slow. The case that was truly a turning point in Massachusetts libel law was *Commonwealth v. Blanding*. In that case the Providence, Rhode Island, *Gazette* published a letter that accused an innkeeper in Rehobath, Massachusetts, of being responsible for the death of a man who died of intoxication. The editor asked that the inkeeper's licence be revoked and that the public refrain from doing business with him.[96] The innkeeper brought a criminal complaint against the editor. The judge refused to allow the defendant to introduce evidence from the coroner's inquest, stating that truth was not a defense in the case.

On appeal, Chief Justice Isaac Parker agreed with the lower court. Parker first determined that this was not the kind of case where truth was admissible. The public interest requires that the press "not arraign their neighbors, exposing them to partial trials in forms not warranted by the constitution or laws." The occasion was not the proper one for a newspaper denunciation because there was no urgent necessity to inform the public, continued Parker. The writer should have taken his complaint to the police, rather than taking the law into his own hands.[97] The existing common law was sufficient to handle this situation, said Parker, and any relaxation of the law would involve the "community, families, individuals in those contentious and acrimonious conflicts which will render the social state little, if at all, better than the savage."

Faced with the obvious contradictions among Parsons, Quincy, and Parker, the Massachusetts Legislature was forced to come up with a reconciliation. With the prodding of Senator S. L. Knapp, one of Buckingham's lawyers, a new libel law was passed that allowed truth to be entered as a justification in all cases of libel.

These new interpretations of libel, which made it almost impossible for public officials to guard their reputations and which forced the affairs of private individuals onto the front pages of newspapers, disturbed former New York Chief Justice James Kent. In 1826, in his celebrated *Commentaries on American Law*, Chancellor Kent examined the various new state laws that allowed truth with good motives as a defense in libel, or that did away with all criminal libels against public officers. He concluded that such laws made it impossible to strike the proper balance between protection of character and protection of a free press. The tendency of such acts, he continued, was to relax too far the vigilance with which the common law guarded personal reputation.[98]

However much it may have disturbed him, the Federalist Kent was witnessing an important change in how people viewed freedom of the press. The new laws and new interpretations recognized that a democratic society functioned at its most efficient when the people are informed about the conduct and character of their public officials. In order for the people to be informed, the press must enjoy the corollary right to publish that information without fear of punishment. The day had long passed when freedom of the press meant only freedom from prior restraints. It now meant that a well-meaning press could publish the truth and be spared from legal prosecutions. It also meant that the gentry would have to find another forum for redressing their reputations.

While these changes manifested themselves in new statutes, in new American interpretations of the common law, or in redefinitions of constitutional rights, their sources can be traced to a better understanding of the political process. With the acceptance of the party system, fewer politicians were determined to burn their opponents on the cross of treason or sedition. Where arrogant politicians such as McKean ignored the intent of the constitution, there were always more sane and sophisticated politicians in the legislature who were willing to make necessary changes.

Notes

1. J. D. Richardson, ed., *Compilation of the Messages and Papers of the Presidents, 1789–1897* 20 vols. (Washington: Government Printing Office, 1907) 1: 322.

2. See, Robert E. Shallhope, "Toward a Republican Synthesis: The Emergence of an Understanding of Republicanism in American Historiography," 29 *William and Mary Quarterly* (3rd ser.) 49–80 (1970).

3. Ebenezer Elmer, *Address to the Citizens of New Jersey* (Elizabethtown, N.J.: 1807).

4. Henry Cabot Lodge, ed. *The Works of Alexander Hamilton* 9 vols. (New York: G.P. Putnam's Son, 1904) 1: 459.

5. "Massachusettensis" [David Leonard], *The Origins of the American Contest with Great Britain* (New York: 1775).

6. Jonathan Boucher, "On Civil Liberty, Passive Obedience and Nonresistance," in *A View of the Causes and Consequences of the American Revolution* (New York: Russell & Russell, 1967), pp. 552-53.

7. Alexander Biddle, ed. *Old Family Letters* (Philadelphia: 1892), pp. 37-38.

8. Adams to F. A. Van der Kemp, March 27, 1790. Library of Congress, The Adams Papers, microfilm, letterbooks.

9. Robert H. Wiebe, *The Opening of American Society* (New York: Alfred A. Knopf, 1984).

10. Robert H. Wiebe, *The Segmented Society* (New York: Oxford University Press, 1975), p. 16.

11. For excellent studies of the Alien and Sedition Laws: Leonard Levy, ed., *Freedom of the Press from Zenger to Jefferson: Early American Libertarian Theories* (Indianapolis: Bobbs-Merrill Co., 1966); John C. Miller, *Crisis in Freedom: The Alien and Sedition Acts* (Boston: Little, Brown and Co., 1952); and James Morton Smith, *Freedom's Fetters: The Alien and Sedition Laws and American Civil Liberties* (Ithaca: Cornell University Press, 1966).

12. Levy, *From Zenger to Jefferson*, pp. lxx-lxxix.

13. *The Virginia Report of 1799-1800, Touching the Alien and Sedition Laws, Together with the Virginia Resolutions of Dec. 21, 1798, the Debates and Proceedings thereon in the House of Delegates of Virginia, and Several other Documents* (Richmond: J. W. Randolph, 1850).

14. Levy, *From Zenger to Jefferson*, pp. lxxvii. See also, Norman L. Rosenberg, *Protecting the Best Men: An Interpretive History of the Law of Libel* (Chapel Hill: University of North Carolina Press, 1986).

15. *Annals of Congress*, 6th Cong., 2nd sess., pp. 975, 1038, 1047-50 (1801).

16. Noble E. Cunningham, Jr., ed., *Circular Letters of Congressmen to their Constituents 1789-1829* 3 vols.(Chapel Hill: University of North Carolina for the Institute of Early American History and Culture, Williamsburg, Va., 1978) 1: 243.

17. Ibid., p. 223, fn. 8.

18. Ibid., p. 238.

19. Ibid., p. 230.

20. John Thomson, *An Enquiry Concerning the Liberty, and Licentiousness of the Press, and the Uncontroulable Nature of the Human Mind* (New York: Johnson & Stryker, 1801), reprinted in part in Levy, *From Zenger to Jefferson*, pp. 284-317.

21. Leonard Levy, *Emergence of a Free Press* (New York: Oxford University Press, 1985), pp. 336-37. Matthew Tindal had made a similar argument in 1704 regarding parliamentary privilege: Matthew Tindal, *Reasons Against Restraining the Press* (London, 1704).

22. Thomas Cooper, *Treatise on the Law of Libel and the Liberty of the Press; Showing the Origin, Use, and Abuse of the Law of Libel* (New York: G. F. Hopkins and Son, 1830).

23. George Hay, *An Essay on the Liberty of the Press* (Richmond: Samuel Pleasants Jr., 1803; reprint ed., New York: De Capo Press,1970).

24. Steven Hochman, "On the Liberty of the Press in Virginia, From Essay to Bludgeon, 1798-1803," 84 *The Virginia Magazine of History and Biography* 431-445 (October 1970).

25. *Ibid.*

26. Hay, *An Essay on Liberty*, p. 28.

27. St. George Tucker, *Blackstone's Commentaries: With Notes of Reference, to the Constitution and Laws of the Federal Government of the United States and of the Commonwealth of Virginia* 5 vols. (Philadelphia: 1803) 1: pt. II, n. G, "Of the Right of Conscience, and the Freedom of Speech and of the Press."

28. John Taylor, *An Inquiry into the Principles and Policy of the Government of the United States,* Loren Baritz, ed., (New York: The Bobbs-Merrill Co., Inc., 1969); John Adams, *A Defence of the Constitutions of Government of the United States of America,* 3rd ed., 3 vols. (Philadelphia: Budd & Bartram, 1797).

29. [James Sullivan], *A Dissertation Upon the Constitutional Freedom of the Press in the United States of America by an Impartial Citizen* (Boston: Joseph Nancrede, 1801), pp. 31, 33.

30. 2 Dall. 374 (U.S. 1798).

31. Sullivan, *A Dissertation,* p. 41

32. 7 Cranch 32, 11 U.S. 31 (1812).

33. Sullivan, *A Dissertation,* pp. 10, 32.

34. Thomas Paine, *The Political Writings of Thomas Paine* 2 vols. (Boston: J. P. Mendum, 1870) 2: 463–65.

35. Jonathan Elliot, ed., *The Debates in the Several State Conventions ... and Other Illustrations of the Constitution* 5 vols. (New York: Burt Franklin, 1966) 4: 540–541.

36. Lester J. Cappon, *The Adams-Jefferson Letters* (Chapel Hill: University of North Carolina for the Institute for Early American History and Culture at Williamsburg, 1959), p. 279. For contrasting views of Jefferson's democratic ideas, see Leonard W. Levy, *Jefferson and Civil Liberties: The Darker Side* (Cambridge: Harvard University Press, 1963) and Frank L. Mott, *Jefferson and the Press* (Baton Rouge: Louisiana State University Press, 1943).

37. Cappon, *The Adams-Jefferson Letters* p. 279.

38. Ibid., p. 276.

39. Ibid., p. 279.

40. Ibid.

41. Philadelphia *General Advertiser and Aurora,* February 19, 1800.

42. *Annals of Congress,* 10th Cong., 1st sess., pp. 111-115 (1800).

43. Ibid., pp. 123-124, 184.

44. Paul Leicester Ford, ed., *The Works of Thomas Jefferson* 12 vols. (New York: G.P. Putnam's Sons, 1905) 9: 257, fn. 1.

45. Ibid. , p. 256.

46. Ibid., p. 259, fn. 1.

47. Ibid., 8: 218–219.

48. Ibid., p. 346.

49. See, H. Trevor Colbourn, *The Lamp of Experience* (Chapel Hill: University of North Carolina for the Institute of Early American History and Culture at Williamsburg, 1965) for a good study of legal education in eighteenth and nineteenth-century America.

50. Taylor, *An Inquiry,* pp. 418-19.

51. Commonwealth v. Clapp, 4 Mass 163, 3 Am. Dec. 212, 213 (1808).

52. See, Paul A. Gilje, "The Baltimore Riots of 1812 and the Breakdown of the Anglo-American Mob Tradition," 13 *Journal of Social History* 547–64 (Spring 1980); and Hugh Davis Graham and Ted R. Gurr, eds., *Violence in America:*

Historical and Comparative Perspectives (New York: The New American Library, 1969).

53. 3 Am. Dec. at 213.

54. Cooper, *Treatise*, pp. 52-53.

55. 16 Am. St. Tr. 40; 3 Johnson's Cases 337 (N.Y. 1804).

56. 16 Am. St. Tr. at 44.

57. 3 Johnson's Cases at 394.

58. 16 Am. St. Tr. at 52.

59. Ibid. at 56.

60. Ibid. at 63.

61. Ibid. at 43.

62. 3 Johnson's Cases at 395.

63. Ibid. at 393.

64. Ibid. at 410–411.

65. Sullivan, *A Dissertation*, p. 23.

66. Ibid., p. 21.

67. Ibid., pp. 29-30.

68. Ibid., p. 23.

69. Ford, *The Works of Thomas Jefferson*, 8: 218–219.

70. *Aurora*, April 23, 1803.

71. Respublica v. Dennie, 2 Am. Dec. 402, 407 (1803).

72. Ibid. at 406–407.

73. A full explanation of the affair can be found in G. S. Rowe, *Thomas McKean: The Shaping of an American Republicanism* (Boulder: Colorado Associated University Press, 1978), pp. 352-355.

74. Ibid., p. 355.

75. *Pennsylvania Archives*, series 4, 4: 579–585.

76. *Journal of the House of Representatives of the Commonwealth of Pennsylvania*, 1806–1807, pp. 35, 64–68, 175–178, 181–186.

77. Law quoted in Commonwealth v. Duane, 1 Binney 601, 2 Am. Dec. 497, 498 (Pa. 1809). The new Pennsylvania law was enacted for a three-year trial period and was not renewed in 1812 when moderates dominated the state legislature.

78. Ibid. at 499.

79. "From the Citizens of Hartford," in Worthington C. Ford, ed., *Thomas Jefferson. Correspondence Printed from the Originals in the Collections of William K. Bixby* (Boston, 1916), p. 137; Andrew A. Lipscomb and Albert E. Bergh, eds., *The Writings of Thomas Jefferson* 20 vols. (Washington, D.C.: Thomas Jefferson Memorial Assoc., 1905) 12: 289; see also, *National Intelligencer*, July 21, 1809 (recollection of Postmaster General Gideon Granger who acted as Jefferson's liaison with Connecticut Republicans).

80. *Annals of Congress*, 9th Cong., 2nd sess., p. 247 (1807).

81. Hartford *American Mercury*, May 1, 1806.

82. Lipscomb, *The Writings of Thomas Jefferson*, 12: 288.

83. Hartford *American Mercury*, April 3, 1806.

84. Ford, *The Works of Thomas Jefferson*, 10: 367–68.

85. *Annals of Congress*, 9th Cong., 2nd sess., pp. 247–252 (1807).

86. *Annals of Congress*, 11th Cong., 1st. sess, pp. 75–89 (1809).

87. 7 Cranch 32 (1812).

88. 5 Am. Dec. 515 (Va. 1811).

89. Commonwealth v. Clapp, 4 Mass. 163, 3 Am. Dec. 212 (Mass. 1808).

90. Ibid. at 213.

91. Joseph T. Buckingham, *Personal Memoirs and Recollections of Editorial Life*, 2 vols. (Boston: Ticknor, Reed, and Fields, 1852) 1: 106–107.

92. Quincy's opinion is reproduced in Cooper, *Treatise*, pp. 85–98.

93. See [Edmund Kimball], *Reflections Upon the Law of Libel, In a Letter* (Boston: Wills and Lilly, 1823).

94. Buckingham, *Personal Memoirs*, p. 115.

95. Ibid., p. 121.

96. 3 Pick. 304 (Mass 1825).

97. Ibid. at 320.

98. James Kent, *Commentaries on American Law* 2 vols., rev. ed. (Philadelphia: Blackstone Pub. Co., 1889) 2: 69.

Chapter 2

Testing the Limits of Tolerance: Mobocracy and the War of 1812

Although lawyers continued into the 1830s to battle the inconsistent and often capricious common law of libel, some progress was evident by the time the United States declared war on Britain in 1812. The rigid test of whether tolerance for criticism and opposition was genuine or illusory came during the prewar period, 1807-1812. Would Republicans, in the face of bitter opposition to their policies, find justification for a new federal sedition law? Would state libel prosecutions mount during this stressful time? Would other methods of censorship manifest themselves?

The War of 1812 has often been called one of America's most unpopular wars because of the questionable motives. for entering into it. This unpopularity was reflected in Congress's vote to declare war on June 18, 1812. The declaration passed in the House by a vote of 79 to 49, and in the Senate by 19 to 13. The vote was split down party lines with the Republicans favoring the declaration and the Federalists believing it was a folly perpetrated by "war hawks."

Nevertheless the war with Great Britain was seen by Republicans as the only salvation for the nation, the party, and republicanism. Without war the country would continue to cower to the belligerence and bullying of the British, the Republican party would be disgraced, and the nation's leadership would once again fall into the hands of Federalists.

To the Federalists, the "War for Free Trade and Sailors' Rights" was an immoral war perpetrated by imperialist Republicans to gain possession of Canada and Western territories. It was also seen as a war against British liberty and the land of America's ancestors. Federalist newspapers and orators spread the word that the war was ruining New England, that Republicans supported the voracious Napoleon in his European conquests, and that the government had no interest in protecting Eastern seaports from the ravages of the British navy.

Of course, the Federalists also saw political opportunities in the Republican sword rattling. Believing that the United States could not win a war against Great Britain, some Federalists recommended that Britain stick hard and fast to its shipping embargoes and restrictions. The administration would either give into the restrictions or lose the war quickly. Either outcome would place the Federalists back in Washington, D.C.

While the war might be considered as much a party war as it was a military effort, the circumstances which led to its declaration were considered real threats to the infant nation. The economy of the country, the sovereignty of American shipping interests, and the world's opinion of the "city upon a hill" were all at stake.

When the Peace of Amiens between France and Great Britain was broken in May 1803, American shipping found itself in the middle of a European war.[1] American ships (850 between 1807 and 1812) were seized, sailors impressed into the British navy, blockades were imposed around European ports, and American commerce was delayed, rerouted, taxed and restricted by both British and French. President Jefferson responded with protests and appeals to the British and the French, all of which fell on deaf ears. A selective embargo on British goods was imposed, but that, too, was an impotent gesture.

In 1807, the Republican-dominated Congress voted for the Embargo Act which prohibited American trade with Britain and France and halted all sailings. Federalists launched a bitter campaign against the Embargo Act and actually won additional seats in the 1808 election because of their active hostility. The Federalist party attracted merchants, exporters, shipping firms, professionals, and large landowners. These groups were the most susceptible economically to the embargo.

Representing the extremist Federalists was Alexander Contee Hanson, editor of the *Federal Republican* in Baltimore. Hanson, reared in a strong Federalist tradition, delighted in heckling and snapping at Republicans, particularly Jefferson and Madison. His associate in the publishing venture was Jacob Wagner, who had served in the State Department during Jefferson's administration. Wagner provided Hanson enough inside information to make the newspaper a thorn in the vulnerable flesh of Republicans.[2] Yet, Hanson did not fare as well as other Federalist editors because his newspaper was printed in the strong Southern Republican state of Maryland. So, when Hanson continued to oppose Republican policies, the Republicans found a away to prick back. On November 7, 1808, Governor Robert Wright, at the request of President Jefferson, called for Maryland's men to volunteer in the state militia. However, many who had served in the volunteer militia from April 1806 until April 1808, failed to re-volunteer since there was no war, no enemy on American soil, and no prospect of foreign invasion.

When the governor's call went out, Hanson wrote an editorial in the *Federal Republican* blasting the call-up as the first step toward "military despotism." In true Federalist spirit, he charged that the Republican president had only one purpose in raising a standing army—"to awe the people into submission, a passive obedience to tyrannical and oppressive embargo laws."[3] Hanson counseled the men of Maryland to think carefully before answering the call, saying that this action "humbled [Americans] into a degrading submission to oppression, an abandonment of the rights of freemen, to gratify a visionary Philosopher."

Rather than bring Hanson into a civil court on charges of sedition, particularly at a time when New England Federalists were fanning the embers of secession, the Republican governor ordered Lieutenant Hanson, a commissioned officer in the 39th Regiment of the state militia, suspended from his rank for one month, imprisoned, and court martialed. Hanson was charged with "offenses pronounced mutinous and punishable by death, and highly reproachful to the President" and the governor. The charges were based partly upon Article 5 of the Rules of War which allowed court martial for use of contemptuous or disrespectful words toward the president, vice president, legislatures, or governors.[4]

The court martial was held on February 24, 1809, at which time Hanson pleaded not guilty to the charges, but guilty of writing the piece. As a qualified lawyer, Hanson presented his own defense, which began with a rebuke against the trial as a "spectacle which ... is equally unprecedented in the history of free government, and alarming to the friends of rational liberty."

Hanson knew the charges were motivated purely by political caprice, and that the governor was taking great license in interpreting military law in order to censure a political opponent. Even the adjutant general in charge of the trial was uncertain whether the court martial was constitutional since Hanson was a volunteer in a state militia that had not been called to active duty.

Hanson argued forcefully that if the Constitution and the Rules or War were interpreted to mean that anyone subject to militia duty was also subject to court martial, then 9 out of 10 men in the state could be court martialed for expressing opinions against the "aspiring and unprincipled demagogue," Jefferson. Article 5 was not meant "to silence political discussion, to overawe the press, and prevent an examination into the measures of government. . . . The bill of rights has been violated ... under the influence of intemperance and misguided zeal, and perhaps of motives still less excuseable."

As for the charge of inciting mutiny, Hanson countered that the November call had been for volunteers, and that it was impossible to incite disaffection in the recruiting process when each man was given a choice of whether or not to volunteer. A volunteer does not surrender his liberties when he chooses to fight for liberty, said Hanson. To do so makes the soldier merely a "slave in livery." The military court found Hanson innocent of all charges. But under instruction of Governor Wright, Hanson remained in jail several days after being acquitted.

Hanson and other Federalist editors in the Northeast were so successful in promoting their anti-embargo views that the Embargo Act was not renewed in 1809. Britain continued to wage an undeclared war on America under the guise of protecting its own sovereignty. In November 1811, after all negotiations had failed, James Madison called for Congress to put "the United States into an armour and attitude demanded by the crisis, and corresponding with the national spirit and expectations."[5]

As the spirit of war was incited, it became evident to some Republicans that the Federalist's anti-war attitude had to be stilled. Massachusetts' Republican Governor Elbridge Gerry was so concerned by the licentiousness of the press that in February 1812, he presented a special report to the state legislature that had been prepared by the Suffolk County Grand Jury and his attorney general. The report showed that in 1811, 236 libels had been published in Federalist newspapers and seventeen in Republican papers. Yet, out of all those occurrences, the courts had succeeded in getting only two convictions.[6]

Gerry blamed the low rate of conviction on the uncertainties of libel in the state and called on lawmakers to pass legislation that would correct the situation. The house promptly passed an act that allowed truth as a defense only when a libel accused an appointed officer of being unfit for office. However, before the senate passed its own version, Governor Gerry was defeated in the 1812 election by a Federalist. One of Governor Caleb Strong's first acts was to declare that Gerry's investigations into libel were a dangerous usurpation of freedom of the press, of the courts, and of juries.

Although the Federalist press of New England continued publishing anti-war and anti-embargo sentiment, no sedition prosecutions resulted. By 1812, almost every New England state had been turned over to Federalists. With Federalist governors and Federalist judges in office, Federalist newspapers were free to continue their opposition. Also, few Republicans were willing to prosecute those who criticized the government's wartime policies.

Barely ten years earlier, the threat of war and the offenses of an opposition political faction had resulted in a sedition law. Yet, in 1812, when the country did go to war, and when the dominant political party was opposed by a strong minority party, lawmakers refused to counter opposition with legislation. There is little doubt that the hard lessons had been learned from the Alien and Sedition Acts.

War was declared in June 1812; the first battle was fought by General William Hull in July; and the first surrender occurred in August when Hull was outnumbered by British and Indians at Detroit. Federalists had ridiculed the war effort and now that their predictions of an early loss seemed to be coming true, they sharpened their attacks on Madison. Several New England states refused to call up a militia, merchants refused to outfit privateers, and the monied population in general was slow to buy war bonds.

Editor Hanson also refused to give up his pen. In January 1812 he wrote:

> As to powder and bullets and swords
> For use they were never intended,
> They're a parcel of high sounding words
> But never to *action* extended.[7]

Yet, his words became more bitter as war neared, and the Republican majority in Baltimore talked among themselves of silencing the traitorous paper. But Hanson refused to be silent. Two days after the declaration of war, he wrote that the war was "unnecessary, inexpedient and entered into from partial personal motives." The editor vowed that he would use all legal means to oppose the war. As to threats against his own newspapers and other Federalist organs, Hanson declared that if authorities would not protect freedom of the press, then Federalists would find their own means of protecting their rights and property.[8]

Two nights later, a group of thirty men gathered in front of the printing office of the *Federal Republican* and began demolishing the building and destroying the press. Although the result was destruction, the mob was orderly and no one was hurt.[9] Officials were reluctant to interfere. Baltimore Mayor Edward Johnson, who appeared at the scene to try to calm the mob, was told by one participant, "The laws of the land must sleep, and the laws of nature and reason must prevail."[10] After pulling down the building, board by board, the mob searched Wagner's house and that of his father-in-law. For the next three weeks mobs scoured Baltimore, destroying buildings and ships, threatening Federalist sympathizers, pulling down houses belonging to blacks, threatening churches, and striking out at any vulnerable target.

After the destruction of the *Federal Republican's* office, Hanson continued to publish in Georgetown. But, in late July, he decided to begin redistribution in Baltimore. Fearing another mob attack, Hanson recruited thirty-five Federalist friends to help defend the newspaper and office. On July 27, the paper was distributed from a Baltimore address with an editorial that blasted the lawlessness that had overtaken the city in the past month and blamed the mobs on Republican influence. The mob action against his own shop was "a daring and desperate attempt to intimidate and overawe the minority, to destroy the freedom of speech and of press."[11]

That evening a mob attacked the office, which was occupied by the Federalist defenders. Men and boys threw rocks at the office, broke windows and shutters, shouted taunts. Hoping to disperse the crowd, General Harry "Lighthorse" Lee instructed his fellow Federalist defenders to shoot a blank volley into the crowd.

Leading the mob was a local apothecary, Dr. Thadeus Gale who stormed the front door. The Federalists responded by firing a live volley, killing Gale and wounding several others. The mob scattered, armed itself, and regrouped in front of the office, this time with a cannon. The commander of the city militia had finally gathered his troops and placed them between the mob and the office with orders to prevent anyone from entering or leaving.

By 6 A.M. the crowd had swelled to 1,500 and the militia commander and the mayor had entreated the Federalists to surrender themselves to authorities. Twenty-three defenders were led under guard to the jail house while the mob heaped insults and rocks on them. During the day, the mob returned to the newspaper office, destroyed the building, and carted off bricks and lumber. Crowds milled around the jailhouse, assuring themselves that the Federalists remained under lock and key. The militia, which had dwindled to forty, was dismissed.

On the second evening, hundreds of men stormed the jail house. While most of the prisoners escaped, several were severely beaten, stuck with penknives, burned with candle grease, tarred and feathered, and had their clothes torn off. One man was killed, and eleven others seriously injured. Both Hanson and General Lee were seriously wounded.[12]

Mob violence was no stranger to Federalist newspapers during the early period of the war. The *American Patriot* of Savannah, Georgia, was forced to close when a mob attacked the editor. A mob assaulted the editor of the *Norristown Herald*, Pennsylvania, and he was forced to quit the business. In 1813, the office of the Elizabethtown, New Jersey, *Essex Patriot* was burned to the ground.[13]

While most Republican newspapers condemned the riots, some praised the action of such mobs or blamed the violence on the Federalist newspapers. Mob action was condoned or at least only mildly condemned because of the strong tradition of mob activity that existed in England and the United States. Law by mob was not new; it had been used effectively before and during the American Revolution to oppose British tyranny. As long as the mob did not appear to threaten life or do undue damage to property, rioting had always been tolerated as a legitimate tool for correcting obvious injustices that official channels were unable to resolve.[14]

Even Jefferson used the rhetoric of mob action, although only half seriously, when he suggested that a bit of mayhem might be the best solution for dealing with opponents of the war. In a letter to President Madison in June, he wrote that the Federalists "are poor devils here, not worthy of notice—barrel of tar to each state South of the Potomac will keep all in order.... To the North...you may there have to apply the rougher drastics of...hemp and confiscation."[15]

Yet, the Baltimore riots were unlike anything yet experienced in the country. As one scholar has noted, the shift from an organized destruction of the newspaper office in June to the massacre at the jail in July represented a "disintegration of the traditional Anglo-American mob behavior and the emergence of a new form of rioting representative of ... a confused democratic society."[16] One person who recognized this confusion was William Ellery Channing, Unitarian minister and prominent religious and political leader in Boston. Following the riots in Baltimore, he preached a sermon entitled "Duties of the Citizen in Times of Trial or Danger," which exhorted tolerance for unpopular views.[17]

Channing reminded his listeners that the government gave to the people two great freedoms—that of voting and that of freely discussing the conduct of government. "Resign either of these, and no way of escape from oppression will be left you but civil commotion.... Freedom of opinion, of speech, and of the press, is our most valuable privilege, the very soul of republican institutions, the safeguard of all other rights."

About the riots, he said, "We have seen a savage populace excited and let loose on men whose crime consisted in bearing testimony against the present war; and let loose not merely to waste their property, but to tear them from the refuge which the magistrates had afforded, and to shed their blood."

Channing warned that during war when public opinion is at its most vulnerable, "we are not to relinquish free discussion, but every man should feel the duty of speaking and writing with deliberation." Yet, he cautioned against agitating people to hatred or writing anything that might "inflame the bad passions. ... It is the time to be firm without passion. No menace should be employed to provoke opponents, no defiance hurled."

Channing was one of the few who viewed the riots as an attack on the First Amendment. Many newspapers themselves were shortsighted in this respect. While most newspapers, Republican and Federalist, condemned the violence, a few condoned it or excused it by placing blame on the *Federal Republican* and its editors. The Baltimore *Whig* and the Washington *National Intelligencer* both excused the mob, claiming that it was retaliating against the enemies of civil liberties and seeking revenge for the death of a comrade.[18]

However, the *Intelligencer* said it would never condone violence, especially when directed against the press. Freedom of the press "is one of the unalienable rights which, as republicans, we will always support, and as conductors of a press ... will not cease to defend to the last extremity."[19] "Cato," in the *Pennsylvania Gazette,* wrote that the riots were the "most disgraceful, alarming and dangerous ... of any event since the adoption of the constitution."[20]

While the lawmakers and courts had learned at the turn of the century to tolerate criticism, the people had not. Where the courts had once stepped in to prosecute "treasonous and monarchist" publications, the people now took the law into their own hands to mete out the proper justice. Public opinion became the censor, and freedom of press and expression disappeared temporarily because the "laws of the land must sleep."

The Federalists and their presses refused to let the Baltimore Riots calm their denunciations of the war, and as the war continued they called for more drastic political action. The most extreme of the party called for secession; and moderate Federalists wanted federal aid to raise their own army to defend the coastline. New England Federalists met in convention at Hartford, Connecticut to talk about their common problems, but their activities became moot when word of the Treaty of Ghent and the victory at New Orleans reached the Eastern Seaboard. Although both Americans and British claimed the victory, it was a pointless war that gained neither side territory and never settled the question of neutral rights on the seas and impressment of soldiers—reasons for war in the first place.

JACKSON AND MILITARY CENSORSHIP

The public learned of the exploits of General Andrew Jackson, Commodore Oliver Hazard Perry, and Captain Stephen Decatur; about the victories of *The Wasp* and *The Hornet*; and of the Battles of Lake Erie, Ft. McHenry and New Orleans from their local newspapers. Most of the information came by way of dispatches from the front, letters from the War Department, and letters from correspondents.

Newspapers had no system of war correspondents, as would develop during the Civil War. Hence, the military found no need to institute censorship systems within its camps although commanders ruled their military zones with the iron fists of ancient military tradition. Occasionally, a "foreigner" would be arrested for "seditious" speech, but the punishment usually was banishment from the camp. Newspapers published near military camps published accounts of battles almost as if they were social affairs—with much description, but little detail.

Hence what the public read of the war was mostly positive and congratulatory—the type of reportage that produced a new generation of heroes for Americans. Greatest among these new celebrities was General Andrew Jackson, hero of the Battle of New Orleans, who eventually rode his wave of public adulation all the way into the White House. As one of America's best military leaders, Jackson carried all the traits of a peculiarly American hero—stubbornness, independence, temper, coarseness, and humanity. Yet, this stuff out of which the Old Hickory myths were hewn was bound to be blemished.

After Jackson's arrival in New Orleans on December 1, 1814, he was briefed on the political climate of the city by several prominent citizens including Attorney Edward Livingston and Governor W.C.C. Claiborne. He was warned about certain dissidents, particularly those in the "politically rotten" legislature, foreign immigrants (French and Spanish), officers in the state militia, abolitionists, spies, and traitors.[21]

On December 16, after seeing the British fleet anchored at his front door in Lake Borgne, Jackson ordered the troops on alert and placed the city of New Orleans and surrounding areas under martial law. Although manpower was in short supply, the general refused to accept the services of the finest group of fighting men in the area—Jean Lafitte's band of pirates and smugglers who lived in the small island village of Barataria. The Louisiana legislature sent a committee composed of American citizens of French descent, including Representative Pierre Louaillier, to ask U.S. District Judge Dominick Hall to order the release from jail of all prisoners including the Baratarians. Hall agreed to do so only after the legislature had adopted a resolution requesting the release.[22]

Although he eventually allowed the Baratarians to serve next to his men, Jackson felt Hall's action was an affront to his own authority as commander of the military district now under martial law. Adding to this insult was Hall's retreat from New Orleans after Jackson had released him from the curfew provision of the General Order.[23] This encounter with Hall and Louaillier, whom he "suspected of communication with the enemy and hatching treason against the country," stuck fast to Jackson's memory and he would reap his revenge against both three months later.

The Battle of New Orleans is hailed as one of America's greatest victories. Although British outnumbered American troops by two to one, Jackson soundly thrashed General Peckham's army, killing 1486. American losses were thirteen killed and fifty-eight wounded. The irony history books remember is that the battle was fought three weeks after the Treaty of Ghent was signed on Christmas Eve 1814.

However, Jackson did not learn of the treaty until February 13, 1815, at which time he received a dispatch from British Admiral Cochran advising him that while a treaty had been signed, "hostilities are only to cease on its ratification by the President and Prince Regent."[24] Word of peace soon spread throughout New Orleans, and the citizens and soldiers alike looked forward to a lifting of martial law.

On February 21, the *Louisiana Gazette* printed a dispatch announcing that Jackson had received word of the peace treaty and that the war was over. Jackson lost no time in instructing editor Godwin B. Cotten that the war had not ended, and that the editor must run a retraction:

Henceforward it is expected that no publication of the nature of that herein alluded to and censured will appear in any paper of this City unless the editor shall have previously ascertained its correctness, and gained permission for its insertion from the proper source.[25]

Angered at this infringement of his rights, Cotten printed the order and retraction but added a personal editorial:

Every man may read for himself, and think for himself— (Thank God our thoughts are as yet unshackled!!), but as we have been officially informed that New Orleans is a camp, our readers may not expect us to take the liberty of expressing our opinion as we might in a free city. We cannot submit to have a censor of the press in our office, and as we are ordered not to publish any remarks without authority, we shall submit to be silent until we can speak with safety—except making our paper a sheet of shreds and patches—a mere advertiser for our mercantile friends.[26]

There was an outcry against Jackson's censorship, particularly since the war was over and martial law would soon be lifted. But, French soldiers found a loophole in military regulations that allowed them to leave the army if they could prove French citizenship. Jackson grudgingly signed their discharges, but countered with another order, banishing all French soldiers from the city.

The removal of French soldiers plus the numerous arrests of citizens under martial law produced a groundswell of criticism from many parts of the city. On March 3, an annonymous letter was published in the French newspaper, *La Courriere de la Louisiane*, which castigated Jackson for his unconstitutional acts as military commandant. The letter read: "When everyone laments such an abuse of authority the press ought to denounce it to the people." The writer said that it was time "the laws should resume their empire, that the citizens of this State should return to the full enjoyment of their rights" and advised all those affected by the general order to disobey it.[27]

Believing the letter to be a direct affront to his authority and evidence of treason, Jackson ordered the editor of the *Courriere* to reveal the name of the letter writer. The author turned out to be State Representative Louis Louallier from Opelousas County, who had once before questioned Jackson's authority.[28]

Louaillier was arrested on March 5, outside of a coffee house, for "exciting mutiny and disaffection."[29] U.S. District Judge Dominick Hall, who had sat on the federal court since 1804 and had a reputation for fairness and informality, immediately signed a writ of *habeas corpus* on the back of the petition and ordered the marshall to serve it on General Jackson the next day. There is some confusion in the testimony about the date that appeared to have been altered on the document. The date may have been changed because of the late hour it was issued and the unwillingness of the marshall to serve it the next day, a Sunday. Or, as Jackson later charged, the change may have been made to make it appear that Hall's arrest occurred before any attempt to exercise his judicial authority in the camp. It is also probable that a mistake was made by the judge, who was noted more for his attention to the bottle than to legal details. Nevertheless the alteration gave lawyer and former judge Jackson a good excuse not to honor what he considered a forged and invalid writ.[30]

Once again Judge Dominick Hall had attempted to usurp Jackson's authority, and this time he would pay. Jackson ordered Colonel Arbuckle to take sixty armed men to arrest Hall on charges of "a[i]ding abetting and exciting mutiny within my camp.... You will [be] vigilent. The agents of our enemy are more numerous than was expected."[31] Jackson was convinced that Hall had been thrown into the arms of "the treacherous and disaffected, and they wielded him as a machine to...disgrace the general, and open a way to the enemy to suddenly return...and make easy conquest of the city."[32]

Contemporary reports stated that a Judge Lewis did attempt to interfere in both the Hall and Louaillier cases, but was arrested along with U.S. District Attorney John Dick.[33] However, twenty-eight years later Jackson denied that he ordered these men arrested because both were serving in the army at the time.[34]

Meanwhile, the case against Louaillier had begun. Charges of mutiny, excitement to mutiny, spying, illegal and improper conduct, disobedience of orders, writing a wilful and corrupt libel, unsoldierly conduct, and conduct in violation of General Orders were brought against the legislator, and Jackson was certain of his authority in bringing the charges.[35] According to his interpretation of martial law, a military court had every authority to punish anyone within the camp for threatening the peace. However, General E. P. Gaines was not as positive about the extent of martial law. He wrote Jackson, in response to inquiries on the question, that the power to try and punish extends only to those citizens accused of treason. Gaines continued:

The seditious citizen is supposed to be within our camp, where he can be confined, or from whence he may be sent to the civil authorities in the interior of the state, where he may be tried and punished. It will but seldom happen that the writing or sedition of a citizen, not in service, or having little opportunity for mixing with the troops, can amount to an offence so onerous as that of "relieving the enemy or corresonding with him."[36]

At his trial, Louaillier argued that his prosecution was illegal because the writ had not been obeyed, because as a member of the state legislature he was not subject to military law, and because he had a right to a trial by a jury. The court refused to accept these exceptions and Louaillier and his lawyer remained silent during the remainder of the trial.[37] General Gaines ruled that the court lacked jurisdiction in six of the charges and acquitted Louaillier of the seventh charge of treason. Jackson, believing that the Frenchman was involved in a conspiracy with other New Orleans Creoles, disregarded the ruling of the military court and kept Louaillier in jail until martial law was lifted.[38]

Several days after the court's decision in Louaillier's case, Jackson ordered Hall to be taken "up the coast beyond the lines" and set free with instructions not to return until martial law had been lifted.[39] On Monday, March 13,

Jackson was notified that the Treaty of Ghent had been ratified. He immediately revoked martial law and discharged his troops. Louaillier was released and Judge Hall returned to the city ready to begin legal action against the general.

On March 21, U. S. Attorney John Dick ordered Jackson to show cause why an attachment should not be awarded against him "for contempt of court, in having disrespectfully wrested from the clerk an original order of the honorable judge...and for detaining Louaillier, also for disregarding the said writ of Habeas Corpus when issued and served, in having imprisoned the judge and for other contempts."[40]

Jackson, with the help of fellow attorneys Livingston and Gaines, prepared a lengthy answer to be read in court on March 24. Although Jackson appeared in court with his response, he left the proceedings, leaving the paper with his aide-de-camp to read. For some reason that is unexplained in the transcript, the aide was not allowed to read the paper although the contents came within the rules laid down for its admission. On the second day of hearings, Judge Hall ruled that no cause had been shown and issued the attachment.[41]

On March 31, Jackson appeared in court to hear his sentence. Angry that he had not been allowed to present his defense and show cause, he refused to answer a sheaf of interrogatories prepared by the District Attorney. Since the court "thought proper to refuse me this constitutional right...I appear before your honor to receive the sentence of the Court."[42]

Acknowledging that passing sentence in this case was an "unpleasant affair," Hall ruled that "the only question was whether the Law should be bent to the General, or the General to the Law." He fined Jackson $1,000 for contempt of court. The judge denied a request to have the answer to the show cause order entered into the record. He also ordered all records of the inquiry expunged from the record.[43]

The thirty-page answer, preserved in the Library of Congress, gives a detailed explanation for the General's refusal to honor the writ. In justifying his General Order of December 15, 1814, Jackson wrote that "personal liberty cannot exert at a time when every man is required to become a soldier."[44]

However, his explanation for arresting Louaillier rings of paranoia, particularly since the lawmaker had been a supporter of the war and had often praised Jackson's military prowess.[45] Jackson supported the arrest by claiming that "unlimited liberty of speech is incompatible with the conduct[?] of a camp and that of the press is more dangerous when it is made the vehicle of conveying intelligence to the enemy or exciting to mutiny."

Although contemporary versions of Jackson's day in court praise his humility and gentlemanly manner, the "tyrannical course" of Judge Hall continued to gnaw at him. President Madison, who had received a number of complaints about Jackson's use of martial law, requested a complete explanation of why "judicial power of the United States has been resisted, the liberty of the press has been suspended, and the Consul and subjects of a friendly Government have been exposed to great inconvenience."[46] Jackson, certain that the president's interest stemmed from malcontents and political enemies, answered the request by sending a copy of his answer to the show cause order. In the fall of 1815, Jackson urged the impeachment of Judge Hall for forgery and conspiracy. With records in hand, Jackson met with the Secretary of War, who said there was no reason to convene impeachment proceedings against the judge. Jackson then approached President Madison, who told him that any decision to impeach the judge would be an executive decision.

When the House Democratic majority leader heard about Jackson's effort to begin proceedings, he asked for the records in the case. Jackson agreed to hand over the documents if a House resolution was passed agreeing to investigate the charges. The representative, however, was made ambassador to Spain and was never heard from again on the matter.[47]

Defeated in his attempts to impeach Judge Hall, Jackson returned to Tennessee to pursue his political career. The affair was continually raised by political opponents and remained a continuous thorn in Jackson's political side for the next thirty years of public service. His actions against Louaillier and Hall surfaced during the campaign of 1827 when Jackson ran against John Quincy Adams, but he was riding such a high tide of popularity that the various charges brought against him failed to make much of a dent in his campaign.

It was not until three years before his death that the matter, like the proverbial dirty laundry, was aired again. In the spring of 1842, a bill was introduced in Congress by Missouri Senator Lewis F. Linn, to expunge Jackson's contempt sentence from judicial records and reimburse Jackson the "unrighteous fine" plus interest. The Linn Bill had a rough passage through Congress. When first introduced, Federalist and Republican senators attached an amendment which would have exonerated the now-deceased Judge Hall. Democrats were forced to vote against the bill with the attachment because it was tantamount to a confession of guilt by Jackson.[48]

The introduction of the bill brought out many of Jackson's old political enemies and prompted Jackson to write letters and articles defending his actions in New Orleans. He wrote friends in New Orleans to search the court records, secure affidavits from friendly Democrats, and send him a copy of a book written in 1827 that was being used to sully his character.[49] He wrote friends such as Francis Blair, Amos Kendall, Sam Houston, and Thomas Hart Benton about the Louaillier-Hall affair, seeking consolation and understanding in the midst of renewed criticism of his heavy-handed rule in New Orleans.

A second bill was introduced in the 1843 session of Congress, but it failed to pass the House of Representatives.[50] Finally, on a third attempt in February 1844, both houses voted to refund the fine and expunge the record.[51] The seventy-seven-year-old, debt-ravaged ex-President used the $2,732.90 to pay off loans.

The censorship of newspapers, the arrest of editors and writers, and the refusal by military officers to honor writs of habeas corpus would be repeated numerous times during the Civil War and the wars of the twentieth century. The basic question—to what degree do constitutionally guaranteed civil liberties yield under martial law?—continues into the present to be a major point of contention between the watchdogs of the press and the military.

NOTES

1. For background on the War of 1812 and its causes: Roger H. Brown, *The Republic in Peril: 1812* (New York: Columbia University Press, 1964); Reginald Horsman, *The Causes of the War of 1812* (Philadelphia: University of Pennsylvania Press, 1962); Bradford Perkins, *Prologue to War: England and the United States 1805–1812* (Berkeley: University of California Press, 1961).

2. "Alexander Contee Hanson," in *Dictionary of American Biography*, Allen Johnson and Dumas Malone, eds., (New York: Charles Scribner's Sons, 1932) 4: 231.

3. "The Trial of Alexander Contee Hanson, esq., on charges...." (Baltimore: J. Robinson, 1809), p. 8.

4. Ibid., pp. 10, 30.

5. Gaillard Hunt, ed., *The Writings of James Madison* 9 vols. (New York: G. P. Putnam's Sons, 1900–1910) 3: 158-165.

6. Clyde A. Duniway, *The Development of Freedom of the Press in Massachusetts* (New York: Burt Franklin, 1969), pp. 153-54.

7. *Federal Republican*, January 21, 1812.

8. Ibid., June 20, 1812.

9. Description of the Baltimore Riot is taken from: Paul A. Gilje, "The Baltimore Riots of 1812 and the Breakdown of the Anglo-American Mob Tradition," 13 *Journal of Social History* 547 (Spring 1980); Donald R. Hickey, "The Darker Side of Democracy: The Baltimore Riots of 1812," 7 *Maryland Historian* 1 (1976); John Lofton, *The Press as Guardian of the First Amendment* (Columbia: University of South Carolina Press, 1980), pp. 51-56; and *Pennsylvania Gazette*, August 19 and 26, September 2, 1812.

10. Hickey, "The Darker Side of Democracy," p. 4.

11. *Federal Republican*, July 27, 1812.

12. See, "An Exact and Authentic Narrative," in *Pennsylvania Gazette*, August 26 and September 2, 1812.

13. Hickey, "The Darker Side of Democracy," p. 14.

14. Gilje, "The Baltimore Riots of 1812," pp. 547-48.

15. Jefferson to Madison, June 29, 1812, in *Papers of James Madison*, Library of Congress, Microfilm.

16. Gilje, "The Baltimore Riots of 1812," p. 557.

17. William E. Channing, *The Works of William Ellery Channing* (1882; reprint ed., New York: Burt Franklin, 1970), pp. 682-83.

18. *National Intelligencer*, August 1, 1812.

19. Lofton, *The Press as Guardian*, pp. 54-55.

20. *Pennsylvania Gazette*, August 5, 1812.

21. Answer to Show Cause, March 28, 1812, *Andrew Jackson Papers*, Library of Congress, microfilm (hereinafter referred to as *Jackson Papers*); "Fine Surposed by Judge Hall," for *The Globe*, February 1843, in John Spencer Bassett, *Correspondence of Andrew Jackson* 6 vols. (Washington: Carnegie Institute, 1926–1933) 6: 194 (hereinafter referred to as *Correspondence*).

22. Resolution of the Louisiana Legislature Concerning the Baratarians, December 14, 1814 in Bassett, *Correspondence*, 2: 114; 6: 189.

23. Bassett, *Correspondence*, 6: 156.

24. Ibid., 2: 163.

25. Bassett, *Correspondence*, 2: 179.

26. Reprinted in A. S. Colyer, *Life and Times of Andrew Jackson* 2 vols. (Alabama: Horseshoe Bend National Military Park, 1967) 1: 351.

27. Tom W. Campbell, *Two Fighters and Two Fines* (Little Rock: Pioneer Pub. Co., 1941), p. 292.

28. A half-dozen versions of the Louallier affair have been published, yet none agree on Jackson's motivations. Early Jackson biographies support his actions, praising his steadfastness in upholding martial law. See, John Spencer Bassett, *The Life of Andrew Jackson* 2 vols. (New York: Doubleday, Page & Co., 1911); James Parton, *Life of Andrew Jackson* 2 vols. (Boston: Houghton, Mifflin & Co., 1887–88); More recent versions chastise Jackson for his heavy-handed control of New Orleans. See, Marquis James, *The Life of Andrew Jackson* (Indianapolis: Bobbs-Merrill, 1938).

29. Bassett, *Correspondence*, 2: 183.

30. Ibid., 2: 156. A copy of the original writ, with the altered date and a note signed by Jackson to the effect that the court clerk had told him the date had been altered, is in the original Jackson papers in the Library of Congress.

31. Deposition of Colonel Arbuckle, *Jackson Papers*; Bassett, *Correspondence*, 2: 183.

32. Bassett, *Correspondence*, 6: 145.

33. New York *Evening Post*, April 11, 1815; Bassett, *Correspondence*, 2: 203.

34. Bassett, *Correspondence*, 6: 166, 195.

35. Louis Louaillier, *The Appeal of L. Louaillier, sen., against the charge of High Treason, and Explaining the Transactions at New Orleans* (New Orleans, 1827).

36. General E. P. Gaines to Jackson, March 6, 1815, in *Jackson Papers*.

37. Louaillier, *The Appeal*, p. 7.

38. Bassett, *The Life of Andrew Jackson*, 1: 226-27.

39. Deposition of Captain Peter Ogden, *Jackson Papers*.

40. Show Cause Order, March 21, 1815, *Jackson Papers*.

41. Opinion in U.S. v. Jackson, March 28, 1815, *Jackson Papers*.

42. U.S. v. Jackson, March 31, 1815, *Jackson Papers*.

43. Ibid.; Bassett, *Correspondence*, 6: 145.

44. Answer to Order to Show Cause, *Jackson Papers*.

45. Louaillier, *The Appeal*, pp. 10-15.

46. Bassett, *Correspondence*, 2: 203-04.

47. Ibid., 6: 158-9.

48. Ibid., 6: 154.

49. Francois Xavier Martin, *The History of Louisiana from the Earliest Period* 2 vols. (New Orleans: Lyman and Beardslee, 1827-29).

50. The Louisiana Legislature passed a resolution April 3, 1843, urging Congress to refund the fine. If they failed to do so, the Louisiana lawmakers would pay the fine, Bassett, *Correspondence*, 6: 216 fn. 2.

51. *Congressional Globe*, 28th Cong., 2nd sess., pp. 280, 284 (1844).

Chapter 3

Schools for Democracy: Civil Libel and the Party Press

Between 1815 and 1850, the United States underwent major political and social transformations that shaped the nation's two-party system, provided the underpinnings of our banking and commerce, molded the country's concepts of judicial power, and established America's foreign policy. After the War of 1812, the nation was filled with pride not only for having survived its first war but also for having gained international respect and prestige. A new westward movement toward cheap land brought optimism and the hope of prosperity to many pioneer families who flooded the Mississippi Valley and the Western territories. This new nationalistic spirit was evidenced by the passage of protective tariffs, a national bank, disposal of public lands and internal improvement; by Chief Justice John Marshall's doctrines of judicial review and national sovereignty and by the Monroe Doctrine.

Political strife temporarily passed from the scene when the Federalist party disintegrated under the odiums of disloyalty, selfishness, and narrow mindedness. It was indeed, as Boston's *Columbian Centinel* labeled it in a headline on July 12, 1817, an Era of Good Feelings—and this from one of the Northeast's strongest Federalist newspapers on the arrival in that city of Repubican President James Monroe. But would it last?

The prosperity and goodwill were marred by a depression in 1819, when state banks collapsed and the Bank of the United States was forced to foreclose on mortgages. Hardest hit was the West, where new settlers had banked on new mortgages to fulfill their dreams. Westerners soon recognized that what was good for the nation, was not necessarily beneficial to them, and they set about looking for better representation in Washington.

The expansion of the West produced clear signals in both the Northeast and South that Western political power could not be disregarded. Both vied for the West's favor by supporting internal improvements and transportation. However, in the 1830s, the South intensified its insistence on states rights and worked to oppose such nationalistic programs as internal improvements and homestead laws. Meanwhile, the courtship of the North and West developed into an engagement as the Northeast offered more manufacturers for the West's raw goods and better transportation to those factories.

The demand for both political and economic equality by all sections brought about an undercurrent of sectional differences that would eventually supercede any party strife. The first indications of these differences surfaced during the debate over Missouri's statehood. Until 1819, Northern and Southern states were equally represented in Congress; but with the slave-holding territory of Missouri seeking statehood, an imbalance in favor of the South was imminent. The manufacturing interests of the North and the agrarian interest of the South worked out the first Missouri Compromise of 1819, which allowed Missouri to enter as slave, Maine to enter as free, and estabished Missouri's southern borders as the northern limit of slavery in the remainder of the Louisiana Purchase. Now equalized, North and South returned, albeit temporarily, to other matters.

By the end of Monroe's second administration, the Republicans had not only absorbed much of the Federalist party, but had broken into factions— National Democrats, Antimasons, Jacksonians. However, none of these factions had coalesced into political parties, nor had sectional differences clarified enough to influence the election of 1824. As a consequence, the election was fought over personalities, inconsequential political intrigues, and broad-stroke issues such as virtue and democracy.

Five of the nineteenth-century's strongest political figures, all claiming birthright to Jeffersonian ideas, vied for the White House. Three—John Quincy Adams, William H. Crawford and John C. Calhoun—held cabinet positions under Monroe; Henry Clay was Speaker of the House; and Andrew Jackson, hero of New Orleans, was Senator from Tennessee.

Because of the lack of real issues or a platform, the nation's party newspapers participated in rather bland electioneering in 1824. Editors kept mudslinging to a minimum, and the lack of any Federalist candidate kept the customary shrillness to a whisper. The party press was still alive, but had little reason to bully or bluster since the platforms of the various candidates were so similar. As a consequence, few libel suits were initiated and no significant decisions in the area of political libel were forthcoming.

Politicians had learned that the more they harassed editors in the courts, the more editors would harass the politicians in the newspapers. Although only three reported criminal libel cases reached state appeals courts between

1812 and 1865,[1] evidence from privately printed journals and reports indicates that criminal libel prosecutions did not stop altogether.[2]

REDRESSING REPUTATION IN CIVIL COURTS

What was occurring was a flight to the civil courts where politicians sought redress when their personal, as opposed to the public, character was assailed. A strongly held theory stated that a politician's private character was not to be equated with his public character, and the only information proper for the public to know pertained to that public character. Whether a man drank too much, whored around, or cheated his neighbor had no bearing, according to politicians, upon how that man conducted the public business. It was this distinction that allowed public officials to find redress in the civil laws.

Thomas Cooper clarified the general feeling of the time concerning private libels: "This is an offense so seldom committed from public or praiseworthy motives...so little moment to the public at large...that this tendency to calumny among neighbors ought to be repressed."[3]

Although officials found it easier to win a libel suit in the civil courts, the rules of evidence, particularly the role of truth, were just as uncertain as they were in criminal courts. Nathaniel Chipman, a Vermont jurist, legislator, and law professor, believed that truth was a good defense in a civil as well as in a criminal prosecution for a libel. "It is in...the interest of all to obtain a full knowledge of the true character of those who may be candidates for the offices of trust." However, since every rule has its exception, there may be an occasion when the "facts may be true, and yet the matter may be expressed in language so grossly indecent as to be an offence against good morals and justly punishable as such."[4]

However, Chancellor James Kent took an even more conservative viewpoint when he wrote that in the case of private libels, courts ought to apply stricter standards when the truth is entered as a justification. The reason: "publications [detailing vice and defects]...are apt to be infected with malice and to be very injurious to the peace and happiness of families."[5]

Kent, always a strict advocate of English common law, believed that if an editor published a libel to expose an individual's misdeeds, the truth of the charge would aggravate rather than lessen the injury. Therefore, the truth ought not to be admissible. "The guilt and the essential ground of action for defamation, consists in the malicious intention; and when the mind is not in fault, no prosecution can be sustained."

Some defense lawyers during this period argued that freedom of the press prohibited criminal libels altogether, leaving any redress up to the civil courts.[6] However, in *Commonwealth v. Whitemarsh*, Boston Municipal Judge Peter O. Thacher responded that civil actions were inadequate and that criminal prosecutions must be retained. Using the *argumentum hor-rendum* so common to jurists of the day, Thacher described the course of what he considered a typical civil libel suit:

He (the plaintiff) may not even arrest the person of the aggressor, unless he will first make oath that he believes that the defendant is about to depart beyond the jurisdiction of the court. He must follow him from court to court, submitting to all the delays and vexations, which malice and ingenuity can devise. He must pay witnesses to attend in his behalf, and lawyers to plead his cause. If at last, he should obtain a tardy declaration of justice, in his favor, and an execution for damages, he must yet levy it at his own expense and risk. If the offending party chooses, he may refuse to pay the debt, and be committed to the freedom of the whole city, still to enjoy all the liberty and impunity, which, perhaps, he may desire, and all en-couragement to renew his slanders upon others. In all this, I confess, I do not see "a certain remedy." [7]

Perhaps the above description is why many journalists of the day con-sidered the libel suit more of a nuisance than a real threat. Horace Greeley, editor of the New York *Tribune*, wrote in his autobiography that "editorial life has many cares, sundry enjoyments, with certain annoyances; and prom-inent among these last are libel-suits. I can hardly remember a time when I was absolutely exempt from these infestations." [8]

Libel suits were far more common in New York than elsewhere, and Greeley blamed this situation on "a perversion of the law by our judges of thirty to fifty years ago." [9] He was referring to *Root v. King*, a widely quoted civil libel suit brought in 1824 by New York Lieutenant Governor Erastus Root against Charles King, editor of the New York *American*. [10] King ac-cused Root of being drunk in the New York Senate chambers and of trying to break up a joint meeting of the two houses when electors for president were being chosen. During the trial, the publisher justified the charge as true by bringing in a number of witnesses. However, the trial took place in Root's hometown before a judge who owed his bench to the Lieutenant Governor. The judge instructed the jury that the preponderance of the evidence was against the truth and that the "unsuccessful attempt at jus-tification" only aggravated the offense. The jury awarded Root $1,400 in damages.

On appeal, the editor argued that the article was true at the time of publication and that he had privilege to report the proceedings of a legislative body as long as there was no knowledge of falsity or willful malice. The New York Court of Errors and Appeals ruled that no such special privilege existed. "The effect of such a doctrine would be deplorable.... No man, who had any character to lose, would be a candidate for office under such a construction of the law of libel." The court also refused to allow belief in truth to be a defense. [11]

One of America's leading constitutional commentators, Thomas Cooley, later noted that because of the decision in *Root v. King*, "the law of New York is not placed by these decisions on a footing very satisfactory to those who claim the utmost freedom of discussion in public affairs." The courts of New York had treated the subject as if there were no middle ground between absolute immunity for falsehood and the application of the same strict rules which prevailed in other cases.[12]

Greeley, who played the role of both plaintiff and defendant during his lifetime, astutely recognized that, win or lose, most plaintiffs were better off not going into court:

If he had tried them and won nominal verdicts, his enemies would have shouted over those verdicts as virtually establishing the truth of their charges; while, if he had been awarded exemplary damages, these would have been cited as measuring the damages to be given against *him* in each of the hundred libel suits thereafter brought *against* him.[13]

For this reason, Greeley eschewed suing two men who falsely accused him of receiving a $1,000 bribe from a railroad company. Greeley said "that man must very badly want to be sued who provokes *me* to sue him for libel." Despite the editor's off-hand comments about libel suits, he did propose that newspapers form a legal "combination for mutual defence." The association would hire one capable lawyer to handle all libel suits against newspapers and would "let no money or effort be spared to baffle and defeat the nefarious attempts [to prosecute]." Such a combination, claimed Greeley, would result "in a substantial and permanent enlargement of the Freedom of the Press."

It was the multiple libel suits brought by James Fenimore Cooper that are credited with finally producing the needed changes in New York's libel laws. Although Cooper's suits are often categorized under literary criticism, they were definitely politically motivated and confirm that most of these early civil suits involved underlying political motivations hidden by a thin veil of vengeance.

Before 1826, Cooper had been well received by the press as a great American author. But during his seven-year sojourn in Europe, his literary attention moved toward politics, and he produced several letters and pamphlets critical of American society. Those writings in turn resulted in an unfavorable reception for Cooper and his work when he returned to America in 1833. Critics spurned his works, suggesting that Cooper stick to writing novels rather than pretend to write about politics.

One of Cooper's severest critics was James Watson Webb, editor of the New York *Courier and Enquirer* and a newly converted Whig. The Whig press was particularly critical of Cooper's turn toward political writing, and a steady stream of criticism came from opposition newspapers.[14] The criticism turned into vituperation and condemnation in 1837 when Cooper became involved in an imbroglio over some park land on his father's estate.

For years, villagers in an around Cooperstown, New York had used Three Mile Point on Lake Ostego as a public picnic and fishing area. When Cooper became the trustee of his father's estate, he ordered the area closed to the public. The local villagers became upset and passed resolutions against the move. Favoring Cooper's side was the local Jacksonian paper, and taking the side of the villagers were the two local Whig papers in Ostego and Chenango. When the latter two papers took up the public's cry, Cooper successfully sued each for libel.[15]

When Webb got wind of the tiff, he too took up the banner, defending his fellow Whig editors and castigating Cooper's "arrogance." Meanwhile, Cooper published two books, *Homeward Bound* and *Home As Found,* which were thinly disguised novels about the Three Mile Point Controversy, about newspaper editors who had been critical of him, and about the vulgar new rich in America. Webb lost no time in reviewing the books with a great deal of invective, going beyond the author's literary abilities and into his personal character and morals. Webb accused Cooper of writing the books in order to appeal to the gentry of England, to reap vengeance against Americans who had taken a dislike to his politics, and to pass himself off as a person of aristocratic blood.[16]

When Cooper answered with a criminal libel suit, newspapers across the state lined up behind the issues according to party affiliations. William Cullen Bryant, a friend of Cooper's, wrote in an understatement that "Cooper had taken a step which would give him a geat deal of trouble, and effect but little good." Cooper had, according to Bryant, "put a hook into the nose of this huge monster, wallowing in his inky pool and bespattering the passersbys; he dragged him to the land and made him tractable."[17]

Webb, who was indicted in Febrary 1839, never let up his vituperation against Cooper during the court fight. In fact, an editorial written after the indictment became the basis for a second prosecution against Webb.

Meanwhile, Thurlow Weed of the Albany *Evening Independent* was convicted for a libel resulting from reviews of the same books. The conviction was by default because Weed was ill and failed to show up for the trial.[18] Weed wrote a letter about Cooper's penchant for libel and the injustice of the conviction, and the letter was published with editorial comment by Horace Greeley in the New York *Tribune.* Cooper sued Greeley for libel and won $200 in damages. Greeley, not one to take Cooper too seriously, published a lengthy and humorous account of his trial and was subsequently sued a second time. This last suit against Greeley was eventually dropped.[19]

Another of Cooper's suits was against William L. Stone, editor of the New York *Commercial Advertiser.* Stone reviewed Cooper's *Naval History of the United States* and questioned many of the facts, particularly Cooper's version of the battle of Lake Erie during the War of 1812. This suit ended up in arbitration, where Stone lost.[20]

In an open letter "To the Famous Litigant" from "Your Most Defensive

Defendants," Stone, Webb, Weed and Park Benjamin, editor of the New York *Evening Sun*, correctly prophesied that "your name will be as great in the books of law as in the books of fiction."[21] The prominence of Cooper's opponents, the opposition by much of the press, the public outcry against the ridiculous verdicts, and Cooper's arrogance throughout the eight years of litigation created the proper atmosphere for a change in New York's libel laws. The new constitution of 1846 allowed truth to be entered as a defense in all civil libel suits. But, as always, this provision led to many interpretations and a new set of uncertainties about the role of truth.

Lawyers and judges spent the first half of the nineteenth century trying to define the basic principles of civil libel as it pertained to both politician and private citizen. Some of the areas that eventually coalesced into an American common law of libel included the extent of privilege to report on judicial and legislative proceedings and reports, proving malice, the role of the jury, and the place of mitigating circumstances such as retraction to reduce damages.

After the Civil War, courts began refining these issues and developing a more uniform body of law from state to state. Belief in the truth, more liberal definition of truth, qualified privilege to report on government meetings and records, the right to comment fairly upon political or nonpolitical issues, retractions and corrections, and guidelines for assessing damages— all had become standards in civil libel law by the opening of the twentieth century.[22]

PARTY PRESS AND THE GREAT DEMOCRATIZER

While civil libel law was developing and changing in the first quarter of the century, newspaper economics remained static. Newspaper editors rarely made large profits from their publishing ventures; in fact, it is a comment upon the power of the press that so many chose a profession that generated so small a monetary reward.

Subscriptions and advertising, the mainstay of twentieth-century newspapers and magazines, brought in very little money. Nineteenth-century newspapers from coast to coast were filled with pleas by the editors to readers to pay for their subscriptions. Advertising, while primarily of the classified variety, paid little. So, newspapers continued to seek financial backing in the same places where editors in England and Europe had been finding it for the past 200 years—the government.

But reliance on government or party support was not motivated solely by pecuniary needs. The United States had always enjoyed a strong, vociferous party press. Since the debates over the Constitution, many newspapers had pledged their allegiance to a certain political party and employed their columns in support of local candidates and national issues. Newspapers were not published in order to provide "objective" reports of social and political affairs; instead, they were published to provide a forum for the political ideas of one party or the other.

In fact, many editors derided the concept of a neutral or independent press. When William Cobbett began his vociferous *Porcupine's Gazette* in 1797, he vowed that the paper would not be impartial, but instead would be an instrument for supporting the causes that he espoused.[23] Joseph Dennie of *The Port Folio* wrote in his prospectus that he had the "deepest abhorrence" for editors who claimed to be neutral, "and for the silly scheme of Impartiality, he cherishes the most ineffable contempt."[24]

Most editors recognized that they were practicing their trade during one of the most important periods of world history. Vital decisions were being made in foreign affairs, domestic activities, and economics by an infant democracy, and editors reasoned that their participation in these decisions was necessary if the democratic experiment was to work.

Federalists under Adams and Jefferson realized early that the political newspaper was an essential adjunct of the party itself because it was the only medium for communicating party messages to a national audience. To this end, the editor and politician worked as partners to ensure that the paper served the party's political and informational needs.

To set the political agenda, the major parties sponsored newspapers in Washington that acted as the center of a network, distributing speeches, editorials, news stories, and various documents to other party newspapers scattered across the nation. These "flagship" papers provided direction to the smaller political papers, but did not mandate total adherence to party line. Sectional and economic differences often required outlying newspapers to tone down certain issues or to gloss over others.[25]

Party loyalty, however, had its price. Editors agreed to devote their columns to disseminate party ideology in exchange for "patronage" dollars. If a newspaper operated in or around Washington, the editor gave his loyalty in exchange for government printing contracts—executive or congressional. Outside of Washington, the party newspaper network was subsidized by federal or state printing contracts. It was also common for 2 party editor to receive an appointment as postmaster.

U.S. Postmaster Generals exercised an unusual degree of independence and autonomy in the federal system which allowed them to nominate postmasters who expressed political sentiments akin to their own. Beginning in the early 1800s, printers formed the most significant political bloc among postmasters.[26] Although financial support from the postmaster position was often insiginificant, the power and opportunity the post offered were significant. As postmaster, an editor was able to circulate his own newspaper free, was the first in the community to receive the latest exchanges from around the country, was often perceived by the community as the local representative of the federal government, and was free to suppress, redirect, open, and even confiscate mail or other newspapers.[27]

The political editor was responsible not only for communicating the party line, but also for discrediting the opposition, for providing a forum for electioneering, and for organizing the local political party. Political hopefuls could remain detached from the messy side of polictics by depending upon the party paper to tout their qualifications, deride the opposition, and get out the vote for the party's favorite son. Robert Weibe describes the politician's use of the party organ as a "ritual dual" or "mock combat" where editors and pamphleteers stood as seconds to defend the honor of their political hero. Through these surrogates, leaders could use vulgar language, slander, and vilify while publicly maintaining the scrupulous decorum of a properly bred gentleperson.[28]

The editor of the *Army and Navy Chronicle*, published in Washington, noted that no publication could succeed for any length of time if it did not assume the partisan character of some party or religion. "The very nature and genius of our political institutions tend to foster, if not to engender," this patronage.[29] The editor described the political press as it existed in the 1830s:

The facility and cheapness with which a press may be established and the modicum of literary acquirement requisite to manage respectably, a newspaper, put it in the power of any person of moderate capital or credit to start a new publication.... Nothing seems easier than to turn editor....The luckless wight who adopts the calling will soon find, to his chagrin, that he has a hard task-master....Such a thing as absolute independence in the press—an independence of party trammels—...is not and cannot be endured in this country. Every publication must espouse some cause, if the proprietors hope to command success.[30]

Because freedom of the press was defined during these early years primarily within the context of libel, the concept of the party press was not considered in its early years to be a factor—good or bad—in press freedom. While a few writers such as John Quincy Adams or the author of the above description were concerned about the need for an "independent" press, their concerns were not joined to any expressions about the *freedom* of an independent press.

It was not until the 1828 campaign that a few contemporaries began seeing a link between the party press and freedom of the press in a participatory democracy. Yet even then, freedom of press was a politically loaded phrase used by Jackson supporters to embarrass Adams.

The early party papers did not play a siginificant role in the outcome of presidential elections. Their role was to support issues and platforms, not men. The candidates' personalities, their abilities, their commitments to certain programs, their outlooks on the American system—all of these remained obscure in the press.

This lack of enthusiasm for the presidential candidates was merely a manifestation of the system that elected presidents, rather than of any real indifference toward the candidates. First, the contemporary view dictated that the office should seek the man and not vice versa. Candidates did not seek publicity during a campaign nor did they make public appearances or travel about the country. Thus, the party newspaper acted as a surrogate, providing the bulk of information about candidates. Second, since 1800, the winning presidential candidates had been hand-picked by Jefferson. This system continued because success depended on two intrigues: favoritism by the president and generous patronage while in government service. If a man had fostered these two elements, his selection was practically guaranteed. Other candidates, usually chosen by state legislatures as favorite sons, were considered interlopers. On election day, electors in most states were chosen by the legislature rather than popular vote.

All of this made for a cozy political monarchy with a minimum of party competition. However, the system began to fall apart in 1824; by 1828, presidential elections had been transferred from the Virginia Dynasty to the people. Since 1815, the nation had been a one-party country with Republicans holding the majority of seats in Congress and most states. However, as factionalism based on economic, social, and sectional interests set in, the one party began to subdivide. This dismemberment produced five candidates in the election of 1824 whose political differences were little more than cosmetic.

Three of the candidates—John C. Calhoun, John Quincy Adams and William H. Crawford—held important cabinet positions (War, State and Treasury, respectively). It was assumed abroad that all enjoyed Monroe's support, and that all had used their positions to dole out patronage to both Congress and the press. But Crawford had the upper hand in both these prerequisites because he not only had Monroe's confidence but also Jefferson's blessing. He also had been the most effective and successful in the patronage game.

Yet, Crawford had his enemies—not the least of which were the anti-Crawford papers which sprang up in Washington, D.C. between 1821 and 1824 to combat his candidacy. Secretary of War Calhoun's official gazette was the *Washington Republican and Congressional Examiner*. Adams waged his political battles in a latecomer, the *National Journal*. All the newspapers accorded Jackson respect because of his military achievements and none paid much heed to Clay.

Yet, Crawford was not without support. As Secretary of Treasury, he had doled out patronage to two Washington newspapers—the *Washington City Gazette* and the *National Intelligencer*, which was only a lukewarm supporter and occasionally gave Henry Clay a sidewise glance.

Newspaper patronage was hardly new, and its place within a democratic system would not be questioned until the end of the Civil War. What did receive criticism was the manner in which politicians used the press, according to Adams, to "vitiate the public opinion and pay for defamation, to receive their reward in votes."[31]

During the campaign of 1824, the party press was still in its infancy and would not grow to maturity until the election of 1828. The method for distributing government printing contracts was a major factor in the upsurge in printing patronage. In 1819, after trying a low-bid system of awarding printing contracts, Congress passed a bill introduced by Henry Clay that established a fixed-rate schedule. Any printer who could produce work at the given rate could be nominated by a congressman. Nominees were then voted on by each house. Thus, not only did the executive branch have its official newspaper, but so too did both houses of Congress.

This diversity in patronage had several advantages. First, it allowed a number of opposition papers to spring up in the capitol. During Jackson's administration, Congress's two papers, the *U.S. Telegraph* and *Intelligencer*, were both Whig organs. Second, it ensured a thorough coverage of the debates and proceedings of Congress. Third, it transmitted a penetrating, if not always scintillating, exchange of views on major issues of the day.

The printing contract rates set in 1819 were generous and allowed a printing house to make a nice profit off government contracts. However, technology eventually outpaced the rates and printers were soon making extravagant profits with faster presses and automated binding and new typesetting methods. It was not until 1840 that Congress recommended reducing the set rates by 20 percent in order to bring printing costs back in line.[32]

With huge profits from government printing to be made by Washington newspapers, it was relatively easy to persuade a newspaper editor to sell his editorial product to the highest bidder. Jonathan Elliot, editor of the *Washington City Gazette*, had laid claim to the lucrative printing contracts of the Treasury Department since Albert Gallatin had been head of Treasury in Madison's administration. He had also done some printing for Adams in the State Department, but after losing the State Department's contract for printing the census, Elliot pledged his paper to Crawford's election because "he could not afford to be [Adam's] friend for nothing."[33]

It was obvious early in the campaign that the anti-Crawford cliques needed a newspaper to defeat the overly ambitious candidate. Calhoun offered War Department printing contracts to Thomas Loraine McKenney, (a former superintendent of Indian Trade who was under investigation for maladministration) if he would establish an "objective" paper to expose Crawford. McKenney agreed and began printing the *Washington Republican and Congressional Examiner* in the summer of 1822. He gave up the editorship in May 1823 because of attacks from prominent Senators regarding the maladministration charges.

Adams, content for the meanwhile to sit back and let his past service, hard work, and dedication represent him to the people, described the adversarial relationship of the Crawford and Calhoun newspapers as "War v. Treasury." Yet, for all of Adams's seeming neutrality, his loyalties were with the *Republican*. He described the *Republican* as a paper written with "firmness and moderation" and "reason, argument and demonstration." Yet, Crawford's *City Gazette*, in its "ruffian-like manner," was filled with "high panegyric," the "foulest abuse," and "scurrility and billingsgate."[34]

Adams humorously portrayed the activities of the party newspapers in Washington during the campaigning of 1822-1824. On the *City Gazette's* announcement that its flag was set for Crawford, Adams noted that the slogan was "Democracy, Economy, and Reform.... Democracy to be used against me, Economy against Calhoun, and Reform against both." Using the language of warfare, he wrote that Calhoun was organizing his *Republican*, and he feared that "these engines will counteract each other, but I shall be a mark for both sides, and, having no counter-fire upon them, what can happen but that I must fall?"

Adams had insisted several times that "I should not purchase the services of any printer, either with public money or my own." He wrote in February 1821, "If that office is to be the price of a cabal and intrigue, of purchasing newspapers, bribing by appointments, or by bargaining for foreign missions, I have not the ticket in that lottery."

Although eschewing the route of a party paper during the early part of the campaign—"I disdain this ignoble mode of warfare, and neither wage it myself nor countenance it in my friends"—Adams was a shrewd observer of how the party press system worked. He wrote the following about the papers that were aligned behind Crawford by September 1822:

The *National Intelligencer* is secured to him by the belief of the editors that he will be the successful candidate, and by their dependence upon the printing of Congress; the *Richmond Enquirer* because he is a Virginian and slave-holder; the *National Advocate* of New York, through Van Buren, the *Boston Statesman* and *Portland Argus*, through William King; the *Democratic Press*, of Philadelphia, because I transferred the printing of the laws from that paper to the *Franklin Gazette*; and several other presses in various parts of the Union upon principles alike selfish and sordid. [35]

After Calhoun dropped out of the presidential race in early 1824 to run for vice president, the *Republican* also withdrew and was sold to a new paper in town, the *National Journal*. The newcomer, which had first appeared in November 1823, offically announced in August 1824 that it would support Adams for president and Calhoun for vice president. By this time the grandfather of Washington's press, the *National Intelligencer*, had become a staunch Crawford defender. Adams and Crawford also had party papers in major towns outside of Washington. It was this gaggle of news-papers that waged the campaign battles, and through their exchanges, supplied almost all of the campaign information and rhetoric that the people outside of Washington would read.

By 1824, there was no doubt that Crawford would win the nomination of the congressional caucus. Yet, the opposition was successful in promoting a boycott of the February caucus. Only sixty-six of 241 Republicans showed up to nominate Crawford. For the first time in over twenty years, the candidate of the Virginia Dynasty was seen as the interloper, and the rest as viable prospects. By the summer of 1824, Crawford was so ill that his backers sought another name to support. Jackson's candidacy gained ground as Crawford newspapers began writing more favorably about the General. Yet Jackson's support in the West was eroded partially by the popularity of the Kentuckian Clay. Few, except Adams, saw Jackson as a serious rival.

Although Adams was the strongest of the remaining candidates, the three-way split among Adams, Clay, and Jackson failed to give any one a clear majority, resulting in the election being decided by the House of Representatives. Clay, in exchange for the Secretary of State post, pledged his backers to Adams, and Jackson lost.

The breakdown of the congressional caucus system and the election falling to the House spelled changes in the traditional party machinery. And these changes had been partly the doing of the party papers in Washington over the prior two years.

Jackson supporters called Adams's election an arrogant veto of the popular will that had been produced by a "corrupt bargain" between Adams and Clay supporters. The next presidential campaign was well under way even before Adams was inaugurated. Also under way was the formation of a new opposition party led by Jackson in the West, Martin Van Buren in the Northeast, and Vice President John C. Calhoun in the South—a coalition of diverse interests with one common purpose—to defeat the Republicans and bring victory to the new Democratic Party. The propaganda weapon would be the pro-Jackson press.

Adam's inaugural address echoed the words of Jefferson when he pleaded for Americans to discard "every remnant of rancor against each other, of embracing as countrymen and friends, and of yielding to talents and virtue alone that confidence which...was bestowed only upon those who bore the badge of party communion."[36] Yet, conciliation was not to be. Adams's nationalistic spirit was too far-sighted for the simple nation, and the badge of a "corrupt bargain" was pinned too tightly on his lapel.

Jackson, heartened by his own showing in the popular election, returned to Tennessee to build a war chest and campaign organization that would ensure him a victory in the next election. Because he viewed the Adams administration as one of corruption and conspiracy, he adopted early in the campaign the slogan, "Jackson for Reform." He would become the champion of the common man by returning democracy to the people.

The platform that was nailed together during the ensuing years promised to reduce the size of government, to clean government of all those who held positions through patronage, to restore the checks and balances required to safeguard the sovereignty of the people, to restore pure republican principles, and to get rid of the extravagant waste of money that marked the Adams administration.

To push this platform, to answer all the abuses that opposition papers heaped upon him, and to popularize his own set of accusations against Adams, Jackson depended upon a large and well-organized campaign committee and a responsive and loyal party press. By 1827, many of America's strongest editors supported his campaign: Thomas Ritchie of the *Richmond Enquirer*; James Watson Webb and James Gordon Bennett of the *New York Enquirer*; Mordecai Noah of the *National Advocate*; Edwin Croswell of the *Albany Argus*; William Coleman and William Cullen Bryant of the *New York Evening Post*; and Dabney Carr of the *Baltimore Republican*.

He also had the support of a former Clay paper, the *Argus of Western America*, edited by Amos Kendall. Kendall had been a close family friend of the Clays, but had broken with the Kentuckian over several major issues. In August 1827, he introduced himself to Jackson, pledging his support to the General's campaign. Kendall and his associate editor Francis Blair, would play a significant role in the campaign and continue to wield great power during both of Jackson's terms in office.

Knowing the importance of a strong press in Washington, Duff Green, a former Calhoun supporter, bought out the old Washington *Gazette*, borrowed $3,000 from Jackson, and pledged his new *United States Telegraph* to the Jackson cause, becoming the flagship of the Jacksonian newspaper fleet.

Despite the "Jackson for Reform" call and the romantic liturgy of the common man and democracy, the election of 1828 has been called the dirtiest presidential campaign in American history. Personalities and personal vendettas overwhelmed contemporary issues such as the national bank, paper money, and tariffs.

The Adams-Clay opposition began early to propagate a list of villainous charges against Jackson in order to counteract his "corrupt bargain" charges against Adams. The opposition press included the Richmond *Whig*, *National Gazette*, Cincinnati *Gazette*, *Niles' Weekly Register*, and Raleigh *Register*. Charges against Jackson included his execution of six soldiers who deserted the militia after the Creek War, the jailing of Judge Hall after the Battle of New Orleans, his tavern brawls and duels, slave dealing, gambling, drunkeness, murder, and, probably the most hateful of all charges, adultery and bigamy because of the untimely marriage to his wife Rachel.

Jackson answered the charges through the Nashville Central Committee and through the *U.S. Telegraph*. While he blamed Clay for starting the rumors, Jackson left most charges and calumnies against his enemies to be advanced by others. In addition to the charges of a "corrupt bargain" between Clay and Adams, the list of charges against Adams included budgetary extravagance, gambling, pimping while Minister to Russia, religious bigotry, and alcoholism.

Press patronage became linked with the issue of press freedom early in the election when Vice President Calhoun, a Jackson supporter, criticized Secretary of State Henry Clay's use of patronage. The charges were made more specific when North Carolina Senator Nathaniel Macon called for a Senate investigation of executive patronage, and Romulus Saunder, congressman from North Carolina, called for Clay to supply the House a list of all newspapers that had received printing contracts for the past several years.[37]

Duff Green's *Telegraph* kept up the verbal mudslinging about patronage during the investigations. Green charged that Adams placed liberty of the press in peril when "the favor of power is essential to the support of the editors," and he warned of a return to the intimidation that flowered under the Sedition Law.[38]

The House investigation showed nothing more than expected—that patronage of Jackson's papers had been reduced while that of the Adams's papers had been increased. The Senate's investigation resulted in several bills to increase the number of papers in each state that published the laws and to place their selection in the hands of Congress rather than those of the Secretary of State. None of the bills were passed.

A year later, in February 1827, a resolution was presented to the House, asking Clay to supply not only a list of papers receiving patronage, but also the reason printing contracts were withdrawn from papers. The resolution was motivated by the withdrawal of patronage from the *National Intelligencer* and the *Argus of Western America*. Although the resolution was never adopted, it was debated for several weeks.[39]

Supporters of the resolution argued that although the law allowed the secretary of state to select the printers of the laws, Clay had abused the spirit of that law by denying printing contracts to capable printers. They insisted that printing patronage destroyed the liberty of press; however, they were never able to specify how that destruction had occurred. It was also charged that the removal of competent printers was "much more effectual and much more dangerous than the Alien and Sedition laws" because patronage operated in such a way that few were cognizant of its effects.

Representative James Hamilton of South Carolina not only drew an analogy between patronage and libel law, but also accused Clay and Adams of establishing a "Government Press" that was more alarming to liberty of press than an army of 6,000 men (an allusion to the dreaded concept of a large standing peacetime army). Hamilton saw the "purity" of the press debased and corrupted by the abuses of patronage particularly when it was used to praise "bad public men and bad public measures."

But Representative Robert P. Letcher of Kentucky refused to buy this high rhetoric of the anti-Adams men. He considered any analogy to the Alien and Sedition Acts ludicrous. The doling out of patronage was not done in secret; it was done publicly and the secretary of state was both praised and abused publicy everytime he changed printers. The power of selection was a two-edged sword; if printing is taken from one friend and given to another, the secretary loses a friend; if he takes it from a friend and gives it to an enemy, he loses a friend and is charged with buying off the enemy. "Whether friend or enemy, selection is still a matter of calculation."

Letcher did not believe that any great harm could come from the power of patronage even when that power was abused. Nor did he believe the American public could be controlled by the newspapers. "I think, on the contrary, that the presses throughout the country will preseve their own course, free from any such influence, and the the people will do the same."

Not all of the papers receiving patronage were pro-Adams, but that mattered little because the real fear of the Jackson forces was that Clay would buy off dozens of papers that would support him against Jackson. In spring of 1828, the House tried again to bridle the patronage dollar, accusing Clay of establishing "a Government press" for the purpose of purchasing loyalty. Calling this action the "pecuniary censorship of the press," the House Committee on Retrenchment proposed abolishing exeuctive patronage altogether because it was worse than any "Star Chamber code of pains and penalties." No action was taken.[40]

Much as the people had once welcomed Jefferson as the savior of the common man over 25 years before, so did they welcome Jackson in 1828. "The scurrilous gutter tactics of unprincipled politicians and journalists,"[41] secured 56 percent of the popular vote and 178 out of 261 electoral votes for Jackson.

Once in Washington, Jackson rewarded campaign loyalty with numerous lucrative patronage positions. The *National Journal* and the *National Intelligencer* reported that fifty-nine editors and publishers were appointed to offices ranging from U.S. attorney and librarian to Congress to minor clerkships and postmasterships.[42] Kendall was chosen as fourth auditor in the Treasury Department, and then promoted to postmaster general during Jackson's second term. He remained as a presidential adviser through Van Buren's administration.

Jackson wished to award Isaac Hill, editor of the New Hampshire *Patriot* with a position as comptroller, but the nomination was voted down in the Senate. Hill later won a seat in Congress and became a central leader in the Democratic party and a Jackson confidante.

When Duff Green's *U.S. Telegraph* lost the president's confidence by being soft on the Bank of the United States and taking Calhoun's direction rather than Jackson's, Francis Blair was invited to Washington in 1830 to begin the Washington *Globe* as the official administration organ. Blair was guaranteed $4,000 annually in printing patronage from the Departments of War and Treasury. Later, that amount climbed to $15,000 as patronage from Congress, the State Department, and other administrative agencies was added.[43] Jackson urged all executive agency heads to award printing contracts to the *Globe*, but when several failed to oblige, Jackson ordered department heads to account for all payments to printers. The order was obeyed and the recalcitrant agency heads soon were contracting solely with the *Globe*. Blair and the *Globe* became so influential that Jackson regularly consulted the editor on all domestic and foreign matters, making the journalist a member of his "Kitchen Cabinet."

Not only did editors receive government appointments and subsidies, but they also received lucrative contracts issued by the Post Office and the Treasury Department. Newspapers often received the contract to furnish office supplies such as twine, printed forms, and wrapping paper for the Post Office.[44] In his first state of the union address, Jackson stated that the Post Office was the vehicle for securing the full enjoyment of the press.[45] To emphasize the importance of the Post Office, the president made the postmaster general a member of the executive cabinet.

It did not escape Jackson's attention that whoever controlled the mails controlled the means by which information was dissimenated across the country. In fact, Jackson appointed twenty-four newspaper editors to positions of postmaster. Nor did the mails escape the notice of Congress. The postal committees in the House and the Senate were among the most important during the first half of the century. The major issues dealt with in these committees included the extension of the post road system, postal rates (including newspaper postage), franking privileges, policies for issuing mail contracts, and establishment of new post offices.

That part of Jackson's state of the union message dealing with the postal service echoed the attitude of every president before him. Each administration had supported the extension of post roads and a generous policy of low rates for carrying newspapers. In his fourth state of the union address, President George Washington called for a study and reconsideration of the newly passed Post Office Act of 1792, hoping that Congress would reduce the rates for posting newspapers. In his fifth annual address, Washington went so far as to ask Congress to abolish all postage for newspapers. Until the overthrow of the Virginia Dynasty, both Federalists and Republicans supported low newspaper postage as a tool for advancing party policy and informing a curious nation.[46]

But, it was 1832 before both the House and Senate took a serious look at the political, economic, and social effects of eliminating postage for newspapers. The bill submitted by Senator George Bibb of Kentucky was prompted in part by the reports of Treasury and the Post Office that showed substantial surplus revenues. It appeared obvious to many from the beginning that if the elimination of newspaper postage might compromise the fiscal well-being of the Post Office, then the Treasury Department could step in and subsidize the privilege.

Administration papers already benefitted from no postage. But whether to grant this privilege to all newspapers was an issue that, not unexpectedly, split down party lines, pitted big city editors against smaller village editors, and later divided along sectional lines.

The elimination of postage would be advantageous to the anti-Jackson papers for it would ensure that all newspapers circulated freely, no matter what their political content or support. As Bibb said, it was "a melancholy fact" that the nation's presses were supported with government patronage; however, Washington's daily papers could not exist without the subsidies. But, with free and cheap circulation an "impartial and independent press might be fostered and established on so firm a basis as to be wholly free from the influence of government."[47]

Said John Clayton of Delaware, "the press which is acting on principle will be as fairly sustained as the press that is pensioned." However, as Senator Isaac Hill of Massachusetts pointed out in his arguments against the bill, the amount of patronage bestowed on the anti-administration papers, the *Telegraph* and *Intelligencer*, was already quite large, and both papers enjoyed franking privileges.

Jackson supporters were concerned that the bill would have a tendency to usurp the traditional role of the village editor. In the Post Office Committee's recommendation to postpone the bill indefinitely, Senator Felix Grundy of Tennessee acknowledged that "there is a prevailing curiosity in the interior to see and read the papers which are published in large cities, and to learn the news and rumors that are circulated there." However, if these city papers were carried free of charge, they would be preferred by the rural reader and eventually the smaller establishments would be supplanted. The ultimate result would be the concentration of political power in the hands of a few.[48]

While the bill would not have been the death knell for rural papers, the perceived disadvantages were not altogether inflated. Because of the distance over which materials had to travel, printing of a weekly paper in a rural town was more expensive than producing a city daily. Also, regional and community news was sparse in small weeklies; most of the space was devoted to reprints about political happenings from city exchanges. If these reports could reach the reader via the original city paper and several days earlier at that, the small weekly had every right to be paranoid about the passage of the bill.

But more than economics was involved in protecting the village editor. Elimination of postage for newspapers meant that the circulation of political information could no longer be controlled by the local partisan editors since those who wanted political information could receive it free from the large city papers. But, Jacksonian Democrats simply did not trust the metropolitan newspapers: "A monopoly of influence in the large cities whose political atmosphere is not always most congenial to a spirit of independence, will be the consequence."[49]

Eventually, the newspaper postage bill was reported unfavorably out of the Post Office Committee. But, Congress kept up a running debate over newspaper postage throughout the 1840s and into the 1850s.

Throughout Jackson's administration, loyal newspapers continued to be carried free by loyal postmasters, and loyal editors were paid a generous sum for advertising of the mail contract and for running the list of uncalled-for letters. Patronage and mismanagement of the Post Office became so bad that Congress began investigations in both houses. In 1834, a Senate committee composed primarily of Whigs investigated the patronage system of the Post Office and reported that large sums of money were being spent "to extend the influence of the department over the public press and through that press over the people."[50]

The excessive use of patronage by the Jackson administration to repay loyal editors brought frequent criticism from friends and opposition. A friend from Virginia expressed concern that freedom of the press would be compromised by the appointment of so many editors to government positions. But Jackson did not believe that just because a man operated a newspaper that he should be discriminated against by the president. Executive patronage and support should be available to everyone "to the rich and the poor, the farmer and printer" as long as "honesty, probity and capability" were the only tests. Such a policy could result only in preserving "freedom of political action."[51]

Republican George Hay, who had written so eloquently about freedom of the press at the turn of the century,[52] wrote that the country was not threatened by violations of the constitution or by oppressive laws, but by "bestowing offices on editors the most profligate and audacious." When the independence of the press "is assailed, not openly and manfully by legislation in face of day," then what has developed is a disease that "touches the vitals of our system. It is a corruption of the public mind and morals, by means placed by the Constitution in the hands of the Executive."[53]

Daniel Webster, Whig candidate for president, linked the party press to freedom of the press when he warned listeners at the 1832 National Republican Convention that political appointments undermined the role of the free press as one of the country's most important "agents and instruments." He likened the "purchased or pensioned" press to a fettered press in other countries, explaining that a manacled press cannot be trusted "because it is under a power which may prove greater than the love for truth." Dependent editors will abstain from speaking the truth for fear of losing their livelihood.

He called the appointment of fifty to sixty editors to public office during Jackson's administration "reprehensive:"

It degrades both the government and the press.... It turns the palladium of liberty into an engine of party.... It so completely perverts the true object of government, it so entirely revolutionizes our whole system, that the chief business of those in power is directed rather to the propagation of opinions favorable to themselves than to the execution of the laws.[54]

While patronage remained a persistent theme among ministers, lawyers, and newspaper editors, few people were genuinely concerned about the lack of independence in the American press. As long as both parties had their spokesmen within the press, few feared that government subsidy would result in a forfeiture of the necessary checks and balances.

Frederick Grimke, an Ohio judge and brother of the Grimke sisters of abolitionist fame, set forth one of the more lucid explanations of how the nineteenth-century mind perceived the party press. Grimke believed, as did Jackson, that no matter how irreconcilable party views seemed, a wide dissemination of these views creates an atmosphere of debate and "increases the intensity of the light by which all parties are enabled to see their sentiments reflected." Through such exposure, the people will adopt wiser and more wholesome opinions, and the seeming chaos of ideas will dissolve into understanding and stability.[55]

To Grimke, the party press was merely an extension of representative government. Like the party, its press was always before the public influencing citizens but not compelling them. Of course, a free press can operate only in a society where the citizens are educated and can discriminate between abuse and truth. He viewed the party press as an equalizer that pointed out licentiousness on all sides of issues. The party press supported freedom of the press because it became the instrument of censorship rather than government—"each newspaper rendering the most vehement and untiring politician harmless and pacific." The check and balance role of the press allowed it to be "vehement and untiring, yet harmless."

Not all of Grimke's contemporaries agreed with him. The *New York Review* acknowledged the necessity of parties in a free country, but warned that the honorable ends of the parties were not being met by the "falsehood, virulence and abuse" that existed in the party papers.[56]

Benjamin Lynde Oliver, a Massachusetts lawyer and author, suggested a solution to the problem of the party press. He recommended that papers become common carriers, open to all willing to pay a reasonable price for the space. Only by such a method would newspapers attain the "highest degree of truth, independence and respectability."[57]

As it stood, explained Oliver, no matter how great a friend the editor is to truth, "it cannot be doubted that he will prefer the interest of what he considers the better part, to wit, his own party." Unlike Grimke, he found censorship of the press a severe limitation because every writer must submit his piece for examination and "license" to the party. "Such freedom of press is hardly worth the trouble of protection." With an independent and public press the demoralizing spectacle "of the most indecent and ungentlemanly opposition, accusing each other of falsehood, bribery and corruption" would cease and no editor "would ever again be compelled to wear the livery of any party."

The aging William Duane of the Philadelphia *Aurora*, who had participated in party journalism since before the turn of the century, wrote an editorial in 1834 berating the Jacksonian newspapers, comparing journalism to the marketplace:

A person who should dare to introduce tainted meat—or rancid butter—or rotten eggs, and put them off as clean articles, would not only be fined or otherwise punished and disgraced, but such an aggressor dare not show his face in the market a second time. Is the putrescence of a dissolute, or the invidious treachery of a hypocritical press, less pernicious, less odious, less detestable, than the retail of poisonous viands?[58]

The "golden shackles" of government patronage continued through Jackson's two administrations, and was carried on in style by Martin Van Buren. But by the time the Whigs took over the presidency with William Henry Harrison, there was a decided move underway to lessen patronage to party newspapers.

In the same year that a Select Committee on Public Printing was studying the feasibility of a national printer,[59] Daniel Webster made brief mention before the Whig convention in Richmond in 1840 of the need for a press that was separate from politics. He called for an independent printer because no man should be compelled to give his money "to pay another man to persuade him not to change the government."[60] However, when Webster became Secretary of State under Harrison in 1841, he continued the tradition of doling out printing contracts to Whig papers.

The idea of an independent printer for government struck the right note with a New York editor Michenor Cadwallader. Soon after Webster returned from the Richmond convention, he received a letter from the editor, who proposed a "national printing establishment." Cadwallader berated the party press as being "devoted to the accomplishment of the most unholy purposes," and a "curse of the first magnitude." The only way to keep this "corrupting power" out of the hands of the president was to separate printing from newspapers. Only then would the "pernicious influence of a partisan press be put off."[61]

Although Harrison made no moves in his short tenure to establish a separate printing office, he did pledge himself not to use his office to manipulate public printing contracts. In his inaugural address he vowed that "the presses in the necessary employment of the Government should never be used to clear the guilty or to varnish crime."[62]

After Harrison's death, John Tyler took up the call and ordered the postmaster general to discontinue appointing editors of political newspapers as postmasters. Tyler insisted that such appointments were "in the highest degree objectionable" and involved too many odious consequences such as introducing politics into the post office, diminishing the revenue, and confering privileges on one editor which all could not enjoy.[63] By the summer of 1846, a joint resolution of Congress provided that all congressional printing be contracted out to the lowest bidder, rather than to whomever was elected by the separate houses. This system cut into profitability and created discontent among the printshops saddled with heavy printing jobs. In 1852, the old system of doling out the contract at inflated fixed prices as a political reward was reinstalled, but the patronage system was now to be overseen by the Superintendent to Public Printing. However, public and congressional concern about scandals involving printing contracts and the difficulty of finding enough printers to carry the increasing printing burden eventually resulted in the establishment of the Government Printing Office in 1860.[64]

Newspaper patronage never became a serious free press issue in the nineteenth century. In fact, it was not until twentieth-century historians like Frank Luther Mott labeled the party press era "The Dark Age of Partisan Journalism" that the era took on its negative aspects. While several recent studies have examined the role of the political press,[65] there is little evidence to indicate any general use of government favors to compromise freedom of the press. As Grimke noted, the party press was actually an equalizer, open to all parties who had a public message. As Representative Letcher said in the 1827 debates on patronage, it was difficult to believe that a printing contract worth $150–200 a year could wield a compromising influence over any newspaper.

One fallacy underlying the charges of a "government press" was the assumption that at some point the newspaper editor had been a politically independent news manager. Then through a variety of inducements, he had been forced to compromise his purity and sell his soul to the highest political bidder. In fact, the party press had been the mainstay of both British and American journalism for centuries. The independent newspaper may have been an ideal, but hardly a reality.

The nineteenth-century editor was a highly visible politician who happened to find his voice in the columns of a newspaper rather than in public speeches or on the floor of a legislature. There is overwhelming evidence in the correspondence of editors and politicians that both worked together to form a communication network to efficiently and effectively spread the party doctrine. An editor was either passive or zealous in his political support, but rarely impartial. And any editor who boasted that his paper was impartial did so for some underlying political reason. And just as politicans in any age, editors fell out with their parties, and either switched party allegiance or fought the party from the inside.

French politician and theorist Alexis de Tocqueville, in his classic *Democracy in America*, commented on America's party press, calling it the "constitutive element" of political liberty. It provided the means for representatives both to listen and to speak to their constituents without ever coming into immediate contact. By ensuring that political ideas circulated throughout the country, the political press of the nineteenth century was a necessary tool for the rapid democratizing of the infant nation. Without it, de Tocqueville's "great democratic revolution" in America may well have only been a backwater skirmish.[66]

NOTES

1. Commonwealth v. Child, 30 Mass. 198 (1832); Commonwealth v. Snelling, 32 Mass 321 (1834); State v. Burnham, 31 Am. Dec. 217 (N.H., 1838).

2. See., *Report of the Case of Timothy Upham against Hill & Barton, Publishers of the New Hampshire Patriot for Alleged Libels* (Dover: George W. Ela, 1830); *The Liberty of the Press Vindicated and Truth Triumphant! State v. Ira Berry, for an alledged libel on Cyrus Weston* (Augusta, 1832); *Trial of the Case of the Commonwealth versus David Lee Child for Publishing in the Massachusetts Journal a Libel on the Honorable John Keyes* (Boston: Dutton and Wentworth, 1829); Thomas Low Nichols, *Journal in Jail, Kept during a Four Month Imprisonment for Libel, in the Jail of Erie County* (Buffalo: Dinsmore, 1840).

3. Thomas Cooper, *Treatise on the Law of Libel and the Liberty of the Press,* (New York: G. F. Hopkins & Son, 1830), p. 2.

4. Nathaniel Chipman, *Principles of Government: a Treatise on Free Institutions* (1833; reprint ed., New York: Burt Franklin, 1969).

5. James Kent, *Commentaries on American Law* 2 vols, rev. ed. (Philadelphia: Blackstone Pub. Co., 1889) 2: 71.

6. Judge Peter Thacher's opinion in Commonwealth v. Whitemarsh (July 1836) is reprinted in "The Law of Libel in Massachusetts," 16 *American Jurist* 93–94 (Oct. 1836).

7. Ibid., pp. 119-120.

8. Horace Greeley, *Recollections of a Busy Life* (New York: J. B. Ford & Co., 1868), p. 260.

9. Ibid.

10. 7 Cow. 613 (N.Y. 1827).

11. King and Verplanck v. Root, 4 Wend. 113 at 138 (N.Y. 1829).

12. Thomas Cooley, *Treatise on the Constitutional Limitations* 7th ed. (Boston: Little, Brown, and Co., 1903), p. 624.

13. Greeley, *Recollections*, p. 265.

14. James L. Crouthamel, *James Watson Webb: A Biography* (Middletown, Ct.: Wesleyan University Press, 1969), pp. 76-79.

15. For a detailed account of the Cooper libel suits: Ethel R. Outland, *The*

"Effingham" Libels on Cooper, University of Wisconsin Studies in Language and Literature, no. 28 (Madison: University of Wisconsin, 1929).

16. Crouthamel, *James Watson Webb,* p. 77.

17. Outland, *The "Effingham Libels",* p. 27.

18. Greeley, *Recollections,* p. 262.

19. Ibid., pp. 264-65.

20. Outland, *The "Effingham Libels",* pp. 226-7.

21. Ibid., pp. 228-31.

22. For a study of the changing law of civil libel: Clifton Lawhorne, *Defamation and Public Officials* (Carbondale: Southern Illinois University Press, 1971), pp. 70-110.

23. *Porcupine's Gazette,* March 5, 1797.

24. Prospectus for a New Weekly Paper, (Philadelphia, 1800). See also, William David Sloan, "The Early Party Press: The Newspaper Role in American Politics, 1788–1812," 9 *Journalism History* 18 (Spring 1982).

25. Richard B. Kielbowicz, "Party Press Cohesiveness: Jacksonian Newspapers, 1832," 60 *Journalism Quarterly* 518 (Autumn 1983).

26. Carl Prince, "The Federalist Party and Creation of a Court Press, 1789–1801," 53 *Journalism Quarterly* 238 (Summer 1976).

27. Ibid.

28. Robert Wiebe, *The Opening of American Society* (New York: Alfred A. Knopf 1984), pp. 100-103.

29. *Army and Navy Chronicle,* July 30, 1840.

30. Ibid.

31. Charles Francis Adams, ed., *Memoirs of John Quincy Adams* 12 vols. (1874-77; reprint ed., Freeport, N.Y.: Books for Libraries Press, 1969) 7: 262.

32. Robert E. Kling, Jr., *The Government Printing Office* (New York: Praeger Publishing, 1970), pp. 1-17.

33. Adams, *Memoirs,* 6: 56.

34. Adams, *Memoirs,* 6: 63-66.

35. Ibid., 6: 61.

36. James D. Richardson, *A Compilation of the Messages and Papers of the Presidents* 20 vols. (New York: Bureau of National Literature, 1897–1917) 2: 296-7.

37. *Senate Journal,* 19th Cong., 1st sess., pp. 132, 137; *House Journal,* 19th Cong., 1st sess., p. 141; House Doc. 41, 19th Cong., 1st sess. (1827).

38. *U.S. Telegraph,* February 9 and March 6, 1826.

39. *Register of Debates,* 19th Cong., 2nd sess., pp. 895-994. (1827).

40. Senate Doc. 399, 28th Cong., 1st sess., p. 43. (1840)

41. Robert V. Remini, *Andrew Jackson and the Course of American Freedom, 1822–1832* 2 vols. (New York: Harper & Row, Pubishers, 1981) 2: 143.

42. *National Journal,* December 3 and 8, 1829; May 11, 1830; *National Intelligencer,* September 27, 1832.

43. Remini, *Andrew Jackson and the Course of American Freedom,* 2: 294.

44. For a comprehensive study of the political press during the Jacksonian years: Gerald J. Baldasty, *The Press and Politics in the Age of Jackson. Journalism Monographs,* no. 89 (August 1984).

45. Richardson, *Messages and Papers,* 2: 460-61.

46. See, Richard B. Kielbowicz, "The Press, Post Office, and Flow of News in the Early Republic," 3 *Journal of the Early Republic* 255-280 (Fall 1983).

47. *Register of Debates*, 22nd Cong., 1st sess., 8: pt. 1, p. 875.

48. Senate Doc. 147, 22nd Cong., 1st sess., p. 5.

49. *Register of Debates*, 22nd Cong., 1st sess., 8: pt. 1, p. 887.

50 *Congressional Globe*, 23rd Cong., 1st sess., pp. 439-474. Senate Doc. 422, 23rd Cong., 1st sess., pp. 25, 31.

51. John Spencer Bassett, *Correspondence of Andrew Jackson* 6 vols. (Washington: Carnegie Institute, 1926–1933) 4: 31–32.

52. See Chapter 1.

53. Charles M. Wiltse, ed., *The Papers of Daniel Webster* 6 vols. (Hanover, N.H.: University Press of New England for Dartmouth College, 1977) 3: 41-42.

54. Daniel Webster, *The Writings and Speeches of Daniel Webster* 18 vols. (Boston: Little, Brown & Co., 1903) 2: 114-15.

55. Frederick Grimke, *The Nature and Tendency of Free Institutions*, John William Ward, ed. (Cambridge: Belknap Press, 1968), p. 398.

56. "Reflections on the Law of Libel," 3 *New York Review* 315 (1838).

57. Benjamin Oliver, *The Rights of an American Citizen* (1832; reprint ed., New York: Books for Libraries Press, 1970), p. 231.

58. "Every Body's Business," *Aurora*, August 22, 1834.

59. Kling, *The Government Printing Office*, p. 13.

60. Daniel Webster, *The Works of Daniel Webster* 6 vols. (Boston: Little, Brown & Co., 1860) 2: 90. The first proposal for a government-owned printing house was made in 1819.

61. *The Papers of Daniel Webster*, 5: 63-64.

62. Richardson, *Messages and Papers*, 4: 13.

63. *Madisonian*, October 7, 1841.

64. Frederick B. Marbut, "Decline of the Official Press in Washington," 33 *Journalism Quarterly* 335 (Summer 1956); Kling, *The Government Printing Office*, pp. 15-16.

65. Sloan, "The Early Party Press,"; Donald Stewart, *The Opposition Press of the Federalist Period* (Albany: State University of New York Press, 1969); William E. Ames and Dwight Teeter, "Politics, Economics and the Mass Media," in Ronald T. Farrar and John D. Stevens, *Mass Media and the National Experience: Essays in Communication History* (New York: Harper & Row, 1971); Culver Smith, *The Press, Politics and Patronage: The American Government's Use of Newspapers, 1789–1875* (Athens: University of Georgia Press, 1977); Gerald J. Baldasty, *The Press and Politics in the Age of Jackson*.

66. Alexis de Tocqueville, *Democracy in America* (New York: Vintage House, 1945), pp. 194-195.

Chapter **4**

"Their Mad and Wicked Schemes": Abolitionists and the Post Office

No issue in American history so embraced all of our traditional liberties as did the controversy over slavery. Far from being a single issue, slavery was a complex problem that challenged the basic economic, social, and political tenets of faith adopted during the prior half century. Those who wrote or spoke out against the "peculiar institution" found themselves inextricably bound up in a struggle to define the bounds of those personal liberties guaranteed by the Constitution.

It was clear to some that slavery and freedom of the press could not coexist within nineteenth-century America. An open letter from the Anti-Slavery Society of Massachusetts in August 1835 asked the central constitutional question:

Admit for a moment that slavery is, as is so confidently asserted, *guaranteed* by the constitution; is not the liberty of speech and of the press also explicitly guaranteed? and if it be found that they cannot co-exist, the question is before the country—which of them is best worth preserving?[1]

In one of the earliest constitutional histories of this country, Hermann Von Holst, explained the dilemma: "A nation that, with full consciousness that it was suffering from a great evil, prohibited and punished any discussion of the means of contending with that evil would be consciously and in principle decreeing away its own capacity to live."[2]

Both fiery abolitionists and moderate anti-slavery reformers recognized that the various attempts made to suppress discussion of slavery carried a menace that would grow beyond the slavery question itself to permeate all areas of political thought. In a speech decrying the Gag Rule, which prohibited anti-slavery petitions from being introduced in Congress, Vermont's Representative William Slade expressed a common fear:

Let it be remembered that the course which may now be adopted to suppress the utterance of hostility to slavery may hereafter be drawn into a precedent to suppress the popular voice on other subjects, and that thus, gathering strength, encroachment may go on from conquering to conquer, until at last it shall sweep away ... all the guarantees of popular rights.[3]

After reading of attempts to prevent the Post Office from delivering abolitionist material in the South, Elijah Porter Barrows, a Presbyterian minister, told his congregation that the tendency of the system of slavery was to "destroy that liberty of the press and freedom of speech and of discussion which are the safeguards of this and every republic." He continued: "Let this freedom guarantied (sic) to every citizen of the United States, by the constitution, be once destroyed *on this point* and it will be an easy work to destroy it on every other point."[4]

No single event created this turmoil. Instead, several conditions and events, stacked one on top of the other like cordwood on a bonfire, appear to have triggered the resounding call for suppression. The fuel included the issue of slavery in new territories, increased slavetrading in the District of Columbia, real and threatened slave insurrections, the debut of the American Anti-Slavery Society, the growth of a strong states' rights party in the South, and Congress's Gag Rule against abolitionist petitions. As Harriet Martineau wrote in 1839, "The surface of society was heaving."[5]

There was very little discussion of slavery in either the Congress or the various state assemblies between the Missouri Compromise of 1821 and 1836. However, the Nullification Crisis of 1828, spearheaded by John C. Calhoun, one of the South's greatest congressmen and Jackson's vice president, would create the first tear in the fabric of nationalism that had pervaded the country since the War of 1812. And although the crisis concerned the Tariff of 1828, at its core was the slavery issue.

For many in South Carolina, the Tariff of 1828 was the final blow to states on the brink of economic disaster, and the only way to protect the honor of the Carolinas was to resist the law. Mass meetings were held; merchants resolved to boycott Northern goods; many Carolinians traded in their woolens for homespun.

Calhoun, who had been a strong nationalist after 1812 and had supported internal improvements, the national bank, and protective tariffs, feared that radical action by South Carolina would tend "to make two out of one nation." Yet, he hoped that the problem could be solved without stepping beyond the constitutional remedies available. For Calhoun, two crucial issues were at stake: preservation of the Union and relief for South Carolina. He secretly worked with South Carolina's radicals to author the South

Carolina Exposition, a document outlining the constitutional methods by which South Carolina could disobey the tariff without splitting from the Union. Calhoun was following the footsteps of Thomas Jefferson who, twenty-seven years earlier, secretly wrote the Virginia Resolution, calling for nullification of the Alien and Sedition Acts.

After outlining the damage the tariff had done to his state, Calhoun argued that it was within constitutional boundaries for any state, not the Supreme Court, to nullify any law which so severely damaged its social and economic interests. And, any nullification vote was binding on both state and federal government.

No one knew better than Calhoun that the real issue in the tariff controversy was slavery. If the majority of Congress could ruin a state's economy without giving that state any redress, the same majority could legislate away slavery and every other institution that the South held dear. Writing to a Maryland friend in 1830, Calhoun warned that if there "be no protective power in the reserved rights of the States, they must in the end be forced to rebel, or submit to have their permanent interests sacrificed, their domestic institutions subverted by Colonization and other schemes, and themselves and children reduced to wretchedness."[6]

The South Carolina legislature refused to endorse the Exposition in 1828. And as nullification fever rose ever higher, even her sister states would not support such an action. But that did not deter the radicals who made up a two-thirds majority in the state legislature by 1832. Eventually Calhoun's hand was forced. In July 1831, Calhoun published the famous Fort Hill Address in which he formally and publicly avowed support for the nullification cause.

He declared that the people of the several states created the Constitution, which was a compact among the states. Each party to a compact has the right to judge for itself what law it will follow. If a law benefits one but harms another, the latter is not subject to that law. Each party has the right to veto the "deliberate, palpable and dangerous" acts of others. He threatened that any action to execute an unconstitutional law would be met with secession.

Jackson answered in his Nullification Proclamation, arguing that the power of any one state to annul a law of the United States was "incompatible with the existence of the Union, contradicted expressly by the letter of the Constitution, unauthorized by its spirit, inconsistent with every principle on which it was founded, and destructive of the great object for which it was formed."

The president warned of the consequences that would befall the state should it dissolve its bond with the Union: "This happy Union we will dissolve; this picture of peace and prosperity we will deface; this free intercourse we will interrupt; those fertile fields we will deluge with blood; the protection of her glorious flag we renounce; the very name of Americans we discard."

To head off bloodshed and disunion, Jackson secured the passage in March 1833 of the Force Bill, which authorized the use of the army and navy, if necessary, to enforce the tariff measures. Meanwhile Henry Clay's Compromise Tariff reduced the tariff over a ten-year period. South Carolina repealed its nullification act.

Although history may look upon the conflict over the tariff as a defeat for the recognition of nullification, it was an important step in developing a radical states' rights doctrine. That the doctrine did not ripen into secession in the 1830s is due in part to the overwhelming denunciation of nullification by all of the Southern states and to Jackson's quick action in getting the Force Bill passed. As the Alabama legislature said in its resolution, "Nullification is unsound in theory and dangerous in practice.... As a remedy it is unconstitutional and essentially revolutionary, leading in its consequences to anarchy and civil discord, and finally to the dissolution of the union."[7]

VIRGINIA AND OPEN DISCUSSION OF SLAVERY

While Calhoun was developing his theories of nullification, at least one Southern state was openly discussing the slavery issue. Virginia had a strong anti-slavery political bloc in its liberal gentry in the east and its freedom-loving Germans and Scots-Irish in the mountains. In the early 1830s, these groups almost succeeded in turning Virginia into a free state.

After the Nat Turner rebellion in Southampton County, Virginia, in August 1831, various bills were presented to the Virginia legislature to deal with the slave problem. Representatives of the liberal gentry and western farmers petitioned the legislature for the abolition of slavery. And in 1832, bills were introduced calling for the colonization of free blacks to Africa and for emancipation.

For the first time in twenty-seven years, the citizens of Virginia were exposed to public debates about slavery. Newspapers not only published the speeches from the House of Delegates about the emancipation and colonization bills, but also participated in the debate by opening up their columns to all viewpoints.

Thomas Ritchie, editor of the Richmond *Enquirer* and a supporter of emancipation, fired the first public volley in the press when he stated that colonization of free blacks solved only one part of the problem. He censured slavery, calling it a "deep seated disease" that could only be cured by "means sure, but gradual; systematic, but discreet."[8]

The first to answer Richie's charges was Senator Nathanial Alexander of Mecklenburg County, who believed that the questions of slavery should not be publicly discussed. He canceled his subscription to the *Enquirer* and called a public meeting to consider "the propriety of discontinuing the use of that paper." Ritchie called Alexander's activities "a bold attempt... to muzzle the liberty of the press," and if allowed to occur the press, "will degenerate into . . . the capricious slave of every popular will without the honesty to speak the truth or the spirit to vindicate the rights of the people."[9]

John Pleasants, editor of the Richmond *Whig*, noted that the people of Virginia had been silent on the subject too long and that the press would be a major instrument for examining the foundations of slavery. The press would also be present to witness the eventual abolition of slavery.[10]

A meeting in Northampton County called on the *Whig* and *Enquirer* to tone down their columns and be more cautious about printing material that may mislead people's perception of Virginia's attitude. In Essex County, a set of resolutions called for Virginians to cancel their subscriptions to pro-abolitionist papers and demanded that editors stop publishing speeches made in the House of Delegates.[11]

But there were occasional supporters of open discussion, if not of abolition. A correspondent, who wrote to the *Enquirer* under the pen name Freedom of Opinion, said that it was impractical to try and stifle the press; in fact, discussions of slavery would have the salutary effect of exposing abolitionists to public censure.[12]

Several weeks later, a letter from "Appomattox" warned that Virginia's abolitionist presses should not be allowed to circulate. The inflammatory material that such papers published "should warn us all of the burning lava yet to be discharged upon us." If newspapers exercise their independence to publish "inflammatory, dangerous, mischevous" material then the reader may exercise his independence by cancelling his subscription. The *Whig* accused "Appomattox" of embarking on the same course as the Sedition Act of 1798, warning that Virginians should not support such threats.[13]

Neither the colonization nor the emancipation bill was passed. However Virginia lawmakers did strengthen the slave code by prohibiting slaves from preaching to slaves and making it illegal to publish material that advised rebellion. This type of legislation not only stopped public discussion of slavery but also played into the hands of Calhoun, whose strategy for uniting the South included the promotion of abolitionism as a wild and fanatical movement that advanced the destruction of social institutions as well as property.

ABOLITIONISTS AND POSTAL CENSORSHIP

Calhoun's rhetoric on the subject of abolitionists was filled with bombastic exaggeration of the danger and overstated characterization of the movement's leaders and purpose. Nevertheless, Calhoun and his supporters succeeded in turning Southern apologists for slavery into ardent supporters of the necessary institution. Even Northern anti-slavery advocates moderated their defense of intemperate abolitionists.

While abolitionist societies had existed in the United States since the

Revolution, it was not until the 1830s that their movement began taking on a decidedly radical bent. William Lloyd Garrison organized the American Anti-Slavery Society in 1832, and it grew rapidly until by 1836 there were over 500 chapters of the society. Martineau described the abolitionists as a body of "men and women of every shade of color, of every degree of education, of every variety of religious opinion, of every gradation of rank, bound together by no vow, no pledge, no stipulation but of each preserving his individual liberty."[14]

With the growth of the society came the increased circulation of abolitionist pamphlets, newspapers, and magazines. In 1835 the society set aside $30,000 to distribute over one million copies of its nine publications throughout the South.[15] This literature, which depicted the horrors of slavery in words and pictures, began reaching Southern cities in the summer of 1835. The publications were met first by mob action and then by laws that prohibited the publication, circulation, and even reading of incendiary material. In the North, they also were met by mobs, public gatherings, and resolutions condemning the wholesale disparagement of Southerners, and warning abolitionists that they were guilty of breaching the sacred compact of states.[16] Yet, the abolitionist societies persisted because, as Calhoun described it, their mission was the emancipation of slaves "through the agency of organized Societies . . . and a powerful press." [17]

To prevent abolitionists from having any substantial effect, the South implemented several measures to forestall distribution of insurrectionist and incendiary information. They included: prohibiting circulation or publication of incendiary publications; calling for the arrest and punishment of any abolitionist carrying incendiary material with them; promulgating awards for the arrest and capture of abolitionist leaders such as William Lloyd Garrison or Arthur Tappan; boycotting businesses owned by Northern abolitionists; seizing shipments of publications as they arrived at the post office; and demanding that Northern states pass laws to prohibit publication of incendiary materials. It was these last two measures which first pitted the Southerners against freedom of the press.

When word reached Charleston, South Carolina, that the mail packet of July 29, 1835 contained hundreds of pamphlets and papers on the subject of slavery, the city became "deeply excited and exasperated; indeed, there is a phrenzied and turbulent feeling," wrote Postmaster Alfred Huger to Postmaster General Amos Kendall.[18]

The *Southern Patriot*, a Charleston paper, warned:

[I]t is a monstrous abuse of the privilege of the public mail, to use it as the vehicle for conveying and scattering in every direction . . . the moral poison with which these publications are drugged. Some mode of prevention should be adopted to abate this nuisance. . . . It is impossible to answer for the security of the mail in this portion of the country.[19]

During the night of July 29, several men broke into the post office and stole a bag of publications. On the following evening, the papers were taken to a parade ground and burned along with effigies of prominent abolitionists.

Postmaster Huger sought advice from U.S. Postmaster General Amos Kendall. Meanwhile he kept the remaining publications, believing that no harm would come if their delivery were delayed. Huger also consulted the local district attorney to get an opinion as to whether the perpetrators could be arrested and whether his own actions in delaying the mail were correct. The postmaster also wrote New York Postmaster Samuel Gouverneur asking him to do everything in his power to prevent "the transmission of these firebrands among us, for God's Sake do so; and let the question of slavery be decided elsewhere than in the P.O. where the Postmaster himself is a Slave holder."[20]

Gouverneur, in turn, asked the American Anti-Slavery Society to suspend the mailing of papers until Kendall had responded to the problem. The Society refused, resolving that while they did not want to unduly burden public officers, "we cannot consent to surrender any of the rights or privileges, which we possess in common with our fellow citizens." Nevertheless, Gouverneur withheld all abolitionist publications from the mail until he received instructions from Kendall.[21]

Finally, on August 4, Kendall answered Huger's letter in a rather obfuscatory manner, leaving all discretion in the hands of the local postmaster. While the Postmaster General has no authority to exclude materials from the mails, said Kendall, he was not prepared to force a local postmaster to deliver harmful papers. Since the post office serves the people of *each* of the states, Kendall could not officially or privately, directly or indirectly, authorize the circulation of such papers. "We owe an obligation to the laws, but a higher one to the communities in which we live, and if the *former* be perverted to destroy the *latter*, it is patriotism to disregard them.... I cannot sanction, and will not condemn the step you have taken."[22]

Kendall received numerous letters, requests, and resolutions during the month of August regarding the distribution of abolitionist material, but his answers remained basically the same. To the chairman of a meeting at Petersburg, Virginia he wrote that he could see no way of remedying the situation aside from having the local postmasters make their own decisions about delivery of the mails. However, he hoped Congress would pass a law that would prevent the use of the mails for such materials and would call on Congress to do just that.[23]

Kendall wrote that Gouverneur had been correct in proposing to the American Anti-Slavery Society that they not use the mails for delivering their materials. While the abolitionists might have the right to distribute their materials within New York, there was no reason why postmasters should force these publications on Southerners before Congress had a chance to react with the proper legislation.

He found legal justification for allowing postmasters to exercise their own discretion in the wording of the Postal Act which only penalized postmasters who "improperly" detained newspapers. A postmaster who, obeying a state law, held up delivery of publications was not acting "improperly." Kendall also argued that no federal law could protect from punishment a public officer who broke a state law. Kendall commended Gouverneur's effort and those of other postmasters for protecting the mails, preventing the interruption of communication, and alleviating excitement.[24]

Kendall kept Andrew Jackson informed of the events in the Southern post offices, sending him copies of his correspondence with Huger and Gouverneur. While Jackson despised the content of the abolitionist papers as well as the mob law that "is becoming too common," he warned Kendall that "we have no power to prohibit anything from being transported in the mail that is authorized by the law." Postmasters should continue to deliver the incendiary publications only to those who are indeed subscribers and take down the names of subscribers and have them exposed. When those subscribers become known, "every moral and good citizen will unite to put them in coventry, and avoid their society."[25]

The outpouring of sentiment for and against the activities at Charleston was overwhelming, but the ensuing debate over freedom of the press lacked any real sophistication or new understandings about the role of a free press in times of social disorder. In fact, most of the debate focused on the states' rights theory and the notion of reserved versus delegated powers rather than on the First Amendment. When it came time to discuss the liberty of the press, the refrains were familiar renditions of the 1800 debates over the Alien and Sedition Acts.

Although the North repudiated the institution of slavery and the South defended it as a necessary evil, the issues raised by abolitionists went far beyond the simple matter of freeing the enslaved. Most Northerners recognized slavery as a moral wrong, but rejected abolition as the proper remedy. Emancipation raised too many terrifying specters in the minds of Northerners, most of whom were racists and who believed that blacks were morally, physically, mentally, and politically inferior to whites. Emancipation meant that the entire Negro population of the South would be set free all at once to wander the streets, rob and burglarize, rape white women, vote, take jobs that belonged to white men, and form political parties. Little wonder that the colonization movement was so popular in the North.[26]

To ensure that immediate emancipation would not occur, non-slaveholders joined with slaveholders to nourish Constitutional theories about states' rights, the compact between states, and separation of powers. Through these vehicles, the non-slaveholder could, without admitting to his racism, protest against the activities of abolitionists and justify extra-legal sanctions against them.

Consequently, it is not surprising that only a handful of Northerners criticized Kendall's support of Southern postmasters. Most, like Harrison Gray Otis of Massachusetts, disliked slavery, but held steadfastly to an interpretation of the Constitution which said that Congress could not legislate away slavery; only the individual states can make that decision. Since it is the state legislatures that must make the decision, said Otis, let the antislavery people present their petitions and their arguments to those bodies, not to the people at large.[27]

William Leggett, editor of the New York *Evening Post*, was one of the few who criticized Kendall while at the same time berating the abolitionists for their ill-intentioned methods. He chastised the postmaster general for not addressing the problem more boldly and manfully. His duty was "single, simple and positive" and ought to have been performed openly and promptly, "without any paltering, shrinking, or evasion." Instead, said Leggett, "he has quailed in the discharge of his duty. He has truckled to the domineering pretensions of slave-holders" and he has shown a "deficiency of courage and independence."[28] The result is the establishment of a *"censorship of the press*... by allowing every two-penny postmaster through the country to judge of what species of intelligence it is proper to circulate." Leggett warned that should Congress prohibit certain materials from being carried in the mail, "not merely will our liberties be destroyed, but the very principles of freedom be extinct within us."

The New York editor had no sympathy for the abolitionists; in fact, he considered their fanaticism "contrary to the unanimous sentiment of the white population." However, as much as Leggett deprecated the conduct of abolitionists, he despised no less Kendall's unlawful way. "They stop the abolition journals to-day: who will insure us that they will not stop ours to-morrow?" After Leggett called for Kendall's resignation, Postmaster Gouverneur canceled the paper's contract to publish the list of uncalled-for letters.[29]

The Albany *Journal* agreed with much of Leggett's assessment and felt that Kendall's instructions would backfire and postmasters could use their power to refuse to distribute newspapers that took the wrong side in politics.[30] The Hartford *Times* called Kendall's actions "a long leap towards anarchy, and subversion of the laws and the constitution."[31]

Unlimited discretion by postmasters troubled one Natchez, Louisiana, editor who wrote that a man would rather receive abolitionist literature and burn it at home, than have his mail rifled by a postal clerk.[32]

William Leete Stone, secretary of the New York Colonization Society and editor of the *Commercial Advertiser*, argued that it was a dangerous assumption of power by the post offices "that may be pleaded in *other* instances. It will be easy to make a pretext, a *precedent* being established."[33]

Supporting fears that postmasters would take discretion too far, the Boston *Atlas* wrote about a Southern postmaster who, while searching the mails for "incendiaries," discovered a love letter written on pink stationery. The editor of the *Atlas* was irate at the behavior: "He not only assumes the responsibility of searching the United States mail, but would make public the contents of a private love letter. Shades of Washington! Where are our liberties?"[34]

In defending its right to use the mails, the New York Anti-Slavery Society told the public that the result of Kendall's action would be to place "throughout the length and breadth of your land, ten thousand censors of the press, each of whom shall have the right to inspect every document you may commit to the post office, and to suppress every pamphlet and newspaper, whether religious or political."[35]

American citizens, said the Society, had the right to express and publish their opinions of the constitution, laws, and institutions of any state and nation. The abolitionists would never surrender the liberty of speech, of the press, or of conscience, all "inherited from our fathers, and which we intended as far as we are able, to transmit unimpaired to our children."

Most editors believed Kendall had acted correctly and well within his constitutional powers as Postmaster General. To the charge that postmasters would have unlimited discretion to rifle through the mails, the Cincinnati *Republican* argued that laws can only be carried out if someone is allowed to exercise a certain amount of discretion. It would be better to allow the postmaster to exercise that discretion than to have the mails filled with incendiary publications.[36]

The Albany *Argus* admired the "prompt, liberal and just reply of the Postmaster General" as the only proper stance for him to take.[37] Webb's *Courier and Enquirer* not only agreed with Kendall's actions but also suggested that the power to censor also belonged to captains of ships and steamboats. He urged these men to refuse any abolition mail.[38]

The duty of all citizens was to avoid this impending dissolution of society, said legal scholar James Kent, and to do whatever was necessary to oppose the interference of abolitionists with the practice of slavery in the South.[39]

Both the North and South feared revolt, insurrection, disunion, and a race war. These fears had been made even more real by Nat Turner's insurrection in 1832, the aborted insurrection of Denmark Vesey in Charleston in 1821, and the Murrel conspiracy in Mississippi in 1835. It was generally believed that the blame for these incidents lay at the feet of abolitionists. If these fanatics succeeded in emancipating slaves, the union would crumble and a race war would ensue.

Calhoun warned a friend in July 1835, that the continuous assaults of the abolitionists would bring about a situation where "we will be compelled to abandon the South and leave it exclusively to the black race."[40] Several days after the Charleston incident, Hezekiah Niles noted in his *Weekly Register* that "it is manifest, we think, that a great simultaneous movement has been made by *Tappan & Co.* to produce an insurrection of the blacks."[41]

The American Anti-Slavery Society refuted charges such in an open letter to the public. President Arthur Tappan explained that the society deplored any slave revolt because it would not only result in bloodshed, but would also bring about harsher treatment of slaves. He denied the charge that publications were being mailed to slaves, saying that they were not intended for slaves, and "were they able to read them they would find in them no encouragement to insurrection."[42] The Anti-Slavery Society of Massachusetts also said that they had no design and no means to address the slaves. "Nothing can be further from our wishes, than to excite the slave population."[43]

Certainly, no one in the South believed these denials, and several editors felt the best way to deal with the threat that the abolitionists posed was to apply a modicum of "lynch law." The Columbia *Telescope* did not care how the matter was dealt with as long as the subject of slavery was not discussed. The moment any one presumed to lecture on its evils, "in the same moment his tongue shall be cut out and cast upon the dunghill."[44]

The *Arkansas Gazette* noted that if the post office did not have the authority to handle the problem, the people of the South would take the law into their own hands and destroy any incendiary publications received through the mails.[45] The Arkansas *Advocate* invited any of Garrison's disciples to visit Arkansas where "they can be accommodated."[46]

In a more moderate vein, a "man of unblemished character, sound judgment and long experience" wrote to the New York *Commercial Advertiser* that while he was no advocate of slavery, he abhorred the methods of abolitionists and praised the recent excitement against the incendiaries. "I care not how rigid the punishment inflicted on offenders, if it has the authority of law and justice."[47]

The best expressions of Southern and Northern sentiment are found in the numerous resolutions passed at public meetings and by legislators following the Charleston affair.[48] These resolutions expressed similar views about the relationship of slavery to the Constitution. All agreed that slavery was an integral part of the American system, that it existed in the states before the adoption of the Constitution, and that its control was not surrendered to the federal government.

The debates forwarded the social compact theory which finds status in the privileges and immunities clause of the Constitution. Under this theory, the states are joined by compact into a union, and each member of the union has an unquestionable right to expect that no interference will take place in its internal matters. Under such a compact it becomes the duty of each state to prevent its citizens from interfering with other states. Any attempt by abolitionists to deny the property right in slaves is a wanton violation of the political compact.

Resolutions passed in Boston read:

That the people of the United States have solemnly agreed with each other to leave to the respective states the jurisdiction pertaining to the relation of master and slave within their boundaries, and that no man or body of men, except the people or governments of those states, can of right do any act to dissolve or impair the obligations of that contract.[49]

Therefore, continued a resolution passed in Philadelphia," we distinctly disclaim any and all right to interfere, directly or indirectly, with the subject of slavery in the southern states."[50] And finally, the citizens of New Haven, Connecticut said:

No man or combination of men have the right to violate the criminal laws of any other state in the union, either by sending publications leading to insurrection in such states, by or in any other manner; and that we hold it to be the duty of good citizens by all lawful measures in their power, *promptly to arrest such proceedings.*[51]

These and similar resolutions usually were prefaced with a statement condemning the institution of slavery as immoral. Southern resolutions added the demand that Northern states pass legislation. Resolutions from Richmond, Virginia, admonished Northerners to "to make all within their borders, and under the influence of their laws, desist from their mad and wicked schemes."[52] But the Richmond *Whig* doubted the efficacy of merely rebuking incendiaries, noting that they have been chastised numerous times, but neither their zeal nor growth had diminished. "Nothing short of [a law] will cure the mischief or satisfy the South."[53] A resolution from Charleston, South Carolina also appealed to Northern patriotism for passage of state laws that would "punish any vile incendiaries within their limits who... discharge their missiles of mischief in the security of distance."[54]

It was also a part of Southern resolutions to call for some form of internal control. A resolution passed by the Charleston City Council, after that city's post office was ransacked, approved a $1,000 award for the apprehension of any person bringing in, publishing, or circulating materials that had a tendency to excite insurrection or disturb the peace.[55] Another town meeting in Charleston resulted in the appointment of a committee of twenty-one. This committee made arrangements with the postmaster that no seditious pamphlets would be issued or forwarded from the post office.

Citizens in Richmond, Virginia recommended that committees of vigilance and correspondence be organized, that police arrest offenders against their own state laws and that every citizen should pledge to inform authorities of dangerous activities.[56]

In the Barnsville District of South Carolina, citizens passed resolutions giving their vigilance committee the power to seize and burn all incendiary papers.[57] In the Pendleton district of western South Carolina, John C. Calhoun joined a committee of twenty-one in urging a committee of vigilance to adopt whatever measures were necessary to prevent circulation of publications. They also advised that the postmaster should cooperate by first delivering questionable materials to the committee.[58]

The self-help program resulted in arrests, beatings, and lynchings through-out the South. The New Orleans *Bee* reported that a person was arrested for disseminating abolitionist materials and turned over for trial. "If convicted the punishment by the laws of Louisiana is death."[59] A young theological student, Amos Dresser, was apprehended in Nashville with anti-slavery papers in his luggage. He was tried, found guilty, and given twenty lashes.[60]

But these internal measures, no matter how harsh, were only temporary. Lasting help could come only from passage of laws in Northern states. Support for Northern cooperation could be found in the social compact theory as well as in the theories of international law, which likened the various states to separate countries that were bound to punish any citizen who infringed on the laws of another country.

A lengthy explanation and defense of the international law theory was put forth by Richard Yeadon, editor of the Charleston *Courier*. Yeadon urged the governor of South Carolina to demand the delivery of abolitionists to the South for trial. He reasoned that "it is treason to the union and the Constitution in any state" to allow any citizen, by word, writing or printing, to disturb Southern rights.[61]

Recognizing the right of free discussion in a Republican land, the editor noted that such discussion must respect the rights of individuals and communities. Any attempt to direct public attention against slavery would be regarded as a direct act of hostility—a "justifiable cause of war." However, international law allows a more reasonable alternative to war—"libel on a government." Citing English and American law, Yeadon argued that abolitionists have committed a crime and were punishable under the laws of sedition for directly tending to create servile war. The South could bring suit in any Northern state for such a libel on government.[62]

The Virginia legislature demanded that non-slaveholding states pass legislation as it was their duty under international law. In his annual message, Governor Swain of North Carolina prompted his state lawmakers to send resolutions to Northern states. The resolutions, based upon theories of international law, respectfully requested Northern states to pass criminal laws to prevent the circulation of material intended to incite slaves to insurrection.[63]

Governor William Schley of Georgia followed suit and also asked the North for laws because they were the best ones to devise and apply a remedy.[64] The Georgia legislature, in turn, adopted resolutions that were forwarded to President Jackson, and the governors of various states.[65]

Governor McDuffie's message to the South Carolina legislature was typical of the sentiment being expressed in state houses across the South. McDuffie, holding that the great principles of international law existed among the sovereign states, demanded of the Northern states the passage of penal laws against abolitionist propaganda:

Every State is under the most sacred obligations, ... to prevent its citizens or subjects from such interference, either by inflicting condign punishment itself, or by delivering them up to the justice of the offending community.... The refusal of a State to punish these offensive proceedings ... makes the State so refused an accomplice in the outrage, and furnishes a just cause of war.[66]

While McDuffie advised that Northern states be approached "with all the fraternal mildness" and with "firmness and decision," he had no sympathy for abolitionists themselves whom he believed should be punished "by death without benefit of clergy."[67]

Governor Lucas of Ohio responded to these Southern appeals by refusing to recommend legislation, leaving matters, instead, in the hands of moral force and public opinion.[68] The legislature of New York supported the appeal of slaveholding states, but felt there was no necessity to pass laws, despite the message from the New York Governor Marcy encouraging the passage of legislation.

The new governor of Massachusetts, Edward Everett, included a severe censure of abolitionists in his January 1836 inaugural address and suggested that the incendiaries were guilty of some offense punishable at common law. Although the conservative Everett was opposed to slavery, he feared that agitation on the issue would result in disunion, and therefore should be checked. That portion of his message, along with memorials and resolutions from Southern governors and legislatures, was referred to a joint legislative committee.

William Goodell, editor of the *Emancipator*, requested an appearance before the committee to explain the abolitionists' side. The interview was granted and nine members of the Massachusetts Anti-Slavery Society, including Goodell and William Lloyd Garrison, appeared.[69] Ellis Gray Loring, a lawyer and officer in the Society, reviewed the various theories forwarded supporting Northern suppression of abolitionists, but found all arguments wanting, particularly that of international law. He noted that both the United States and Massachusetts Constitutions forbade restrictions on freedom of the press.

He asked the legislature to "stand neutral between us and our opposers. Give us a fair field and no favor, and if we do not prevail, it is because the right is not with us." While the legislators would be unlikely to actually adopt new penal laws to deal with incendiaries, abolitionists feared that lawmakers might pass resolutions censuring abolitionists. Such a censure would, in the eyes of the abolitionists, be worse than any law because it would be extra-judicial, with no opportunity for redress in court. Also, a censure might be construed as being preparatory to some future legislation.

It was also argued that a public censure would be seized upon as a "warrant for mobs to react." At that point, the committee chairman insisted that such statements linking the legislature to mob violence were out of order and impermissible at the hearing. The hearing then broke up when it became uncertain what the Society's members would be allowed to say.

However, another hearing was held the next week at which the abolitionists were able to complete their arguments. Samuel Sewell noted that the resolutions from the Southern legislatures were a direct interference with the domestic affairs of Massachusetts and that no state could dictate what another could do. He called the language of the resolutions "arrogant and insulting" for their attempts to punish Massachusetts citizens for holding opinions which were guaranteed by the Constitution. After considerable debate, the legislature refused to pass any law, but did admonish its citizens to refrain from interfering in the institutions of other states.[70]

Mr. Hazard of Newport, Rhode Island, presented resolutions favoring legislation and was elected chairman of a committee to report a bill that would hold abolitionists legally responsible for incendiary expression. However, the bill was defeated.[71] A meeting of citizens in Philadelphia resolved that the legislature of Pennsylvania enact at the next session whatever provisions were necessary "to protect our fellow citizens of the south from incendiary movements without our borders."[72]

Mordecai Noah, editor of the New York *Evening Star*, urged that it was the duty of the North to adopt immediately measures "against the base wretches who are the authors of these treasonable schemes.... It is our imperious duty to make common cause against and to apprehend these incendiaries."[73] He formulated a law that would make the printing or publishing of writings or pictures that are intended to cause insurrection or breach of peace among the slaves a misdemeanor. It would also require a grand jury investigation of any charges from a Southern state that a citizen of a Northern state had published the same kind of material.[74]

James Watson Webb, editor of the *Courier and Enquirer*, also urged legislation, arguing that if it is right to prevent publications with a licentious tendency, surely it is proper to stop "publications calculated to destroy the foundation of society." A letter from "Camden" went even further to say that states could make the publication of incendiary materials a capital crime.[75]

The call for legislation concerned many Northerners and while a great deal of debate ensued, no laws were passed to curb abolitionists. The rhetoric of international law and the compact theory of states was well rehearsed, but when it came to acting decisively upon the obligations such a compact imposed, the non-slaveholding states were more likely to look out for their own sovereignty than that of the slaveholding states.

While Northern states willingly chastised, castigated, and verbally flogged the abolitionist firebrands, they opposed the passage of actual legislation. As Russell Nye noted in his *Fettered Freedom*, "American journalism possessed a powerful tradition of freedom of expression.... Editors were extremely jealous of their prerogatives, and reacted swiftly to real or imagined attempts to infringe upon them."[76]

A meeting in Portland, Maine, simply noted that it was the duty of all good citizens to avoid all interference with the institutions of other states. A meeting in New York resolved that sending of incendiary publications was a gross infringement of the rights of states. And in New Haven, Connecticut, citizens were urged to promptly arrest such interference. Citizens who use the mails to distribute incendiary publications, "are deserving of the reprobation of all good and patriotic men."[77] Generally, the tool for suppression of abolitionist sentiment should be public meetings and the press.[78]

Despite a lively meeting in Boston's Faneuil Hall that protested against the abolitionists, there was no resolution calling for specific laws. This lack of action upset the *Southern Patriot*, which had hoped that Boston "would have taken the lead and the credit of having *first* suggested to the legislature of Massachusetts that series of measures that would have put an end to discussions on the subject of slavery, within her limits, by the *strong arm of the law*." [79]

When word reached Southern states that the citizens of the North were not living up to their pledge of protection, they called for reconsideration but added serious warnings: "[S]hould the non-slaveholding states omit or refuse . . . to put a final stop to the proceedings of their abolition societies . . . it will then become the solemn duty of the whole south . . . to withdraw from the union."[80]

Despite warnings from the South, the citizens of Lowell, Massachusetts turned down a set of resolutions that would have required the citizens "to muzzle the press, to shut up their halls and churches against the discussion of the subject, and to prevent all over whom they have any control from attending meetings of such discussions."

If Northern states subscribed to the separation of powers and the compact theories, supported the right of the South to protect its own institutions, and acknowledged the real danger that abolitionist fever was stirring up in that section, why were they so reluctant to even suggest legislation to curb the incendiaries? The answer seems to lie in just what Northern states were willing to give up in order to service their obligations and duties to their Southern states. Was it possible to secure the free press rights of abolitionists while at the same time securing Southern states from their dangerous influence?

Every Northern constitution had its own free press clause, and abolitionist publishers would be protected by those clauses until such time as they created a significant breach of peace in their home states. So far, the only violence that had occurred in the North resulted from the mobbing of speakers, not newspaper offices. Even then, state sedition laws were sufficient to handle whatever problems occurred.

The non-slaveholding states were not ready to abandon the constitutional rights of their own citizens just to quell hysteria in the South. Nor were they ready to believe that the danger to the Union was so great that the time had come to harness freedom of expression in the name of preserving the republic. The Boston *Advocate* recognized the impasse and warned that the Southern states were as much bound by the compact to protect the freedom of press of Northern states as Northern states were bound to protect slavery.[81]

William H. Seward, then a young lawyer and unsuccessful nominee for governor of New York, wrote to Thurlow Weed, editor of the New York *Evening Journal*, that the very fact that "no honorable, or high minded, or reputable man in the North" lent his sanction either to the legislation against abolitionists, or the conduct of the Post Office Department, proved that "if the South persists, the issue will be changed, fearfully changed for them."[82]

The Massillion, Missouri, *Gazette*, exasperated at the South's tendency to cry foul every time things did not go their way, did not believe the threat to the republic was real enough to warrant censorship: "It is time for us of the free states ... to let the south understand that we will discuss every subject that may present itself, as fully and free as we have always done; when we cease to do so, we shall cease to be a free people."[83]

Thomas Ritchie, editor of the Richmond *Enquirer*, agreed that the talk of disunion was self-defeating. He advised that entreaties to the North should be carried out "firmly and frankly, but calmly, respectfully and affectionately." However, it should be left to the Southern legislatures to appeal to their Northern counterparts for laws and resolutions.[84]

The Richmond *Enquirer* warned that if Southern meetings and resolutions failed to accomplish the desired end, then more efficient measures could be adopted: put the abolitionists "under the ban of society," close meeting houses to their agents, throw every difficulty in the way of their holding meetings and establishing presses, and suspend business with them.[85] This last recommendation was quickly adopted by more radical Southerners who suggested a general boycott of Northern businesses, particularly those operated by known abolitionists.

In August 1835, storekeepers passed a resolution pledging themselves not to deal directly or indirectly with abolitionists. The theme was picked up by the Richmond *Whig* and the Richmond Committee of Vigilance in mid-September. According to Peter Daniels, when the circulation of publications was first detected in Richmond, the committee was formed (composed primarily of Whigs), and a member asked for a convention of Southern merchants to devise a plan for boycotting Northern businesses. The idea was adopted, but more moderate Democrats such as Richmond *Enquirer* editor Ritchie voted against it, hoping that the North would find its own efficient means of preventing the distribution of incendiary materials.[86]

The New Orleans *Bee* supported some type of economic pressure: "Let the south then be true to herself and diminish the dangers of such an intercourse, by diminishing as far as practicable, and even at the temporary sacrifice of her own interests, the commercial intercourse with the north." The editor recommended as the first step redirecting European trade to Southern ports, and storing cotton and rice in Southern seaboard communities rather than in New York. "It may starve some of the restless spirits of fanaticism out of their present purse-fed insolence."[87]

The New York *Herald* responded to the call for a boycott as just one more step toward final separation. The editor contended that a non-intercourse action by the South would punish many friends and few enemies. "Where there is one abolitionist among the merchants north of the Potomac, there are one hundred against the fanatics."[88] There is no way to measure the effect of these non-intercourse activities. However, it would not be presumptuous to speculate that they had little effect.

By December 1835, the debates over how to control incendiaries shifted from urging state control to promoting federal control. Jackson had earlier told Kendall not to stop the mail, but certainly to take down the names of subscribers to the suspect publications. When Kendall filed his annual report on the Post Office, he suggested that there was a mutual obligation of states to suppress attacks by their citizens on the institutions of other states. While the federal government was prohibited from passing laws prohibiting discussion, it could prevent its agents from breaking state laws. Therefore, it was up to Congress to pass a law to prevent postal employees from violating state laws.[89]

In his annual message of December 1835, Jackson reproached the abolitionists for their "unconstitutional and wicked" attempts to inflame the slaves to insurrection and to promote disharmony between the states. While noting that most interferences with Southern interests could be dealt with through state law, Jackson placed the question of the mails directly into the hands of Congress. Specifically, he called on Congress to pass a law to prohibit the circulation through the mails in the Southern states, of "incendiary publications intended to instigate the slaves to insurrection."[90] Although there was some disagreement about what Jackson's directive meant, most interpreted his message to allow Congress the power to decide what types of materials could be passed through the mails and what punishment to inflict on anyone placing such materials into the mail stream. Southerners in Congress lost no time responding to Jackson's message. On December 12, Senator Calhoun moved to have the president's recommendation referred to a special committee rather than to the Northern-dominated Committee on the Post Office and Post Roads.[91] Uppermost in Calhoun's mind was the need for a committee to endorse a solution that would not at the same time extend federal power into the Southern states.

In the senator's opinion, Jackson's proposal to allow Congress the power over what content circulated in the mails was merely another attempt to push the federal government into areas where it did not belong. As Calhoun became more states' rightist, he began examining issues only in terms of their effect on the power of states and on the Southern states. He opposed any bill that gave the federal government greater powers, or that protected the majority against the minority.[92]

At the same time that Calhoun railed against the extension of federal power, he was becoming almost hysterical about the abolitionist influence across the country. His letters show a frenzy that borders on the fanatical. His rhetoric was exaggerated, magnifying the dangers out of proportion. He sincerely believed that the continued distribution of abolitionist material would "shake the political fabric to the center, if not rend it asunder," "result in the impoverishment and prostration of an entire section of the union," "destroy the security and independence of the white race," "burst asunder the bonds of this union," and "engulf [the Union] in a sea of blood."[93]

The dual hatred of Jacksonian federalism and abolitionist interference would seem to leave Calhoun in a quandary since Jackson's proposal would indeed reduce the amount of incendiary material reaching the South. But, for the South Carolinian, Jackson's proposal had too many long-term consequences. Calhoun more than anyone saw freedom of press and slavery as entwined and inseparable areas reserved to the states. As long as the states reserved sole authority over freedom of the press and slavery, the South would be secure; but, to allow Congress to claim authority over the freedom of the press would threaten slavery. After hearing Jackson's message, Calhoun wrote that "the Government has no right to determine what kind of materials can be carried by the mails. Such a power is odious and dangerous."[94]

The Select Committee made its report during the first week of February 1836. Accompanying the report was proposed legislation that would prohibit any postmaster from knowingly receiving and putting into the mail any material touching on the subject of slavery and intended for delivery in a state where such material was forbidden by state law. Any postmaster violating the law would be fined and dismissed.[95]

Had it not been for the tie-breaking vote of Vice President Martin Van Buren, wrote Senator Thomas Hart Benton of Missouri years later, the bill never would have been engrossed. Benton speculated that Calhoun had manipulated a tie vote in order to force Van Buren, Democratic candidate for the presidency, to show his true colors on the issue of abolition. Benton explained that "Calhoun had made the rejection of the bill a test of alliance with Northern abolitionists, and a cause for the secession of the Southern States; . . . the whole responsibility for its loss would have been thrown upon (Van Buren) and the North" at a time when many were questioning the vice president's true feelings about abolition.[96]

Abolition was not a popular cause across the country, nor was it supported by the Democratic Party. It would have been politically fatal for Van Buren to openly favor abolition; he had no choice but to cast the tie-breaking vote in favor of engrossment, "although it was a bad bill, as it was known it would not pass," wrote Benton.[97] William Jay of the American Anti-Slavery Society wrote several years later that Van Buren gave his vote for the slave-holders "and received from them, at the ensuing election, 61 electoral votes, by means of which he became President of the United States."[98]

To Southerners, Van Buren's vote was "worth all the pamphlets and Reports that can be written, to open the eyes of the South," wrote the Richmond *Enquirer*. Although all of the Northern senators and all of the arguments for freedom of the press, rights of discussion, and property in the mail were thrown against him, Van Buren's vote "called for the firmest nerve and soundest principle, and his vote shows . . . how much of both he possesses." The vice president had voted for engrossment of a bill "which prevents the great organ of communication between the North and the South from being converted into a poisonous and offensive weapon."[99]

While Calhoun and other Southerners may have seen the bill as a test for Northern Democrats, the ensuing debate did not meet those expectations. In fact, unlike the continuing debates over the acceptance of petitions against slavery, very little was said about the merits of slavery or its abolition. Consequently, the final vote on the bill, while certainly sectional, could not be used by Calhoun as a weapon to denounce Northern abolition-loving senators.

While there was little debate on the issue of slavery during the consideration of Calhoun's bill, there was a good deal of speech-making about the meaning of the First Amendment, the extent of Congress's power over the Post Office, and the legitimacy of using the Post Office to support state laws.

Despite the diversity of opinions on these issues, there appeared in the debates two areas of consensus: that abolitionists were using the mails to distribute materials that had an evil tendency and were aimed at alarming slaves to revolt, but that the First Amendment prohibited Congress from passing any law that punished a publisher for what he printed or circulated. For this reason Jackson's message, which condoned interference, was not welcomed by many members of Congress.[100]

By the mid–1830s there existed a strong tradition that Congress had no authority to define what types of content could and could not be published. However, for the first time since 1801, this concept, which had only been a sentiment lodged in rhetoric, would now be tested in a different arena to see if it could stand up to the stress of practice. It appears to have survived the test, for Whigs and Democrats, slaveholders and non-slaveholders, Northerners and Southerners alike held firmly that Congress could not prohibit publication or circulation of materials based on their content. This concept, while not legally defined, had become a fixture on the landscape of free press tradition and practice.

Calhoun repeatedly warned that any attempt by Congress to control the publication and circulation of publications was tantamount to a reenactment of the dreaded Sedition Act. According to the report, it would be equally unconstitutional for Congress to prohibit publication of a newspaper as it would be to prohibit its circulation—"The object of publishing is circulation, and to prohibit circulation is, in effect, to prohibit publication." Congress's power over the Post Office does not extend to the political, moral, and religious content of the mails. The report warned that if Congress were given the power to decide what was incendiary and to prohibit its circulation through the mails, then Congress could also decide what other institutions were harmful and move to abolish them.[101]

Daniel Webster agreed with Calhoun that liberty of the press meant the liberty to print as well as to circulate, and he feared that if an exception were made for publications about slavery, then the law could be applied to any other publication. Congress might, under this example, be asked to suppress the circulation of political, religious, or any other publications that might produce excitement.[102]

While most agreed that Congress had no power under the First Amendment to censor publications, not everyone agreed with Calhoun's assessment of Congress's postal power. Senator John King of Georgia argued that the purpose of the postal system was to "keep up a social, friendly and commercial intercourse among the people of the States," and under this power Congress could pass all laws which carried into effect those objects.[103]

Senator James Buchanan of Pennsylvania said Congress can decide what will and will not be carried in the mail. However, the future president warned that "unless in extreme cases, where the safety of the republic were involved, we should never exercise this power of discrimination." And this, said Buchanan, was one of those extreme cases.

Buchanan saw no contradiction between the First Amendment and the postal power. While any citizen may publish even that which aids the enemies, it did not follow that government was bound to carry such publications through the mails. Buchanan saw the actions as entirely different—"one is merely passive, the other is active."[104]

Senator John Davis of Massachusetts challenged Buchanan's argument, saying that the use of the postal power to censor the mails was an old argument that had been used whenever it was thought necessary to censor licentiousness. Given the choice of a corrupt press or a free press, those who favored liberty had always decided that it was better to put up with a lesser evil than to see the press destroyed.

Interestingly, the real issue for Calhoun was not censorship per se, but censorship by the federal government. In fact, most believed that censorship was legal as long as it was exercised by the states. Just as states continued to prosecute for seditious libel after the repeal of the federal Sedition Act, it was within the power of states to pass laws prohibiting circulation of incendiary materials when Congress could not do the same. States may pass any laws, without restriction or limitation, to stop "the introduction and circulation of papers calculated to excite insurrection," said Calhoun. In fact, Southern states would be compelled to revise their laws in the face of the inroads being made by abolitionists.[105]

Thomas Morris of Ohio, a strong Jackson supporter, simply could not support the president because "to punish injuries done to individuals belongs exclusively to the States."[106] Henry Clay of Kentucky warned that "the States alone had the power, and their power was ample for the purpose."[107]

But Calhoun countered that state law was not always ample for the purpose. If a state prohibited the circulation of certain publications, then the federal government and other states states must cooperate and even modify their own acts so as not to impinge on a state's protectionist moves.[108]

The only means to force that cooperation was through federal legislation. Rather than allowing Congress to punish persons for placing certain types of materials in the mail, Calhoun's bill placed the burden of censorship on the deputy postmasters who would be required to pull anything from the mail that contravened existing state law. Thus, each state, not Congress, would define the content to be suppressed. The materials could be placed in the mails with no consequences to the publisher, but when the mail reached its point of delivery, illegal materials could be withdrawn with Congress's blessing. But to say that Congress had no power over the content of the mails and then to say that Congress can direct postmasters to withdraw materials was a contradiction many senators could not reconcile.

Clay noted that the law attacked the problem at the wrong end. Rather than placing the burden on the postmaster, why not place it on the recipient of the material? Once the recipient has taken the materials from the stream of mail, a state could compel its own citizens to hand over the materials.[109]

Webster contrasted Calhoun's bill to the Sedition Act, claiming that the latter may have been even better (it "*was* the old law of liberty") since the decision to punish an editor had been made by the courts. Under the present bill, the withdrawal of material from the mails rested not in the courts, but in the hands of deputy postmasters who were unschooled in either the constitution or the law.[110]

Georgia's Senator King failed to see any contradiction for he felt that the freedom of the press could not be used as a cloak to protect against wrongdoing. The First Amendment was simply a prohibition against congressional interference with how a state chose to define freedom of press. If a state defined freedom of the press to exclude incendiary publications, then Congress was required to ensure that itself and other states did not interfere with the execution of that state's definition. To carry out its passive role, it was necessary for Congress to pass legislation such as that under consideration.[111]

Calhoun "asked nothing" except that the federal government stop violating laws essential to the peace and security of the South. Since the South had failed to convince Northern states to pass legislation prohibiting publication of incendiary materials, Calhoun saw this bill as the only way to protect the South. "To refuse to pass this bill would be virtually to cooperate with the abolitionists." Should the Senate refuse to pass the bill "and conflict should ensue between you and our law, the southern States will never yield to the superiority of yours."[112]

Waving the old flag of nullification, Calhoun added that "it should be fixed in every Southern mind that the laws of the slaveholding states are paramount to the laws of the federal government . . . and that the latter must yield to the former in the event of conflict. If the Government should refuse to yield, the States have a right to interpose."[113]

Thomas Morris of Ohio refused to take seriously Calhoun's ranting that the security of the Union rested on the passage of the "strange, wild and visionary" bill. "For my own part", I . . . believe, that persons who make such threats, desire what they threaten.[114]

Clearly, the lack of consensus as to the breadth of Congress's power over the content of the mails resulted in the defeat of the bill on June 8, by a vote of twenty-five to nineteen. The vote split along sectional lines. Only four Northern senators voted for it; three Southern senators (two from Maryland and Benton of Missouri) voted against it.

It is unlikely that any bill touching on freedom of the press would have survived examination by the Senate. At least one historian has argued that the Jackson proposal may have had a better chance of survival than Calhoun's if the menace were to the federal government and not just to the South. Or, if the materials had proposed to abolish slavery by illegal means, then censorship would have been legitimate.[115]

The Senate debates also reveal that the legacy of the Sedition Act was too close to the memories of these legislators. Nor did they want to be seen as drawing kinship lines between themselves and the old aristocratic Federalists. Jefferson was still a hero to these men, and the Kentucky and Virginia Resolutions were quoted by nullifiers and nationalists alike. No matter how federal censorship was clothed—with the cloak of the postal power or the undergarment of state law—it would not be condoned at this point in American history. It would take another generation and a war before Congress would allow itself to "incidentally" limit freedom of the press in its exercise of delegated powers.

While the Senate debated Calhoun's bill, the House of Representatives took up the same issue within its regular Post Office and Post Roads Committee. The majority of the committee (six of nine) had concluded that Congress did have constitutional powers to act in this matter, but the committee could not agree on any particular set of recommendations, preferring to wait until the Senate acted.[116] However, an amendment to the pending

Post Office reorganization act was introduced that read much like Calhoun's bill. It too was defeated.[117]

Neither Calhoun nor Jackson carried the day, and the issue of postal censorship of abolitionist materials was ended in Congress—with an ironic twist. Buried deep in that year's postal reorganization law, at paragraph thirty-two, was a provision that federal postmasters were prohibited from unlawfully detaining or delaying delivery of letters, pamphlets, and newspapers, on pain of $500 fine, maximum six months in jail, and forfeiture of job.[118]

Several months after the defeat of his bill, Calhoun wrote a friend: "From all that I saw and heard during the Session, I am perfectly satisfied that we must look to ourselves ... for safety. It is perfectly idle to look to the non-slaveholding states to arrest the attacks of fanatics." Several days later he wrote another friend: "If possible let us save the liberty of all; but, if not, our own at all events."[119]

William H. Seward probably summed up the sentiments of some of those senators who voted against the bill when he wrote: "Those laws bring a question of awful import home to every man's understanding and heart, and no party in the North can sustain itself after enacting such measures."[120]

Any discussion in the public presses about Calhoun's proposal was quickly overshadowed by the noisier debates on the gagging of abolitionist petitions. Nevertheless, a few voices, mostly of abolitionists, were heard on the topic of press censorship. The Massachusetts Anti-Slavery Society's Fifth Annual Report noted that there was a great deal of apathy toward the question. The president's message and Calhoun's report ought to have "excited in the minds of the people, the liveliest emotions of astonishment and alarm; but neither of them disturbed the nation or elicited a single burst of indignation from any body of men but the abolitionists." Under other circumstances, such a proposition "would have convulsed all the political and moral elements in the land and created a hurricane excitement."[121] Yet, even the Society's report said little about the First Amendment or freedom of the press.

One of the more interesting public commentaries about the bill came from former New Hampshire Senator William Plumer. He published a pamphlet in early 1836 that labeled Calhoun's report and bill as the "most ingenious and able attempt ever yet made in this country ... to interweave with the fabric of our government the principles of ruthless despotism." He also took note of the indifference: "They condemn and abhor the Bill ... but content themselves with the belief that it will not pass."[122]

Plumer's major argument against the bill was its cavalier attitude toward the state constitutional guarantees of free speech and free press. Those senators who spoke out against the bill never disputed the contention that states had full power over their presses. That the states alone had the power to define freedom of the press for their citizens was originally put forward in the Kentucky and Virginia Resolutions, and was found as well in the various arguments against the Sedition Act. But Plumer placed a new interpretation on these "reserved powers." He noted that almost every state had a press guarantee similar to that found in the federal Constitution. While Congress was forbidden by the First Amendment to interfere with free speech and press, "Does not a similar article in each state Constitution place the same right beyond the encroachment of the state legislature?" Freedom of speech and press were not rights "reserved from" Congress and vested in the state legislatures, but were reserved from both Congress and state legislatures, by the United States Constitution and by the state constitutions. No state legislature can alter those documents without the permission of the people.

Plumer compared Calhoun's bill to the "well-known policy of tyrants" who single out one objectionable act, exaggerate its character, and then call on restraints of the press to remove the evil. "Instead of leaving truth and error alike free to combat, till truth gain the ascendancy, they enchain both, and in so doing . . . abridge the freedom of all in the community, excepting those only who are free to hold the chains."[123]

The editor of the Richmond *Compiler* agreed with Plumer's interpretation. The paper produced extracts of various state laws, state constitutional guarantees, and the U.S. Constitution "from which it will be seen that no law can constitutionally be passed for the purpose of restraining the fanatics of the north in their crusade against our rights."[124]

The abolitionists who spoke out against the bill appeared more concerned with their image and with slavery itself than with freedom of the press. For example, the Massachusetts Anti-Slavery Society Report spent most of its fourteen pages talking about that part of Calhoun's report which touched upon the institution of slavery and the duties of one state to another.

The *Anti-Slavery Record* came the closest to approaching the question of a free press when it quoted the editor of the Essex *Gazette* on the Senate bill's prohibition against materials "touching the subject of slavery":

Let Daniel Webster then keep his Plymouth speech at home. Let no negligent postmaster suffer the Constitution of Massachusetts to slip through his fingers. Let him look sharply for the Declaration of Independence. It is an incendiary document, written by a pernicious old incendiary, by the name of Jefferson. [125]

Although his comments were not directed at the post office bill specifically, at least one anti-abolitionist did question the constitutionality of such organizations as the American Anti-Slavery Society. Many criticized the abolitionists for their inflammatory spirit and destructive nature, but Calvin Colton actually found a niche in the legal system where the abolitionists might be prosecuted.[126] Colton, a former journalist and an Episcopal minister turned politician, was an advocate of colonization who wrote several books decrying the nature of reform movements, specifically abolitionism.

Colton went beyond the typical rhetoric that accused abolitionists of threatening the Union and proceeded to demonstrate that the American Anti-Slavery Society's purpose was to overthrow the government. He described the organization as "a grand and permanent political organization, self-erected, self-governed, independent, and irresponsible." He contended that no license existed for a permanent political organization to act independently of the federal government. Once another political society becomes active "the healthful balance of power is lost. Such an unconstitutional organization...assails the Constitution and laws of the country, with no rival influence to counteract it."

The normal modes of popular action—public presses, public assemblies, petitions, addresses and remonstrance to Congress and the ballot box—are all that is comprehended in the First Amendment. By adhering to the authorized modes of effecting change, wrote Colton, there is always a balance of influence against attempts to overthrow government. Because freedom of speech is guaranteed to all, the speech of one man is balanced by that of another on the other side of the question. The same applies to the press.

However, continued Colton, once a political machine is allowed into the discussions, the balance of power is lost. The organization has usurped the business of state, and "neither the public, nor the Government, seem yet to know which end, or how, head or tail, to take hold of the monster."

The setback produced by the defeat of Calhoun's Post Office Bill and the refusal of the North to cooperate in suppressing abolitionist publications was only temporary. Unable to stop this noxious literature at its Northern source, Southern states turned to their own legislatures for new or amended laws to deal with incendiary publications.

Each of the slave-holding states had an extensive set of Slave Codes that regulated the actions of slaves and the relationship of slave to master. The South used these laws to counterattack the onslaught of incendiary publications. Many of the laws already punished persons found guilty of inciting slaves to insurrection; however, these laws were aimed more toward the John Browns and Nat Turners than the Tappans or Garrisons. Therefore, legislatures either amended old laws or passed new laws aimed directly at abolitionists and at keeping the South free of outside meddling.

For example, Virginia had an old law that punished expression that had a tendency to produce discontent or excite insubordination among slaves. But, in 1832, the law was modified to make it a crime for any person to circulate incendiary publications. The penalty was thirty-nine lashes for the first offense and death for the second offense. Four years later, the law was amended to forbid any agent of an abolitionist society to enter Virginia to express anti-slavery views or to circulate material that tended to incite revolt. The penalty was two to five years in prison.

The Richmond *Whig* criticized the 1836 law as being far worse than "Lynching and Lynch's Law, and a reflection on the legislators of the state that such deformed crudities are submitted in the shape of bills."[127] Again, in 1849, Virginia made it punishable to merely deny the right to own slaves.[128]

In 1835, Maryland made it a crime for anyone knowingly to circulate or assist in circulating any material that tended to incite slaves to revolt. And in South Carolina, an 1820 law set a $1,000 fine for anyone bringing incendiary publications into the state. This law was strengthened in 1835 with the additional provision that penalized anyone bringing into the state slaves who had been north of the Potomac, in Mexico, the West Indies or in Washington, D.C. Such laws were intended to prevent unnecessary infection from abolitionists.[129]

At least ten states passed new laws or amended old ones between 1830 and 1838 to deal directly with the problem of antislavery publications and abolitionist agents. Most of these laws were merely thinly disguised sedition laws, using language similar to the older laws used against political seditions in the earlier part of the century. The laws often required a finding of "criminal intent," "tendency to incite," or "willful intent to incite."

No more than a handful of cases under these laws were ever officially reported, indicating perhaps that few arrests were made or that zealous local courts dispatched justice too quickly for defendants to appeal. There was also very little discussion of these laws in the press, although *Niles Weekly Register* did report on developments in several of the cases.

Michael Reid of West Feliciana, Louisiana, had stated publicly before several whites that Negroes were as free as whites and that the Negro had no obligation to call any man master. Reid was indicted under an 1830 law that made it punishable by up to twenty-one years at hard labor or death to express ideas that had a tendency to produce discontent or excite insubordination among slaves. Reid was found guilty and sentenced to five years hard labor. The Louisiana Supreme Court overturned the conviction, relying on established precedent in criminal libel. The court noted that no person could be held criminally accountable unless the exact words are given in the indictment, which they were not in Reid's case. The court also ruled that although the law punished for words that had a "tendency" to produce an evil, any reading of past cases and the state guarantee of freedom of speech would also require "criminal intent" on the part of the speaker. And finally, the court was reluctant to find any tendency to produce discontent or incite insubordination since the words were not spoken in the presence of slaves.[130]

In 1836, one defendant was spared a flogging because the law punishing anti-slavery publications was directed only at members of abolitionist societies. Lysander Barrett was attempting to get signatures on a petition to Congress for the abolition of slavery in the District of Columbia. The petition, which was distributed and signed by ten people, stated that slavery should not exist and that it was a sin against God. Barrett and the ten signees were arrested for circulating incendiary material. The Supreme Court of Virginia ruled that the defendants were not guilty because the law they were accused under applied only to abolitionist societies, their agents, and members. There was no evidence that Barrett or any of the other ten persons were members of any abolitionist society.[131]

The case of Dr. Reuben Crandall of Washington, D.C., created quite a stir in the Atlantic states. Crandall, a physician from New York, moved to Washington, bringing with him over a dozen copies of anti-slavery publications. He apparently read them, found them of some interest, and noted on at least one "please to read and circulate." However, the papers were never passed on.[132]

While Crandall was unpacking his belongings in a shop that he had rented in Georgetown, the newspapers were spotted by the son of a local physician. Crandall lent the young man a copy, which he later left at a nearby apothecary shop. A month later, Crandall was arrested in the presence of a large pro-slavery crowd that had gathered outside of his home. He was charged with circulating incendiary publications among blacks.

Fearful of the hostile crowd outside, Crandall turned over to the constable several abolitionist publications he had brought from New York. Urged on by the constable, the crowd followed Crandall to the city jail where a riot broke out. The next day, Crandall was arraigned in the jail rather than at the office of the justice of the peace because there was a fear that Crandall might be taken from constables and lynched. During the arraignment and interrogation, Crandall admitted he sympathized with abolitionists although he was not a member of any abolitionist society.

Denied an opportunity to lynch Crandall, the Washington mob destroyed the restaurant and saloon of a local mulatto, vandalized black churches, burned a house of prostitution, and burned tenement houses where blacks lived. The riots lasted several days despite armed patrols.

Crandall's arrest and the ensuing mob violence occurred within several weeks of the mobbing of Charleston's post office and at the peak of the propaganda war by abolitionists. Also, Crandall was the brother of Prudence Crandall, a school mistress in Connecticut, who had tried to open a school for black girls. After several years of fighting Northern racism in the courts and at the school, she eventually was forced to give up the idea of educating black girls. However, her brother had not supported her efforts and had spoken to her often about shutting down the school. Had all of these factors not come into play, Crandall's case would not have received as much publicity.

Francis Scott Key, U.S. Attorney for the District of Columbia, ordered Crandall held for trial on five counts of seditious libel—"publishing malicious and wicked libels, with the intent to excite sedition and insurrection among the slaves and free colored people of this District."[133] In January 1836, a grand jury indicted Crandall on all five counts. Bail was set at $5,000—a sum Crandall was unable to raise. He remained in jail eight months before the trial was held in April 1836.

At the trial, Key was unable to meet the demands of seditious libel law. He failed to convince the jury that mere possession of incendiary material was tantamount to publication or that reluctantly allowing a friend to borrow one copy of such material amounted to publication. Nor was he able to convince the jury that personal possession of incendiary material was evidence of malicious intent. After listening to ten days of testimony, the jury took one hour to acquit Crandall.

Neither ringing defenses of First Amendment rights nor new insights into free speech for unpopular ideas were forthcoming from the handful of cases involving the distribution of anti-slavery ideas. Defense lawyers stuck closely to the precedents for seditious libel; courts usually found the indictments to be so impaired that they were unable to find against the defendants.

NOTES

1. *Niles' Weekly Register*, August 29, 1835.

2. H. Von Holst, *The Constitutional and Political History of the United States* 8 vols. (Chicago: Callaghan & Co., 1879) 2: 117.

3. *Congressional Globe*, 26th Cong., 1st sess., pp. 128-130 (1840).

4. Elijah Porter Barrows, *A View of the American Slavery Question* (New York: J. S. Taylor, 1836), pp. 32, 38.

5. Harriet Martineau, *The Martyr Age of the United States* (1839; reprint ed., New York: Arno Press, 1969), p. 5.

6. Gerald M. Capers, *John C. Calhoun—Opportunist* (Gainesville: University of Florida Press, 1960), pp. 119-120.

7. See Herman V. Ames, ed., *State Documents on Federal Relations: The States and the United States* (Philadelphia: 1902; reprint ed., New York: Da Capo Press, 1970).

8. Richmond *Enquirer*, January 7, 1832.

9. Ibid., January 12, 1832.

10. Richmond *Whig*, January 2 and 17, 1832.

11. Richmond *Enquirer*, January 22, March 1, May 4, 1832.

12. Ibid., January 12, 1832.

13. Richmond *Whig*, February 6, 1832.

14. Martineau, *The Martyr Age*, p. 3.

15. W. Sherman Savage, *The Controversy over the Distribution of Abolition Literature, 1830–1860* (New York: Negro Universities Press, 1968) p. 13.

16. Ibid., pp. 31-33.

17. Report from the Select Committee, in Meriwether, *Calhoun Papers*, 13: 62.

18. Richmond *Enquirer*, August 25, 1835. Descriptions of the incident at Charleston can be found in the following: Savage, *The Controversy*; William M. Wiecek, *The Sources of Antislavery Constitutionalism in America, 1760–1848* (Ithaca:

Cornell University Press, 1977); Martha Hall Medford, *The Controversy Over Use of the Mail for Distribution of Abolition Literature*, (Thesis, University of Texas, 1940); Lindsay Rogers, *The Postal Power of Congress: A Study in Constitutional Expansion* (Baltimore: Johns Hopkins University Studies in Historical and Political Science, 1916) ser. 34, no. 2; Dorothy Canfield Fowler, *Unmailable: Congress and the Post Office* (Athens: University of Georgia Press, 1977); Russell Nye, *Fettered Freedom: Civil Liberties and the Slave Controversy* (Ann Arbor: Michigan University Press, 1963).

19. *Niles' Weekly Register*, August 4, 1835.

20. Fowler, *Unmailable*, p. 27.

21. Correspondence between Gouverneur and the American Anti-Slavery Society was published in the New York *Evening Post*, August 15, 1835, reprinted in Theodore Sedgwick, ed., *A Collection of the Political Writings of William Leggett* (New York, Taylor & Dodd, 1840), pp. 20-23; also printed in *Niles' Weekly Register*, August 15, 1835.

22. *Niles' Weekly Register*, August 22, 1835.

23. Savage, *The Controversy*, p. 22; *Niles' Weekly Register*, September 5, 1835.

24. *Niles' Weekly Register*, September 5, 1835.

25. Bassett, *Correspondence of Andrew Jackson*, 5: 360-361.

26. See, Lorman Ratner, *Powder Keg: Northern Opposition to the Antislavery Movement, 1831–1840* (New York: Basic Books, Inc., 1968).

27. *Niles' Weekly Register*, September 5, 1835.

28. Sedgwick, *Political Writings of William Leggett*, pp. 14-15.

29. Nye, *Fettered Freedom*, pp. 58-59; *Niles' Weekly Register*, September 19, 1835.

30. Albany *Journal* in Auburn *Journal and Advertiser*, August 26, 1835.

31. *Niles' Weekly Register*, September 19, 1835.

32. Natchez (La.) *Courier*, reprinted in *The Anti-Slavery Record*, December 1836.

33. *Niles' Weekly Register*, August 22, 1835.

34. Boston *Atlas*, reprinted in *Niles' Weekly Register*, August 29, 1835.

35. Address of the Anti-Slavery Society to the Public, *Niles' Weekly Register*, September 12, 1835.

36. *Boston Globe*, October 3, 1835.

37. See, Nye, *Fettered Freedom*, pp. 75-76; Nehemiah Adams, *A Southside View of Slavery* (Richmond, Va.: 1855), pp. 1-10; Savage, *The Controversy*, pp. 10-14.

38. New York *Courier and Enquirer*, August 10, 1835.

39. Ibid., p. 10.

40. Meriwether, *Calhoun Papers*, 12: 516.

41. *Niles' Weekly Register*, August 8, 1835.

42. *Niles' Weekly Register*, September 12, 1835.

43. *Niles' Weekly Register*, August 29, 1835.

44. *Niles' Weekly Register*, October 3, 1835.

45. *Arkansas Gazette*, September 8, 1835; Richmond *Whig*, July 31, 1835.

46. *Niles' Weekly Register*, October 3, 1835.

47. *Niles' Weekly Register*, October 10, 1835.

48. A description of the numerous resolutions can be found in Savage, *The Controversy* , pp. 2934.

49. *Niles' Weekly Register*, August 29, 1835.

50. Ibid., p. 456.

51. *Niles' Weekly Register*, October 3, 1835.

52. *Niles' Weekly Register*, August 22, 1835.

53. Reprinted in the *Liberator*, August 22, 1835.

54. *Niles' Weekly Register*, August 22, 1835; *Philanthropist*, January 15, 1836.

55. *Niles' Weekly Register*, August 22, 1835.

56. Ibid., p. 445.

57. *Philanthropist*, January 15, 1836.

58. Meriwether, *Papers of John C. Calhoun*, 12: 548–554. See, Nye, *Fettered Freedom*, pp. 178-182.

59. *Niles' Weekly Register*, October 3, 1835.

60. Amos Dresser, *The Narrative of Amos Dresser, with Stone's Letters from Natchez* (New York, 1836).

61. Richard Yeadon, *The Amenability of Northern Incendiaries, as well as to Southern as to Northern laws, Without Prejudice to the Right of Free Discussion* (Charleston: T. A. Hampton, 1835; reprint ed., J. B. Nixon, 1853), pp. 14-15.

62. Ibid., pp. 6-10.

63. *Niles' Weekly Register*, January 2, 1835.

64. *Niles' Weekly Register*, November 21, 1835.

65. *Niles' Weekly Register*, December 12, 1835; a description of the various legislative resolutions is found in Savage, *The Controversy*, pp. 43-49.

66. Albert B. Hart and Edward Channing, eds., *American History Leaflets, Colonial and Constitutional* no. 10 (New York: A. Lovell & Co., 1893), p. 12.

67. Ibid., pp. 3-4.

68. *Niles' Weekly Register*, December 26, 1835.

69. William Goodell, *An Account of the Interviews which took Place on the Fourth and Eighth of March Between the Committee of the Massachusetts Anti-Slavery Society and the Committee of the Legislature* (New York: 1836).

70. Savage, *The Controversy*, p. 53.

71. Henry Wilson, *A History of the Rise and Fall of the Slave Power in America* 3 vols. (Boston: James R. Osgood & Co., 1869) 1: 322, 327.

72. *Niles' Weekly Register*, August 29, 1835.

73. Reprinted in Richmond *Whig*, August 11, 1835.

74. *Niles' Weekly Register*, October 10, 1835.

75. New York *Courier and Enquirer*, August 10 and 27; September 8; October 22, 1835.

76. Nye, *Fettered Freedom*, p. 118.

77. *Niles' Weekly Register*, August 29, September 5, October 3, 1835.

78. New York *American*, September 12, 1835.

79. *Niles' Weekly Register*, October 3, 1835.

80. *Niles' Weekly Register*, October 3, 1835.

81. *Niles' Weekly Register*, October 3, 1835.

82. Frederick W. Seward, *Autobiography of William H. Seward* (New York: D. Appleton & Co., 1877), p. 291.

83. Ibid.

84. Richmond *Enquirer*, September 29, 1835.

85. Richmond *Enquirer*, September 29, 1835.

86. Martin Van Buren Papers, vol. 21, Library of Congress microfilm, ser. 2, reel 14. Letter to Van Buren from Peter V. Daniels, September 25, 1835.

87. *Niles' Weekly Register*, October 3, 1835.

88. Ibid., pp. 74-77.

89. House Executive Doc. 2, 24th Congress, 1st sess. (1835).

90. Fred Israel, ed., *The State of the Union Messages of the Presidents, 1790–1860* 3 vols. (New York: Chelsea House Publications, 1967) 1: 442–43.

91. Debates in Congress, 24th Cong., 1st sess., p. 46 (1835).

92. See, Gerald M. Capers, *John C. Calhoun—Opportunist.*

93. Meriwether, *Calhoun Papers*, 13: 42, 62, 64, 70.

94. Ibid., 13: 13.

95. Ibid., p. 11-12.

96. Thomas Hart Benton, *Thirty Years' View* 2 vols. (New York: D. Appleton and Co., 1854) 1: 587.

97. Ibid.

98. William Jay, *A View of the Action of the Federal Government in Behalf of Slavery* (New York: American Anti-Slavery Soc., 1839), p. 205.

99. Richmond *Enquirer*, June 7, 1836.

100. Jackson's view of Congress's power over the mails would eventually be held constitutional by the Supreme Court in *Ex parte Jackson*, 96 U.S. 727 (1877).

101. Senate Doc. 118, 24th Cong., 1st sess. (1835).

102. Debates in Congress, 24th Cong., 1st sess., pp. 1721-22 (1835).

103. *Congressional Globe*, 24th Cong., 1st sess., Appendix, pp. 285-86 (1835).

104. Debates in Congress, 24th Cong., 1st sess., pp. 1723-24 (1835).

105. Debates in Congress, 24th Cong., 1st sess., p. 1146 (1835).

106. *Congressional Globe*, 24th Cong., 1st sess., Appendix, p. 284 (1835).

107. Debates in Congress, 24th Cong., 1st sess., p. 1729 (1835).

108. Senate Doc. 118, 24th Cong., 1st sess. (1835).

109. Debates in Congress, 24th Cong., 1st sess., pp. 1728-29.

110. Ibid., pp. 1721-22; 1732 (1835).

111. *Congressional Globe*, 24th Cong., 1st sess., Appendix, pp. 285-86 (1835).

112. Debates in Congress, 24th Cong., 1st sess., pp. 1145, 1147-48 (1835).

113. Ibid., p. 1148.

114. *Congressional Globe*, 24th Cong., 1st sess., Appendix, p. 284 (1835).

115. Lindsay Rogers, *The Postal Power of Congress* (Baltimore: The Johns Hopkins Press, 1916), pp. 109, 114.

116. *Congressional Globe*, 24th Cong., 1st sess., pp. 291-292 (1835).

117. *Congressional Globe*, 24th Cong., 1st sess., pp. 481-82 (1835).

118. 5 *U.S. Stat.* 87 (July 2, 1836).

119. Meriwether, *The Papers of John C. Calhoun*, 13: 275, 279.

120. Seward, *Autobiography*, p. 291.

121. *Fifth Annual Report of the Massachusetts Anti-Slavery Society*, January 25, 1837.

122. "Cincinnatus" [William Plumer], *Freedom's Defence; or, a Candid Examination of Mr. Calhoun's Report on the Freedom of the Press to the Senate, February 4, 1836* (Worcester: Door, Howland, 1836), pp. 3-4.

123. Ibid., pp. 23-24.

124. *Niles' Weekly Register*, December 5, 1835.

125. *Anti-Slavery Record*, December 1836.

126. Calvin Colton, *Abolition a Sedition* (Philadelphia: George W. Donohue; reprint ed., Freeport, N.Y.: Books for Libraries Press, 1970).

127. Richmond *Whig*, April 1, 1836.

128. Savage, *The Controversy*, p. 56.

129. Ibid., pp. 55-57.

130. Helen Catterall, *Judicial Cases Concerning American Slavery* 5 vols. (Washington: 1929) 3: 613–614; Savage, *The Controversy*, pp. 116-117.

131. Catterall, *Judicial Cases*, 1: 195–196.

132. Description of the Crandall case comes from Neil S. Kramer, "The Trial of Reuben Crandall," 50 *Records of the Columbia Historical Society* 123–129 (1980); *The Trial of Reuben Crandall, M.D. Charged with Publishing Seditious Libels, by Circulating the Publications of the American Anti-Slavery Society* (New York: H. R. Pierce, 1836).

133. *The Trial of Reuben Crandall*, p. 3.

Chapter 5

"The Savage Populace": Violence Against Abolitionists

Attempts to censor abolitionist materials from the mails and the concurrent congressional debates over the right of citizens to petition for the abolition of slavery had the potential of affecting everyone, no matter what a person's politics were. Northerners, even those disposed against the fanaticism of abolitionists, soon realized that the questions being posed did not have so much to do with the abolitionists, as they had to do with the rights of all those who lived in the North. But it would take the polarizing effect of violence to focus the North's attention on this broader impact of the contemporary debates. As Rev. William Ellery Channing, a respected Boston Unitarian minister, predicted in his 1836 treatise on slavery:

One kidnapped, murdered Abolitionist would do more for the violent destruction of slavery than a thousand societies. His name would be sainted. The day of his death would be set apart.... His blood would cry through the land with a thrilling voice, would pierce every dwelling, and find a response in every heart.[1]

Although the majority of Northerners were alerted by the violence that occurred in the mid–1830s against abolitionists, it would be another fifteen to twenty years before they were sufficiently alarmed to actively support abolition. Unlike Southerners who were at peace with slavery and all its inherent baggage, Northerners were trapped by their own contradictions. For most Northerners, slavery was a moral evil. But the abolition of slavery was an even greater political evil that threatened the very foundations of the nation. This fear sprang from the deeply rooted belief that the Negro was inferior—a certainty that was reflected in both legal discrimination and widespread racism.[2] Deep seated was the fear that abolitionists might actually succeed in loosing a population of illiterate, immoral, and depraved people into Northern communities.

When abolitionists' rights were threatened by the actions of Postmaster General Amos Kendall, many Northerners supported the infringement. Also, when anti-abolitionists resorted to violence, many blamed the abolitionists or simply ignored the violence. Beriah Green, abolitionist and president of the Oneida Institute at Whitesboro, New York, wrote that the greatest obstacle to abolition was apathy. Appeals to the population at large were met with closed minds; everyone was too engrossed in their own concerns to be interested in others. According to Green, there was no time for charity or philanthropy that might disgrace the wealthy and prosperous.[3]

However, several incidents occurred between 1835 and 1837 that helped build a bridge between Northerners and abolitionists and bring about a coalition that, in the following twenty-five years, would do battle in Congress, in the press, and in the streets against the Southern interests. Once it was settled that the federal government could not tamper with rights of abolitionists, anti-abolitionists resorted to mob violence. Leonard Richard's study of the *Niles' Weekly Register* of that period indicates that thirty-one anti-abolitionist riots occurred between 1834 and 1837.[4] This was a significant increase over the previous five years—an increase directly related to the rise of abolitionist activity.

Mobs found their most fertile ground where anti-slavery agents were organizing in colonizationist strongholds and in the border states where commerce and migration brought slavers and abolitionists together into the same communities. In both areas, the threat to the status quo was met with violence from citizens who defended their actions as those of the guardians of liberty. In the name of liberty they broke up anti-slavery meetings, burned churches, vandalized businesses, destroyed presses, and killed. Less than a handful of these riots directly affected the press. Yet, it was these few but violent attacks on the press that did the most to spark anti-slavery sentiment and bring slavery and the defense of liberty into a single issue.[5]

It seems historically fitting that the man who was the bane of anti-abolitionists and who was both blamed and cursed for spreading anti-slavery agitation should be one of the mob's first victims. William Lloyd Garrison and his *The Liberator* were barely known in the early 1830s. But, with the organization of his American Anti-Slavery Society and his open attacks on the American Colonization Society, Garrison soon became a household word. His polemics were shrill and his efforts were resolute; few historians deny that he deserved most of the abuse flung at him. The difficulty was that many people failed to distinguish between the intemperate Garrison and the more moderate abolitionists.

As the anti-slavery movement grew, it received vocal support from the British anti-slavery movement which was led by George Thompson. When he visited America, violence followed him everywhere. Thompson was scheduled to end his American tour in Boston in mid-October, 1835, by addressing the Boston Female Anti-Slavery Society.[6] On the day he arrived in Boston, several hundred anti-abolitionists went to the anti-slavery head-quarters to wait for the speaker. Thompson did not show up, but Garrison, who also was to speak that evening, did attend. He was chased out of the building and hid in a nearby carpenter's shop, where he was found by the mob. With a rope tied around his neck, Garrison was led toward the Commons where, presumably, tar and feathers had been prepared for Thompson. But fearing for Garrison's life, several men led him into the city hall where he agreed to be charged with breach of peace and placed in the custody of the sheriff. On the way to the jail, the carriage was mobbed, but Garrison made it to the jail where he stayed overnight before leaving town.

Mob action was encouraged—either directly or indirectly—by newspapers like James Watson Webb's New York *Courier and Enquirer*. Webb raised the specter of amalgamation, cursed the presence of foreign meddlers, and frightened the public with tales of slave revolt.[7] Some of the more ardent anti-abolitionist papers actually supported violence as the only solution to the problem. For example, the Boston *Transcript* offered a $100 reward to "the individual who shall first lay violent hands on Thompson."[8]

In 1833, the New York *Courier and Enquirer* asked those contemplating action against Arthur Tappan and Garrison, "Are we to tamely look on and see this most dangerous species of fanaticism extending itself through society?" Or, continued Webb, was it the citizen's duty to crush "this many-headed Hydra in the bud?"[9] Soon afterwards, 1,500 New Yorkers mobbed an empty building where abolitionists were scheduled to meet, and then moved on to another empty chapel, once again to find that the abolitionists had already conducted their business and left. Frustrated, the mob seized an elderly black man and forced him to preside over a mock abolitionist meeting.

Two years later, Webb demanded that the New York convention of the Anti-Slavery Society not be allowed to convene in Utica, and that it be "put down." However, Webb did not recommend violence this time; instead, he urged New Yorkers to "drown the howlings of Fanaticism by a voice too loud and too emphatic to be misunderstood" and "peacefully" stop people from entering the assembly.[10] The Utica riots disrupted the convention, attacked the local paper that supported the abolitionists, and marched on the homes of two leading abolitionists.

Rev. Channing, reflecting on the violence, chastised the general press for its want of moral independence: "one result of this state of things is, that the newspaper press fails of one of its chief duties, which is to stem corrupt opinion, to stay the excess of popular passion. It generally swells, seldom arrests, the violence of the multitude."[11]

THE CINCINNATI RIOTS

Until 1836, mob action directed at newspapers or their editors was infrequent. But as the American Anti-Slavery Society's mail campaign increased during 1835 and 1836 and more abolitionist newspapers and societies cropped up in border states, editors like James Gillespie Birney were no longer immune from violence.

Birney was a former Alabama slaveholder who at first believed in "gradual emancipation," but soon began supporting "immediate emancipation."[12] To spread the word of abolitionism, Birney proposed publishing a newspaper in Danville, Kentucky, in July 1835. The newspaper was to be called the *Philanthropist*. However, he found Kentuckians ill-disposed toward his abolitionist aims. After announcing plans to begin publication, Birney received a resolution from Danville's citizens asking him to delay until the Kentucky legislature had considered regulating abolitionist publications. Birney replied that no state had the authority to restrain his freedom of press, and he would not acquiesce in the face of public pressure.[13]

But pressure from Danville's citizens did force Birney to abandon his Kentucky publication and move to Cincinnati, "where it will be difficult to mob it—yet it may be done.... But let them mob it—as sure as they do, it will instantly make throughout this State five abolitionists to one that we now have."[14] The *Philanthropist*, published outside of Cincinnati, in New Richmond, Ohio, was a mild newspaper with none of the harshness that characterized Garrison's *Liberator*. Nevertheless, the paper did raise local eyebrows. A mass meeting was called in January by the Cincinnati *Whig*, and despite Birney's defense of himself, the members voted to censure him and the paper.

A month later, Birney received another set of resolutions calling for the suppression of the paper. The editor's answer struck at the very heart of the issue:

[I]f the right ... to speak and write and print be maintained, slavery must come to an end; or the alternative, if the right of slaveholders to oppress be maintained, the right to speak and write and print in the free states must come to an end. You have placed yourself in this dilemma—you have the power of choosing either horn of it.[15]

After several months of calm, Birney moved the paper into Cincinnati where it became the official organ of the Ohio Anti-Slavery Society. Numerous civic meetings were held in the city to protest the paper's presence. Not only were the citizens concerned about amalgamation, but they were also disturbed by the effects that anti-slavery activity might have on the economy of the city. Predominant among the citizens attending these meetings were businessmen and city leaders, whose livelihoods depended, directly or indirectly, on slave labor.

Cincinnati was a major trade link between New York and the Mississippi Valley. Almost all manual labor on the river between Cairo, Illinois, and Pittsburgh was carried on by slaves, and most of the food stuffs, cotton, and tobacco shipped on the Ohio River were the products of slave labor. In addition to disturbing the river trade, anti-slavery activity might jeopardize plans for a proposed railroad link with Charleston, South Carolina.

On July 12, 1836, a group of men broke into the office of Birney's printer and destroyed some equipment. A placard was posted around the town the next day stating that the incident was only a warning and any attempt to restart the *Philanthropist* would be viewed as an act of defiance. Birney reestablished his press and continued to print despite growing excitement against him.

On July 21, Birney received another set of resolutions demanding that he cease publication and warning of violence. The Ohio Anti-Slavery Society refused to comply with the demand, replying that it was a denial of freedom of the press and that they would not submit to the slave power of the South. The committee that adopted the resolutions met again two days latter to consider the Society's answer and warned, a third time, that it would be unable to stop any violence that might occur.

On July 30, a more unruly meeting passed resolutions to destroy the *Philanthropist* and chase Birney out of town. The meeting turned into a mob that attacked the print shop, dumped the press into the Ohio River, and scattered type in the street. Birney was out of town on a speaking tour. The mob advanced on his home and Birney's young son convinced the men not to burn the home. From there, the mob broke into several Negro homes and wrecked a saloon.

Thus ended the first major attack on the abolitionist press in the North and began a nationwide debate on the meaning of freedom of press and speech that would reach a crescendo a year later when Elijah P. Lovejoy, editor of the Alton, Illinois, *Observer*, was killed by anti-abolitionists. Although news of the "Cincinnati Mob" was quickly replaced by news of upcoming national elections, many newspapers reacted to what had occurred. But according to Rev. Channing, the "newspaper press, with few exceptions, uttered no genuine indignant rebuke of the wrong-doers, but rather countenanced, by its gentle censure, the reign of force."[16]

One of those who used only "gentle censure" was the New York *Journal of Commerce*, which echoed the common sentiment that Birney carried some of the blame for the violence. The Albany, New York, *Argus* also blamed the abolitionists, who were waging an "irritating and merciless warfare against the domestic institutions, the property and the lives of the people of the Southern States." Abolitionists, insisted the *Argus*, brought their own trouble, and violence was merely the "frequent and legitimate fruit of abolition discussions."[17]

Locally, the Cincinnati press had little sympathy for Birney. The Cincinnati *Republican*, a prime mover behind the violence, called the participants "a well-behaved mob," and the Cincinnati *Whig* held that few sympathized with the sufferers, blaming Birney as the "wicked cause of a reproach to our city. . . . The heartless fanatics have sinned with their eyes open," refusing to heed the warnings.[18] But, William Leggett of the *New York Evening Post* said it was ridiculous to blame Birney: "It was the folly and madness of the mob and their leaders which have brought this reproach on Cincinnati." [19]

But the *Post*'s nemesis, the *Courier and Enquirer*, reprinted a note from the Cincinnati *Whig* to prove Birney's culpability. The story alleged that a package of money had been sent to Birney by Arthur Tappan, "being no doubt sent to pay him for disturbing the peace and welfare of Cincinnati."[20]

The Richmond *Enquirer* condoned the mob's action: "If ever a mob could be justified, it is in the case of the Fanatics of Cincinnati. If ever a mob of this description conducted themselves with any moderation, it was the Mob of Cincinnati."[21] The conduct of the mob itself was often commented upon because it was publicized early that many of Cincinnati's best known citizens participated in it.

Like many others, the *Western Reserve Chronicle* felt Birney had failed to exercise discretion by not heeding the numerous warnings from the citizens of Cincinnati. While freedom of expression must not be surrendered, said the editor, "there may be times and places, when and where the exercise of this prerogative on particular subjects, may be obnoxious to the community: in such cases the will of the people should undoubtedly be obeyed."[22]

The Emancipator chaffed at this narrow view of First Amendment protection: "In plain English, you must not discuss any subject which the majority of the people are not willing to hear; and if you do so, and get mobbed for it, the blame is your own." *The Emancipator*, edited by William Goodell and one of the oldest abolitionist newspapers of its day, set forth a view of the First Amendment that would receive attention after Lovejoy's death, but would not gain widespread acceptance until after the Civil War. Eschewing a majoritarian interpretation, the editor explained that the First Amendment was written to protect the rights of the minority against the majority. The majority can take care of itself; in fact, a constitutional guarantee that protects only the majority would be a nullity. "Under our government, the right of one man to the exercise of free discussion is as clear and perfect as the right of a thousand."[23]

Goodell's more democratic concept of freedom of expression had not received much attention to date because the struggle for a free press in America had been carried on by mainstream editors, or the "majority," against violations by state or national government. Even the abolitionist press, which had been in existence since the early 1800s, did not see itself as a "minority voice" operating apart from the press of the day. The abolitionist newspaper was merely another political organ, joining those of the Whigs and Democrats in espousing particular political philosophies.

But the 1830s was a decade of reform when certain individuals and groups began to expose the underbelly of American society such as poverty, disease, and crime. This altruism set them apart from the average American. Reformers and their organizations' concerns, such as anti-slavery and temperance, were identified by some as a "minority" because they searched for answers outside of the cogs and pulleys of the traditional political system. Their attacks on social problems were radical and their solutions, which called for extensive change, created great discomfort for the majority of Americans.

Greatly affected by the violence against Birney's newspaper was Rev. Channing, who afterwards showed a great deal more sympathy toward the men whom he had earlier referred to as "fierce fanatics." Channing's expressions of contempt following the Cincinnati riot were eloquent and forceful. Yet, his concepts of the role of free expression, while wide-ranging, were generally typical of the time.

In a letter to Birney, Channing addressed "the spirit of violence and persecution which has broken out against the Abolitionist through the whole country." Like Birney, he referred to the "deliberate, systematic efforts" being made to wrest liberty of speech and press from Abolitionists. He warned that the violence was just a symbol of a greater evil that was abroad. "The abolitionists then not only appear in the character of champions of the colored race. In their persons the most sacred rights of the white man and the free man have been assailed. They are sufferers for the liberty of thought, speech, and the press."[24] Alluding to the same principles as the *Emancipator*, Channing said that the defenders of freedom were not people from the mainstream who were adept at well-turned compliments to liberty but were the non-conformists who stood up for the rights that mobs and conspiracies put in jeopardy.

Of all the powers, the last to be entrusted to a majority is the decision about what questions will be openly discussed. "The greatest truths are often the most unpopular and exasperating; and were they to be denied discussion till the many should be ready to accept them, they would never establish themselves in the general mind." And if the multitude is once allowed to dictate or proscribe subjects of discussion, society would be blinded.

To the argument that abolitionism tends to stir up insurrection and threaten the safety of the Union, Channing replied that almost all men saw ruinous tendencies in ideas they oppose. "Exclude all enterprises which *may* have evil results, and human life will stagnate." Despite his eloquent words in defense of Birney, Channing could not reconcile himself to the "intolerance, sweeping censure and rash, injurious judgment" of some abolitionists, which had resulted in many good men being repelled by the movement.

Channing's words were echoed in several newspapers. The Salem, Ohio, *Landmark* wrote that "it is a licentious mob not a free press which threatens our liberty and social happiness. The press must be free...with a moral freedom, maintaining with unflinching fidelity the rights of man and the supremacy of the laws."[25] The Louisville *Daily Journal* rejoiced at Birney's escape: "Although we believe that his writings upon slavery, are pernicious in their tendency, we never had a doubt of the goodness of his heart or his perfect sincerity in the expression of his opinions."[26]

But there were those who refused to acknowledge that the violence had anything to do with freedom of expression. The *Liberator* quoted from "a New York paper" that the purpose of the mob was to put an end to ideas and activities that threatened the business interests of the city. "It was a business measure, standing distinct from the principles of political freedom, individual security...law, or morals, or religion. Hence the business press only was affected by it." [27] However, the *New York Evening Post* stated that even if the mob activity were aimed at protecting business interests, the resort to violence was indefensible.[28]

THE MARTYRDOM OF LOVEJOY

Many of the same newspapers that carried the account of the Cincinnati riot in late July also carried a brief report about a printing press, recently delivered to Alton, Illinois, that had been shoved into the Mississippi River by anti-abolitionists from Missouri. This press, belonging to the newly formed Alton *Observer*, had just been shipped from St. Louis to be used by Elijah P. Lovejoy to continue his abolitionist work in Illinois.

Elijah P. Lovejoy, a classically educated schoolmaster from Maine with a strong Puritan sense of morals and an even stronger need to bring reform to the Western frontier, would become the first American to die defending a newspaper. He would be hailed as the "Martyr of a Free Press," "Saint to all Journalists," and he would become a symbol for a society gone berserk.

After graduation from Princeton University, Lovejoy was invited by St. Louis's Presbyterian businessmen to edit the St. Louis *Observer*, a Presbyterian reform newspaper. The *Observer* was a conventional religious organ with a small readership. Lovejoy bolstered interest in the paper by adopting some of the radical reform stands being pushed by the Presbyterians in the East, including anti-Catholicism and anti-slavery.

While Lovejoy was committed to anti-slavery, he was not as sure about how to deal with the problem—colonization, gradualism, or immediatism. He had little respect for Garrison and the American Anti-Slavery Society. He believed abolition was a danger and that Garrison was an "incendiary fanatic" and "sick brained."[29] But, over the years, Lovejoy moved slowly from being a colonizationist to a gradual abolitionist, finally embracing immediatism before his death.

Lovejoy had correctly assessed the impact of the issues he chose to focus on. People began talking about the *Observer* and about Lovejoy. But as circulation grew, so too did threats of violence. His final commitment to abolition came when he published a statement of the principles of the American Anti-Slavery Society in Fall of 1835. He was criticized for his hostility toward slavery, but he defended his right to discuss slavery, saying "I cannot surrender my principles, though the whole world besides should vote them down—I can make no compromise between truth and error, even though my life be the alternative."[30] He made a successful plea for the right to express his ideas, and his tormentors backed off temporarily.

But peace between the *Observer* and St. Louis would not last forever. In May 1836, a free Negro who had knifed two lawmen was chained to a tree, burned to death, and then decapitated. Lovejoy condemned the mob for destroying the law.[31] When the grand jury was impanelled, the judge blamed the Negro's actions on abolitionists and pointed particularly at Lovejoy. The *Observer*'s offices were burglarized and vandalized three times within a week of the judge's criticism of Lovejoy.

The grand jury failed to bring in an indictment against the mob leaders. The judge had charged the panel not to bring an indictment if they found that the violence had been precipitated by "congregated thousands seized upon and impelled by that mysterious, metaphysical and almost electrical phrenzy."[32]

Lovejoy blasted the judge's "Papist" explanation, saying that it opened "the door for the perpetration, by a congregated mob calling themselves the people, of every species of violence."[33] That night, a mob of 200 men broke into the *Observer* office and destroyed printing materials. This incident forced Lovejoy to move the press up river to Alton, Illinois. When the press arrived in Alton on Sunday, July 24, it was set on the wharf unattended, a ready target for vandals from St. Louis who dumped the press into the Mississippi River.

The people of Alton, sympathetic to Lovejoy's plight, ensured the editor that such vandalism would not happen again, but resolved that they would prevent in a lawful manner the publication of any abolitionist paper. Assured by the nonviolent attitude of the citizens of Alton, Lovejoy agreed to temper his anti-slavery remarks and devote more space to religion.

"But gentlemen," continued Lovejoy, "as long as I am an American citizen, and as long as American blood runs in these veins, I shall hold myself at liberty to speak, to write, and to publish whatever I please on any subject, being amenable to the laws of my country for the same."[34]

After purchasing a new press, Lovejoy began printing the Alton *Observer* on September 8, 1836. He did curtail his anti-slavery writings for a while but remained an active abolitionist, receiving support from a number of churchmen and reformers throughout northwestern Illinois. Lovejoy's connection with abolition made him the ideal person to organize a state anti-slavery convention in Alton.

But as word of the convention spread throughout the summer of 1837, the voices of colonizationists and pro-slavery advocates rose. Among those voices was the *Missouri Republican*, published in St. Louis. The newspaper attacked Lovejoy and baited Alton residents into taking action against Lovejoy, saying that if they valued their own and their neighbor's property, they would stop the *Observer*. [35]

Two days after the *Observer* announced that a state anti-slavery convention would be held in Alton, the people of the town met to censure Lovejoy, who had broken his pledge to avoid abolitionism and print only religious materials. Lovejoy answered that no public committee of citizens could set a newspaper's editorial policy.

By the end of August, Lovejoy had lost a good deal of his local support. The American Colonization Society had sent representatives into town, and the major issue in the mayoral election was Lovejoy and his *Observer*. Finally, talked boiled over into violence when a small group of men destroyed the *Observer* press, type, and materials. The mob left the building only to encounter Lovejoy as he was returning to town. They surrounded him, shouting "Damn him!" "Rail him!" "Tar and feather him!" but he was eventually released unharmed.[36]

A month later a new press arrived in town and was stored in a warehouse. Watched over by the mayor, ten or twelve "respectable ruffians" broke into the warehouse, removed the press, dismantled it, and threw it into the river.[37] Lovejoy continued to publish the *Observer*, using the presses of the Alton *Telegraph*.

A growing tide of unrest spread throughout Alton as the town waited for Lovejoy's fourth press to arrive from Cincinnati. Some of Alton's most respectable citizens met in the first week of November to seek some compromise that would still the talk of violence. Lovejoy's friend, Edward Beecher, president of Illinois College, presented a set of nine resolutions accompanied by an appeal to the citizens' respect for human rights. Beecher argued that free communication was one of man's basic rights and any attempts to prosecute for its evil tendency must rest solely in the hands of civil authority, not mobs.[38]

But, the meeting was soon overtaken by anti-abolitionists who proposed a set of substitute recommendations, including one advising Lovejoy to sever his connection with the *Observer*. Lovejoy once again asserted that no public committee had the authority to decide whether or not he could publish a newspaper. The only authorities that he was subject to were the laws of God and the laws of civil authorities. As if aware of the fate that awaited him within the next few days, he vowed "You can crush me if you will;

but I shall die at my post, for I cannot and will not forsake it.... There is no way to escape the mob, but to abandon the path of duty; and that, God helping me, I will never do."[39]

But this time his plea was ineffective. Lovejoy asked the mayor to protect his new press. The mayor refused but gave Lovejoy permission to form a company of armed security guards. The press arrived early on November 7 and was stored in a guarded warehouse. In the early evening, the first contingent of the mob left the town's saloons and marched to the warehouse. They began throwing stones and suddenly someone outside of the building fired a shot; the shot was answered and one man was dead.

The mayor called for the mob to remain calm until he could negotiate with the men inside the warehouse. But Lovejoy and his allies were determined to exercise their right to defend their property. By this time 200 people had gathered outside the warehouse and the roof of the building had been set on fire. Lovejoy and another man come out of the warehouse, aimed their rifles at a man holding a torch to the roof. But before either could get any shots off, Lovejoy was shot 5 times. He crawled back into the warehouse where he died.

Despite two deaths, numerous injuries, and a burned out warehouse, no one was ever found guilty. But the incident brought revulsion from every part of the country. As Rev. Channing had predicted almost two years earlier, "His blood would cry throughout the land with a thrilling voice, would pierce every dwelling and find a response in every heart."[40]

The death of Lovejoy had a profound effect on the anti-slavery contingent in the North who had not yet made any commitment to abolitionism. As Edward Beecher wrote in his narrative of the event, "the nation was asleep: and nothing but an earthquake shock could arouse her to life. God would use this event to arouse and to save the nation, slumbering on the brink of ruin."[41] The abolitionists now had their martyr, a saint who would cry out from the grave to warn the country that this was only the beginning. As the Boston *Courier* noted: "The question, whether slavery shall be much longer tolerated in the United States, we apprehend will very soon become one that will swallow up nearly every other one of a political character."[42]

The murder also increased the distance between abolitionist and anti-abolitionist. No longer did the word "abolition" necessarily bring to mind the fanatical Garrison; now it also conjured up the memory of a martyred Lovejoy. At the opposite pole were the "murdering, cutthroat pro-slavery forces." William Goodell, now editor of the Utica, New York, *Friend of Man* spoke the rhetoric that typified this polarization:

Northern freemen will be compelled to ask themselves whether they are living under the constitution and the laws of their country or under the lash of the slave-holder,... whether they will become slaves or abolitionist—whether despotic anarchy on the one hand or civil order and emancipation on the other shall hold the supremacy of our republic.[43]

This battle between good and evil, saint and sinner evoked a great deal of sympathy, respect, contempt, and indignation—all of which made it easier for some people to choose which side of the struggle they would commit to. This is not to say that there was a rush to pay annual dues to the American Anti-Slavery Society. But the sentiment was changing.

None of this could have been accomplished, however, without newspapers, abolitionists, and enemies of violence coming forward immediately to condemn the murder in loud and strident voices. Unlike the reaction to the Cincinnati mobs, most newspapers reacted swiftly and with conviction. As the *Pennsylvanian* noted, the affair had a wholesome consequence because it had "swept away that strange apathy which has heretofore kept the press silent upon the subject of tumults and outrages."[44]

But the *Emancipator*, now edited by Joshua Leavitt, was not going to let the press get away with past misdeeds so easily. The editor blamed the press and the clergy for winking at violence and thus being "chargeable with the violence and desperation of the opposition." He also charged the "inactive, niggardly and cowardly abolitionists" themselves with the crime of neglect for having done nothing to check the mobism.[45] Beriah Green also criticized the Northern press for refusing to publish the horrors of slavery; instead, the press had been an apologist for slavery, protecting and encouraging "the monster, while gnawing with wearies tooth upon the vitals of the nation."[46]

The news of Lovejoy's death spread rapidly throughout the country, hastened by numerous letters to Northern abolition editors from men who claimed they either were with Lovejoy or were in Alton, and by the St. Louis papers that had been keeping careful watch on Lovejoy's activities since he had left that city. The best measure of the spread of news is the number of newspapers that commented on the incident. Garrison's Boston *Liberator* and the New York *Emancipator*, the nation's largest abolitionist papers, reprinted editorials from over 170 newspapers spread across the North from Portland, Maine to Jefferson, Iowa. Only a scattering of articles from Southern newspapers were reprinted. However, this absence of Southern reaction indicates only that Southern newspapers did not participate in exchange with Northern newspapers. The majority of articles reprinted came from Abolitionist, Free Soil, and Whig papers, which were more likely to be sympathetic toward anti-slavery activities.[47]

One newspaper that refused to comment on the incident or to run any reprints of editorials was the Alton *Telegraph*. The editor insisted that, as a political paper, the *Telegraph* could not be involved with the abolitionist problems in town because they were "subjects of minor importance." He refused to run reprints from other papers, hoping that the people would "let it rest."[48]

Lovejoy's death provided a unique context for the debate on freedom of expression. Until the mid–1830s, discussion and debate had centered upon government action against the liberty of press—the Alien and Sedition Acts, libel laws, and censorship by the post office. However, the debates in 1836–1837 dealt with the question on a broader and more fundamental level, raising questions about each person's duty under the First Amendment.

While some writers and speakers expanded on the concept of the First Amendment as an instrument to protect minorities from majorities, the traditional arguments were still the strongest and found parallel application in this new situation. For example, the earlier argument that postal censorship would lead in turn to censorship of religious and political materials was renewed when talking about mobs. The editor of the Peoria, Illinois, *Register*, the owner of slaves in another state, wrote that to establish the principle that the mob is the law would result in as many mobs as there were opinions. Mobs would be allowed to murder pro-slavery men in towns with strong abolitionist sentiments; to burn theatres where puritanism prevailed; to demolish churches where infidels were strongest; and to tear down coffee houses where temperance was dominant.[49]

The Philadelphia *Commercial Herald* noted that even though editors and ministers were the targets of violence "an Anti-Masonic or a Masonic editor may be murdered tomorrow—a Jackson or Van Buren or a Whig editor the next; and so it may go."[50]

One new element to the discourse was the argument that the mob had totally rejected Lovejoy's right to due process and equal protection of the laws. This had never been a free press issue before because any real or proposed government action would have been cloaked with due process.

For Lovejoy, not only was his personal liberty of expression taken from him without due process, but so were his life and property denied him while civil authorities looked on. That Lovejoy and his friends were forced to take up arms to defend the right to own and operate a printing press was symbolic of something even more fearful than the specter of sedition laws or postal censorship—the destruction of democracy.

This denial of life, liberty, and property by a mob raised unresolved contradictions in the minds of many Northerners. Hostility, both in the North and South, toward abolitionism had been based in part upon the fear that if the federal government could deny a slave owner his property, so could it deny other sacred liberties. But with the death of Lovejoy, a mob, led by respectable pro-slavery forces as well as colonizationists, had snatched away those very same liberties of property and life that the North had been safeguarding for the slaveowners.

Many people in the North quickly realized that Lovejoy's death represented much more than just the controversy over abolition, but went to the very heart of those issues "vital to the liberties of the entire union." While there may be differences of opinion about abolition, noted the New York

Evening Post, it would be uncanny to believe there was a difference of opinion about freedom of discussion. "Whether they erred or not in their opinion, they did not err in the conviction of their rights as citizens of a democratic government, to express them; nor did they err in defending their right with an obstinacy which yielded only to death."[51]

The New Hampshire *Herald of Freedom* agreed: "Not only has an editor been murdered for publishing his opinion, but the press throughout the country has had an outrage committed on it, and the rights which every editor possesses have been rudely and ruthlessly violated."[52]

For Rev. Silas McKeen, who delivered the eulogy for the Lovejoy family in Oldtown, Maine, the danger was not confined just to the press, but to all of men's liberties. "Those balls which pierced his heart were aimed at the heart of Liberty! Your liberty and mine."[53] Rev. David Root, in his eulogy to Lovejoy delivered in Dover, New Hampshire, summed up the extent to which Lovejoy's death had touched basic liberties: "He stood as the representative . . . of the freedom of speech, liberty of the press, the rights of conscience, the obligation of civil government and the claims of suffering humanity."[54]

Others refused to see the long-term effects of Lovejoy's death, believing that Lovejoy had in fact broken the law himself when he took up arms to defend the press. In fact, some editors went so far as to state that it was perfectly legal for slaveholders to protect their property with arms against the incursions of abolitionists, but it was illegal for Lovejoy to defend his press.

One reason Lovejoy was not granted the same rights as others to defend his property was the perception of him as an outsider, an interloper, a troublemaker. Robert Wiebe in his *Segmented Society* described the nineteenth-century community as a well-ordered group of like-minded individuals whose behavior and appearance were regulated by a core of honorable and respected persons. And in those communities, peace (or the absence of conflict) was the highest value. No one engendered more hatred than the "troublemaker." While communities rarely used violence against their own members, it was legitimate against outsiders like Lovejoy. No protection was provided Lovejoy because law enforcement's duty was to protect the community, not the troublemaker.[55]

The Boston *Atlas*, which early had expressed sympathy for Lovejoy and outrage at the mob, changed its tone after a letter published in the New York *Observer* detailed how Lovejoy and his allies had taken up arms and had killed "an innocent onlooker." The *Atlas* saw the Alton riot as just another municipal riot, having about as much to do with slavery and liberty of the press as it had with phrenology and animal magnetism. Lovejoy "was no martyr to the liberty of the press; *but a martyr to his own folly, insubordination and independence of the laws.*"[56] According to many, including Rev. Channing, Lovejoy was to blame for not calling upon the law for protection. However, as was eventually revealed at the trial, Lovejoy had indeed sought protection of the law and was refused.

The multitude of voices that spoke out after the death of Lovejoy can be placed into three camps: those who grieved for Lovejoy and his cause and decried the act of the mob; those who grieved for Lovejoy, but not his cause; those who grieved neither for Lovejoy nor his cause, and censured the mob only lightly. Most, fell into the middle category, insisting as did the New York *Evening Post*, that "to say that he who holds unpopular opinions must hold them at the peril of his life. . .is to strike at all rights, all liberties all protection of law."[57]

Leading off the sentiment against Lovejoy was the St. Louis *Bulletin*, which termed Lovejoy's action "imprudent." This word was to pop up over and over again in newspapers, speeches, and sermons. According to the *Bulletin*, Lovejoy was tempting his fate and in the end he paid the penalty for disregarding the admonition of so many people.[58] The Missouri *Republican*, which had dogged Lovejoy for many months, agreed that while it was an "unfortunate occurrence," the guilt would rest forever on "those who madly and obstinately persisted" in establishing an abolition press in Alton. Because Lovejoy turned a deaf ear to the warnings, "public opinion will hold them responsible for the fatal consequences."[59]

In his analysis of community violence, Wiebe notes that "with very few exceptions, the magnet of disturbance attracted the blame" and violence was judged less by the underlying substantive issues—such as slavery and abolition—than by the degree of conflict it drew.[60]

The *Courier and Enquirer* reminded readers that he had again and again predicted that if the abolitionists continued their crusade, it would lead to rioting and bloodshed and the eventual downfall of the Union. The editor believed that freedom of expression operated at its freest when those who did not conform to the existing body of shared beliefs moved on to other communities. This majoritarian view stressed conformity over diversity, immediate peace over confrontation; the majority over the minority.

Such a philosophy was quite at home in the homogeneous American society of the early nineteenth century. Settlers, primarily of Anglo-Saxon descent, had a large store of shared values that brought them together into close-knit communities. There was no need for persons to settle where there was no kinship of beliefs. Catholics lived in Catholic communities; Anglicans, in Anglican communities; slaveholders, in slave states, and so forth. When confrontation did develop, the farmer or merchant could move on. Homogeneity was also enforced by the family structure, church, education, and the press.

Yet, in the early nineteenth century, narrow cracks appeared in America's homogeneous society, particularly in the rapidly growing trade centers such as Boston, Philadelphia, Cincinnati, St. Louis and even Alton, Illinois. While such communities became economically, religiously, and even ethnically diverse, the central core of citizens, the "gentlemen of property and standing," were unwilling to make room for diversity of ideas, especially those ideas that would threaten economic and political positions.

A letter to the New York *Courier and Enquirer* typified the attitude toward conformance. The writer insisted that while Lovejoy may have had the legal right to voice his opinions, the exercise of that right should have been postponed to some more propitious occasion when it would not result in violence. "The freedom of the press is abused to bad purpose when it becomes the instrument of dissension and murder."[61]

The Charleston *Observer* wrote even more sharply of the folly of diversity noting that it was little short of madness for a man to expose himself to personal violence and his property to ruin by running counter to public opinion. And the Charleston *Mercury* labeled Lovejoy "a traitor to religion, honor and the peace of society."[62]

But the New York *American* was indignate at the tone of those newspapers that sought to extenuate the crime's atrocity by dwelling on Lovejoy's obstinacy and rashness. "To maintain the freedom of the press, no perseverance can be obstinate—no daring rash." Anyone not prepared to defend freedom of discussion against mobs was unworthy of the privileges which the American Constitution secures to all.[63]

The Boston *Atlas* also countered the majoritarians:

In other words, if a man chooses to publish a newspaper in which he advocates sentiments disagreeable to a certain portion of his fellow citizens, they are not only at liberty to destroy his printing press but if in the course of the operation, they should happen to kill the editor, the "guilt" of the "unfortunate occurrence" will rest not upon the murderers, but upon the victim! Who would choose to publish a newspaper upon these terms?[64]

Although there were those who preached tolerance as a noble challenge of democracy, few outwardly championed the dissenters or willingly aligned themselves with unpopular reform causes. Toleration was encouraged as long as it could be done from afar. But the Alton murders did force many to come from the sidelines and preach toleration.

The New York *Observer*, a Presbyterian organ, insisted that individual liberty, the right to control our own judgment, and lawful conduct, was not up for bids. It was the only liberty worth contending for, "and he who has the heart to abandon it, is unfit for freedom and should have a master."[65]

The *New Yorker* offered a guide for toleration, instructing Americans that if the views are in error, let them be refuted; if the motives are corrupt, let them be exposed; if the actions are unlawful, let them be lawfully punished. But right or wrong, better or worse, no opinion should die just because it is unacceptable to the majority.[66]

The *Boston Daily Advocate*, an Anti-Masonic paper, insisted that the

Constitution was written to protect minorities because majorities can always protect themselves. "The liberty of the press, confined to publishing none but the doctrines approved by the majority, is no liberty at all."[67] And the New York *Evening Post* insisted that the right to discuss all political questions and to examine all political institutions "is a right as clear and certain, so interwoven with our other liberties, so necessary, in fact, to their existence, that without it we must fall at once into the despotism of anarchy."[68]

Of course, any man who would die defending those liberties would quickly be promoted to the rank of martyr or saint, and the abolitionist movement would be, as Gerrit Smith said, "baptized with blood." Rev. Root reminded his listeners that no great cause had ever been carried forward against prejudice, legislative sanction, violence, or persecution without the sacrifice of some victims. And from Lovejoy's blood would spring a "formidable association in defence of liberty and truth." And, wistfully reflecting on the older Puritan belief that God and man would work together to create the City on a Hill, Root predicted that thousands would rally around universal emancipation and the event "will open the eyes and rouse up the old puritan spirit of the nation."[69]

The Providence, Rhode Island, *Journal* noted that Lovejoy's martyrdom was more important to the abolition cause than any other event. It would do more for advancing the cause than all the papers, pamphlets, meetings, speeches, and appeals that had been made on behalf of liberty and humanity.[70]

But while many were raising Lovejoy to martyr status, the New York *Journal of Commerce* refused to give the editor such a lofty place, fearing that martyrdom would legitimize the abolitionist movement. "He was no martyr to the liberty of the press, but a martyr to his own folly, insubordination and independence of the laws." The Boston *Evening Gazette* concurred, "while we lament his death, we can no more regard him as a martyr than we can excuse the means chosen to put him down." And a letter in the *Courier and Enquirer* signed "Anti-Fanatic" said that while Lovejoy may be canonized as a saint and martyr by others, "I cannot but consider him as a hot-brained fanatic."[71]

Martyr or not, Lovejoy's death was seen by many anti-abolitionists as the beginning of more serious efforts by abolitionists. The New York *Journal of Commerce* accused the mob of making a great mistake when it killed Lovejoy—not because they had put down a man, but because they had raised up a martyr. "The old maxim that 'the blood of the martyrs is the seed of the church' is just as true in the case of abolition and for similar reasons."[72]

But it was the Southern papers that spoke most often of the consequences of the murder. The Louisville *Herald* warned that spilling the blood of Lovejoy was worse than sowing dragons's teeth. "Every drop will, as it were, spring up into a new Abolition Society, that will, hydra-like, lift its head in the land, and we fear no Hercules will be found who can vanquish it."[73]

The Charleston *Observer*, a Presbyterian paper, noted that the abolitionists would make a strenuous effort to turn the event to their advantage, rather than use it as a lesson to stay out of matters that did not concern them. However, the Alexandria, Virginia, *Gazette* insisted that abolition "will never raise seed from the blood of such martyrs as Mr. Lovejoy, however freely it may be poured on the ground."[74]

While editors disagreed on Lovejoy's martyrdom, there was general agreement about the implications of the murder on world opinion. Abolitionist and anti-abolitionist alike believed that the mob violence would be a message to the world that the "Great Experiment" was not working. One paper predicted that the United States would become a laughing stock of the world; another said the murder would be "trumpeted through Europe as an unanswerable evidence of National anarchy, barbarism, and approaching dissolution—of the utter futility of all republican theories and pretensions." The New York *Express* warned that Europe's despots would hear of the event and hold up the violence as evidence of the incapacity of man for self government.[75]

Most of the comment upon the Lovejoy murder appeared in newspapers during November and December of 1837. Concurrent with this newspaper comment were sermons, which were later reprinted. The Rev. Hubbard Winslow, pastor of the Bowdoin Street Congregational Church in Boston, noted that his Thanksgiving sermon was reprinted in the hope of "adding a humble mite towards the propagation of what the author believes to be sound and wholesome doctrine."[76] Other preachers who spoke out from the pulpit on the Lovejoy affair were probably similarly motivated to put their sermons in print. Winslow's Thanksgiving sermon, which he titled "Rejoice with Trembling," was an eloquent statement of the majoritarian view of conformity and concession. He was skeptical of Lovejoy's martyrdom, believing that it had been obscured by the fact that Lovejoy's fate was the "legitimate result" of unchristian principles and measures.

Supported by scripture, Winslow argued that Christ admonished his disciples to go to other places if the civil authorities would not protect them: "If they persecute you in one city flee ye to another." As for Lovejoy, instead of arming himself and opposing the mob, he should have realized God was against him for the present or that his cause was to be furthered by other means.

To the argument that abolitionists were working on behalf of the liberty of the press, Winslow answered that in fact they were putting that liberty into bondage. There is no quicker way to undo a good cause than to overdo it. "We should always be careful to keep at a prudent distance *within* our acknowledged rights, if we would be sure to retain them."

And in a comprehensive summary of the rights of the majority over the minority, Winslow explained the duties of citizens in a democratic society, concluding that even in a republican society, the right to express one's self irrespective of the prevailing will and voice of the people "exists only in theory," never in fact. "We must remember that republicanism implies *concession* on all sides... that *republican* liberty is not the liberty of an isolated *individual*, or of a *despot*... but liberty to say and do what the prevailing voice and will of the brotherhood will allow and protect."

A good deal of the debate about freedom of press also occurred during public meetings, such as that at Boston's Faneuil Hall. The Boston meeting is significant in that it implicated not only the rights of Lovejoy himself, but also the rights of those wishing to publicly express their sentiment about the incident at Alton. On November 27, less than three weeks after the murder at Alton, a number of citizens, led by Rev. Channing, petitioned the Boston Board of Aldermen for use of the historic Faneuil Hall. The petition was rejected on the ground that any resolutions that might be passed would be pro-abolitionist and result in a mob incident.

Channing wrote an open letter to the citizens of Boston, answering the aldermen. The possibility of a mob had not even entered his mind. Instead, the petition was presented so that the citizens of Boston might have an opportunity to demonstrate their "abhorrence of the spirit of mobs... and particularly might express their utter, uncompromising reprobation of the violence which has been offered to the freedom of speech and press."[77] Channing charged the aldermen with condoning the violence at Alton: "Boston now says to Alton, go on; destroy the press; put down the liberty of speech; and still more, murder the citizens who assert it; and no united voice shall here be lifted up against you."

The Aldermen reversed themselves and allowed the public meeting to be held. Resolutions were offered to the gathering, which, without mentioning Lovejoy or Alton, condemned violence and murder and supported freedom of the press, the right of legal redress, and the right of citizens to be protected in their pursuit of legal activities. Speaking for the resolutions were George W. Hilliard and the young Wendell Phillips. Speaking against the resolutions was Massachusetts Attorney General James T. Austin, an outspoken anti-abolitionist and critic of Channing.[78] Austin's speech, echoing sentiments similar to those of Rev. Winslow, is another comprehensive statement about the Alton incident from the majoritarian viewpoint.

Austin described the slaveholder as living in a state of alarm, distress, and constant fear that his family may be murdered and his home burned. People like Lovejoy, continued Austin, should be aware of this fear of insurrection and refrain from exacerbating the condition. With his racism on display, Austin likened the situation to a zoo with "lions, tigers, hyenas, an elephant a jackass or two, and monkeys in plenty." Now here comes a man who wants to free the animals. The slaveholders, like the humans in his analogy, would have every right to dread the outcome.

Although he regretted that the mob action resulted in murder, Austin saw nothing in Lovejoy's actions to deserve any sympathy. He repeated the charges already expressed by several editors that Lovejoy should not have taken up arms but should have sought protection from the law.

Austin then argued another analogy, that the mob of Alton was no different from the mob that tossed tea into Boston's harbor 60 years earlier. Those citizens of Alton, like those of Boston, said Austin, urged that harmful actions be stopped. But when all entreaties were found to be in vain "and there was no law that could protect them, and no middle path between ruin and resistance," the "orderly mob" reacted.

The only way to stop mobs, warned Austin, was to do nothing to excite a mob. Echoing Winslow, Austin urged that peaceable men should not demand "extreme rights." If liberty of press is to be preserved, then we must not abuse it. No law ought to control it, but the law of self-respect and self-restraint. "If the press becomes an incendiary to put the passions of mankind in a blaze, who but its conductors are to blame, if it perishes in the conflagration it has made?"

According to the report in the *Liberator*, Austin's speech "produced great excitement throughout the Hall" and when Wendell Phillips stood to address the crowd, those sympathetic to Austin were so boisterous that he was unable to proceed until the crowd was silenced. Phillips speech, while a great example of public address, contained no ringing defense of toleration or liberty of expression; rather, it was an extemporaneous patriotic rebuttal to Austin's speech.

Phillips, only twenty-six when he spoke in Faneuil Hall, attacked Austin's Boston Tea Party analogy. "To draw the conduct of our ancestors into a precedent for mobs ... is an insult to their memory." The men of Boston were rising to sustain the laws and constitution; the rioters of Alton were doing nothing more than sustaining their own wills, right or wrong. He defended Lovejoy's right to take up arms, and the fact that he fired a gun did not lessen his claim to sympathy or destroy his title to martyrdom.

To charge that Lovejoy was imprudent because he chose to publish opinions disagreeable to the community was, according to Phillips, to sanction mob control over our freedoms. "It deprives not only the individual and the minority of their rights, but the majority also, since the expression of *their* opinion may sometimes provoke disturbance from the minority."

Rev. Channing's role in the Faneuil Hall meeting was minor; however, a few days before Christmas he wrote a lengthy open letter to abolitionists that was published in the *Liberator*.[79] His original outrage at the Board of Aldermen for its disallowing the use of Faneuil Hall had been somewhat moderated by the time he wrote the letter. Although the reverend sympathized with the majority of those who toiled in the abolitionist vineyards, he remained uncomfortable with the more fanatical among them like Garrison and Lovejoy. He was never able to reconcile their radical politics with the need for a peaceful abolition of slavery. Consequently he was criticized by many of his own parishioners as an abolitionist, and repudiated by abolitionists as mercurial at best.

Central to the letter was what Channing termed the "peace principle," or the "unwillingness to use physical force for self-defence." He was disappointed that Lovejoy had not chosen the peace principle, but instead, had taken up arms in a "mistaken conception of duty." Because the abolitionists were organized into large and fervent groups that were hated and distrusted by many, the only way they could gain legitimacy was to appeal to moral sentiment and the law; "by resolute patience and heroic suffering."

This admonition was not intended to extenuate the guilt of Lovejoy. Instead, Channing was disappointed at the apathy which had greeted Lovejoy's death. "Here we learn how little the freedom of the press, considered as a *principle* is understood by our citizens, and how few are prepared to maintain it on its own ground." Freedom of the press was always put in jeopardy when unpopular ideas were involved; and unless those ideas were tolerated, that freedom was always in jeopardy. The abolitionists themselves had done great honor to the principles of freedom, steadfastly supporting the right of men to publish their convictions. Just as he had thanked Birney for his stewardship to the principle of free press, he also thanked the abolitionists.

Channing reflected on the days when freedom of press needed no defense because it was an immutable principle, an inalienable right, the conservator of all institutions. But the times had changed and the great principle was dying out, as demonstrated by the public's refusal to give it to dissenters. "To refuse it to a minority, however small, is to loosen every man's hold of it." Espousing a cyclical view of history, Channing demonstrated that throughout history many great principles had faded into hollow cants. But when that occurred, it was for every citizen to restore life to those principles. It might be disheartening to some that the battle for liberty never ends and that its first principles must be reestablished many times over, but it is the law of mankind "that no true good can be made sure without struggle; and ... to struggle for the right is the noblest use of our powers and the only means of happiness and perfection."

Liberator editor Garrison saw little good in Channing's letter; it was "defective in principle, false in its charity, and inconsistent in its reasoning." He accused Channing of retreating from his earlier statements respecting the use of Faneuil Hall and from a recent letter to Henry Clay warning of the dangers of extending slavery through the annexation of Texas.

While it is difficult with any certainty to draw conclusions about the debates that followed Lovejoy's death, the intensity of the discussion and the territory over which they ranged provide some general clues about contemporary thinking. There was certainly a general and widespread outrage against the taking of Lovejoy's life. And, whether contemporaries believed Lovejoy imprudent or not, they generally acknowledged that his death affected more than just his abolitionist mission—that it touched upon one or more liberties common to all people. There was also general agreement that, for good or bad, Lovejoy's death somehow legitimized abolitionism as a reform movement, thus promoting its growth.

The event also sparked, at least temporarily, a resurgence of nationalism. The irony was that many reform movements, including abolitionism, had criticized the spirit of Jacksonian nationalism because it blinded people to the system's flaws or it obligated people either to defend, rationalize, or even deny those failures. Anti-abolitionism's greatest argument to rationalize slavery was that its abolishment would destroy the Union and the Constitution. But now it had been demonstrated in blood that slavery also could threaten the Constitution. The flaws were set out on center stage in very simplistic terms that made denial difficult.

As Henry Ward Beecher summarized the issue almost twenty years later: "Ignorance is right if slavery is right. Free speech is wrong if slavery is right. A system of slavery is imperiled by the natural conduct of a system of liberty. It is the necessity of slavery to make freedom dumb."[80] While this characterization may have made Northern defense of slavery impossible and denial difficult, it could not clear the muddy pool of racism that continued to persist. The choice was not easy; fear overcame reason, and apathy seemed to be the easier road.

Although the majoritarian interpretation of freedom of expression appeared to dominate at least the written reports, a tendency toward toleration and temperance following Lovejoy's death could be seen. There was a rapid decline in mobism and violence.[81] Newspapers were more cautious in their denunciations of abolitionists for fear that they might be condemned as promoters of hatred and violence. Also, anti-abolitionist newspapers prayed for self-control, believing that riots and murder served rather than disserved the abolitionist movement. There also must have been some concern that the stability of the nation, despite its nationalistic spirit, might be undermined by increased lawlessness.

Significant change in Northern attitude would manifest itself slowly over the next 20 years. Abolition would become institutionalized and Southern "slave power" would be seen as a growing specter threatening the North. Consequently, more respectable names appeared on behalf of abolition. While the mid–1830s may have engendered a greater intensity over the issues of freedom of speech and press, no basic change in people's understanding of those freedoms evidenced itself in contemporary discussions. As always, the existence of competing realities such as racism, property, and slave revolt meant that some would opt for more restraint of licentiousness and imprudence. However, some early statements about toleration and the rights of the minority in the face of an overwhelming majority surfaced that would eventually see more thorough discussion by Britain's John Stuart Mill in his 1859 essay *On Liberty*.

This concept of toleration is distinguishable from that enunciated by Jefferson, Hay, and others during the years of the Alien and Sedition Acts. At that early date, toleration was to be exercised by government and its officers in an effort to stave off legal remedies against a licentious press. This newer version of toleration that was pushing up through democratic theory made it incumbent on all citizens—poor and rich, educated and uneducated, employed and unemployed, slaveholder and freeman, religious and irreligious—to practice toleration for threatening ideas. This novel form of toleration would be difficult to instill in a nation that clung to its homogeneous roots while society was becoming more diverse.

NOTES

1. William Ellery Channing, *Slavery*, 3rd ed. (Boston: James Munroe & Co., 1836), p. 182.

2. Lorman Ratner, *Powder Keg: Northern Opposition to the Antislavery Movement, 1831–1840* (New York: Basic Books, Inc., 1968), pp. 7-14.

3. Beriah Green, *The Martyr. A Discourse in Commemoration of the Martyrdom of the Rev. Elijah P. Lovejoy* (Utica, N.Y.: American Anti-Slavery Society, 1838), p. 12.

4. Leonard Richards, *"Gentlemen of Property and Standing"* (New York: Oxford University Press, 1970).

5. Russel B. Nye, *Fettered Freedom: Civil Liberties and the Slavery Controversy, 1830–1860* (Ann Arbor: Michigan State University Press, 1963), pp. 152-53.

6. The following narrative comes from John L. Thomas, *The Liberator: William Lloyd Garrison* (Boston: Little, Brown & Co., 1963), pp. 202-205; New York *Courier and Enquirer*, October 24 and 26, 1835.

7. See, New York *Courier and Enquirer*, July-October 1835.

8. Theodore Lyman, Jr., *Papers Relating to the Garrison Mob* (Cambridge: Welch, Begelow & Co., 1870), p. 14.

9. New York *Courier and Enquirer*, October 2, 1833.

10. New York *Courier and Enquirer*, October 1 and 7, 1835.

11. William E. Channing, *The Works of William Ellery Channing* (1882; reprint ed., New York: Burt Franklin, 1970), p. 751.

12. Information on the "Cincinnati Riots" comes from numerous sources: William Birney, *James G. Birney and His Times* (New York: 1890); Dwight L. Dumond, ed. *Letters of James Gillespie Birney, 1831–1857* 2 vols. (Gloucester, Mass.: American Historical Association, 1966); *Philanthropist*, January 8, 1836–February 27, 1836; *Narrative of the Late Riotous Proceedings Against the Liberty of the Press, in Cincinnati* (Cincinnati, 1836); Richards, *"Gentlemen of Property and Standing"*; and Nye, *Fettered Freedom*.

13. Dumond, *The Letters of James Gillespie Birney*, 1: 204–210.

14. Ibid., p. 311.

15. *Philanthropist*, February 26, 1836.
16. Channing, *Works*, p. 744.
17. Reprinted in Richmond *Enquirer*, August 19, 1836.
18. Cincinnati *Republican*, August 1, 1836; Cincinnati *Whig*, August 2, 1836.
19. Reprinted in the *Philanthropist*, October 7, 1836.
20. New York *Courier and Enquirer*, August 13, 1836.
21. Richmond *Enquirer*, August 12, 1836.
22. Reprinted in the *Emancipator*, August 30, 1836.
23. Ibid.
24. Channing, *Works*, pp. 743-744.
25. Reprinted in the *Philanthropist*, October 7, 1836.
26. Louisville *Daily Journal*, August 3, 1836.
27. *Liberator*, August 27, 1836.
28. New York *Evening Post*, August 8, 1836.
29. Dillon, *Elijah P. Lovejoy*, p. 48.
30. St. Louis *Observer*, November 5, 1835.
31. Ibid., May 5, 1836.
32. *Missouri Republican*, May 26, 1836.
33. St. Louis *Observer*, July 21, 1836.
34. Lovejoy, *Memoir*, p. 221-222.
35. *Missouri Republican*, August 17, 1837.
36. Lovejoy, *Memoir*, pp. 232-234.
37. Ibid., pp. 250-251; *Philanthropist*, September 22, 1837.
38. Alton *Telegraph*, November 8, 1837; Beecher, *Narrative*, 52–59.
39. Lovejoy, *Memoir*, pp. 278-81.
40. Channing, *Slavery*, p. 182.
41. Beecher, *Narrative*, p. 61.
42. *Emancipator*, December 7, 1837.
43. *Liberator*, December 15, 1837.
44. *Emancipator*, December 14, 1837.
45. Ibid., November 30, 1837.
46. Green, *The Martyr*, p. 13.
47. Because there is no census of 1837 newspapers, it is difficult to state what percentage of newspapers in 1837 were Democratic, Whig, Independent or even Free Soil. However a census of 1850 newspapers does show that 53 percent of newspapers counted were Whig papers. J. G. C. Kennedy, *Catalog of Newspapers and Periodicals Published in the United States* (New York: 1852).
48. Alton *Telegraph*, October 11, and November 29, 1837.
49. *Emancipator*, December 14, 1837.
50. Ibid., November 30, 1837.
51. New York *Evening Post* in *Emancipator*, November 23, 1837.
52. New Hampshire *Herald of Freedom*, December 12, 1837.
53. Beecher, *Narrative*, p. 310.
54. David Root, *A Memorial of the Martyred Lovejoy* (Dover, N.H. 1837), p. 12.
55. Robert H. Wiebe, *The Segmented Society* (New York: Oxford University Press, 1975), pp. 83-84.
56. *Liberator*, December 8, 1837.

57. *Emancipator*, November 23, 1837.

58. *Liberator*, November 24, 1837.

59. Ibid.

60. Wiebe, *The Segmented Society*, p. 81.

61. New York *Courier and Enquirer*, November 20 and 27, 1837.

62. *Emancipator*, December 14 and 21, 1837.

63. Ibid., November 23, 1837.

64. Ibid., December 7, 1837.

65. Ibid., December 7, 1837.

66. Ibid., November 30, 1837.

67. *Liberator*, December 1, 1837.

68. *Emancipator*, November 23, 1837.

69. *Emancipator*, December 14, 1837; Root, *Memorial*, p. 12.

70. *Emancipator*, December 7, 1837.

71. *Emancipator*, December 14, 1837; *Liberator*, December 15, 1837; and New York *Courier and Enquirer*, November 27, 1837.

72. *Emancipator*, November 30, 1837.

73. Ibid.

74. Ibid., December 14 and 21, 1837.

75. *Emancipator*, November 30, and December 14, 1837.

76. Hubbard Winslow, *Rejoice with Trembling: A Discourse Delivered in Bowdoin Street Church* (Boston: Perkins and Marvin, 1838).

77. New York *American*, December 5, 1837.

78. The following account of the meeting in Faneuil Hall and the speeches are found in the *Liberator*, December 15, 1837.

79. The letter was published in the *Liberator*, December 22, 1837.

80. Henry Ward Beecher, "On Which Side is Peace?" in *Patriotic Addresses* (New York: Fords, Howard & Hulbert, 1891), p. 197.

81. Richards, *"Gentlemen of Property and Standing* , pp. 15, 157, 160-61.

Chapter 6

"Watchmen on the Wall": Civil War and Military Censorship

When it became apparent that the South had no intention of abolishing slavery and that Congress had no authority to do so, the interest in abolition as a political movement abated. But the anti-slavery movement was by no means dead; indeed, it became more prominent in the 1840s and 1850s as it attacked slavery in a more restrained and hopeful manner. The acquisition of over one-half million acres of Western lands moved the anti-slavery spotlight away from the fanaticism of abolitionism and placed it on Free Soilers and Republicans who opposed the extension of slavery into the Western territories.

The first test of Congress's ability to bring about harmony was the Compromise of 1850, which allowed California to bypass territorial status and submit a state constitution prohibiting slavery, which it had already passed. New Mexico and Utah would enter as territories with no restrictions on slavery. Since neither of these territories wanted slavery, this was a safe concession to Southern interests. Congress also agreed to pass the Fugitive Slave Law, another important concession to slaveholders. In addition, domestic slave trade was abolished in the District of Columbia.

In the North, abolitionists and Free Soilers decried the Fugitive Slave Law for its immoral concession to the slaveholder. They also used the Compromise as an opportunity to expose the slaveholders' domination over cherished liberties.

In an address to California and New Mexico, William Jay, an abolitionist, urged citizens to adopt a free soil constitution because although all of the constitutions of slaveholding states guaranteed freedom of press, there was one exception—the discussion of slavery. The very instant that the press ventured beyond that limit, the constitutional barriers erected for the preservation of the press "sink into the dust." Jay warned that if slavery were allowed to take hold in the new territories, the slaveholder would not hesitate to abolish liberty of the press.[1]

In 1854, Congress passed the Kansas-Nebraska Bill, which allowed slavery to be decided by popular sovereignty. Because the bill opened up Nebraska, which lay above the 36° 30′ north latitude, to slavery, it angered many Northerners, even those who had earlier endorsed the popular sovereignty formula. Kansas and Nebraska held a certain attraction to slaveholders, and the influx of both pro-slavery and anti-slavery "immigrants" into Kansas before election time resulted in voter fraud and bloodshed.

The Kansas-Nebraska Bill, the Compromise of 1850, and the Fugitive Slave Law splintered the Democratic party into the Free Soilers, Know Nothings, and Native Americans. The Democrats, who had managed to retain national strength for over twenty-five years because of their willingness to accommodate sectional differences, were now finding accommodation to be the party's downfall.

The Whigs also were split over the Compromise of 1850 and the Fugitive Slave Law. Southern Whigs eventually joined Southern Democrats, who had coalesced into a conservative political force dominated by Southern planters.

The Kansas-Nebraska Bill also precipitated the formation of a new Republican party in 1856, which would eventually attract the Anti-Compromise of 1850 Democrats, Anti-slavery Whigs, Know Nothings, and Anti-Nebraska Bill Democrats. John C. Fremont, the Republican's first presidential candidate in 1856, ran against Democrat James Buchanan, who campaigned on a platform of non-interference with slavery.

Henry Ward Beecher, an abolitionist and Republican, reacted to the Buchanan candidacy, berating the Democrat's conciliatory attitude toward the South and warning that a Democratic victory would result in a curtailment of personal freedom. In Beecher's view, the only way Southerners could keep anti-slavery sentiment from spreading was to suppress liberty of speech and press both among slaves and whites. "A system of slavery is imperiled by the natural conduct of a system of liberty. It is the necessity of slavery to make freedom dumb." Therefore, warned Beecher, unless the North is willing to give up its liberties, the election of Buchanan "will be the beginning of an excitement and a warfare such as has never been dreamed of hitherto. Every vote for him is a vote for war."[2]

The Dred Scott decision of 1857, which legitimized slavery and the property rights of slaveowners, added further damage to the efforts of Democratic compromisers in Congress. By making slavery legal in every state and territory, the decision hamstrung Congress's ability to prescribe popular sovereignty as a formula for admission of states.

Despite this blow to popular sovereignty, the Democrats continued their fight to save the Union, their control of Congress and the presidency. The strongest Democratic candidate for the presidential race in 1860 was Stephen Douglas, who first had to keep his Senate seat against the opposition of Republican Abraham Lincoln. The famous Lincoln-Douglas Debates of 1858 reflected the basic philosophical differences between Republicans and Democrats. The Republican Party was the first major party to establish a platform on the moral wrong of slavery and the duty to prevent slavery's extension. On the other hand, the Democrats supported the right of voters in any state or territory to extend slavery. Douglas won his Senate seat, but the Democratic hold on Congress continued to slip.

In 1859, the Republicans continued to build their party, supporting such popular expansionist projects as the Homestead Bill, the Pacific Railroad Bill, Great Lakes Navigation Bill, and protective tariffs on manufactured goods. These measures were resisted by the South because they aggrandized the role of the federal government. By setting itself against progress in exchange for protecting slavery, the South would suffer economically.

The National Democratic Convention of 1859 dealt the final death blow to the party. Northern Democrats refused to support a pro-slavery platform that called for active protection of slavery in all territories and a declaration that slavery was right. Southern Democrats walked out of the convention and nominated their own presidential candidate, thus guaranteeing Republicans a victory in 1860.

Alienated from the North by Lincoln's election, the Southern States drew closer together, knit by a common commitment to defend their institutions and beliefs even if it meant declaring the South an independent nation. Between December 20, 1860 and January 8, 1861, seven states, mostly in the deep South, elected delegates to secession conventions; all had voted for secession by February 1. On February 7, the constitution of the Confederate States of America was adopted in Montgomery, Alabama, and two days later, Jefferson Davis was elected president.

Whether it was hysteria over the election of Lincoln or a logical conclusion to decades of sectionalism, secession had been implemented. However, many hoped it had not been finalized. Congress rushed to negotiate, offering revised concessions that were defeated by Republicans.

Meanwhile, lame duck president Buchanan was faced with the question of whether to defend or surrender Fort Pickens in Pensacola and Fort Sumter at Charleston, the only forts in the South not yet surrendered to the new Confederate government. Buchanan had no wish to fan the flames of secession with military action nor to thwart the efforts of compromise that were underway in Congress.

Lincoln, however, was not convinced that surrendering the two forts would bring the South back into the Union. After the inauguration, he authorized an expedition to reinforce Fort Sumter. Jefferson Davis and his cabinet ordered Confederate forces at Pensacola and Charleston to seize the forts. On April 12, General Pierre G. T. Beauregard opened fire on Fort Sumter; on April 14, 1861, Major Robert Anderson surrendered. No one was killed in the thirty-hour bombardment, but by April 14, 1865, 540,000 men would be dead. Predictions made as early as 1820 had finally become reality.

THE NORTHERN PRESS PREPARES FOR WAR

From the very beginning, the American press was present at almost every battle and minor skirmish of the Civil War. Bradley Osbon, a reporter with the New York *World*, watched the bombardment of Fort Sumter from the U.S. revenue cutter *Harriet Lane*. He was also the first to give American readers Major Anderson's first-hand account of Fort Sumter's fall.[3]

And just as quickly as the American news media began gearing up to cover the war, the government began struggling to define the press's boundaries. The government had a number of major obstacles to hurdle in this endeavor. First, the Northern press had grown into a powerful political and economic force. Northern editors clung close to their political roots, cherishing their roles as opinion makers and opinion leaders. The result was a diversity of political opinion that sprang from the equally diverse political, economic, and social philosophies of the Northeastern cities and Midwestern farmlands. Not surprising, this editorial dissemblance produced and even encouraged a certain amount of opposition to the war. Dissent ranged from the outright pro-slavery, pro-secession Confederate papers in border states, and the pro-Union, anti-administration Copperhead papers in the Midwest to the pro-peace, pro-Union Democratic papers in the Northeast. Backed by strong circulations and rising advertising revenue, neither loyal nor opposition papers shrank from their perceived duty to criticize the war effort and those in charge

Second, newspapers had advanced technologically to the point that large steam presses could produce special issues within hours. The telegraph could relay stories instantaneously across the country.

Third, newspapers relied on numerous sources, some more reliable than others. The newspapers adopted a unique combination of letter writers, Associated Press dispatches, exchanges, and correspondents to feed their columns. Whatever the source, the reporters were typically non-professionals who wrote more opinion than news. Ethical behavior often took a back seat to the "scoop"; stories were filled with gossip, speculation, hero worship, exaggeration, bias, and misinformation. And when the better reporters were able to gather accurate information, it often was so precise that it provided the enemy with vital military information. These detractions were not the sole property of correspondents. Editors printed the rubbish. Rumors from the front were not verified and many times stories run on the front page were contradicted by stories elsewhere in the newspaper. Maps, the trademark of many Northeastern papers, were so detailed that they revealed troop placements, camps, and artillery types and placements—all to the chagrin of the military.

Despite and because of these characteristics of the wartime press, the federal government did not hesitate to repress this irrepressible American journalism. But, like the newspapers, the government was dealing with a novel situation, with only European experiences to provide some guidelines. As a result, the various efforts to control the press were unsophisticated, arbitrary, hasty, and heavy-handed. No federal legislation censoring or restricting the press was passed during the war.[4] Thus, suppression was instigated with no legislative direction, by a variety of civil and military agencies, usually in an arbitrary manner without proper concern for due process. Consequently, the war was pockmarked with dozens of incidents that ranged from the arrest and imprisonment of a crippled newsboy, to the military seizure and suppression of the Chicago *Times*.

Generally, wartime censorship took three forms: arrest and expulsion of correspondents in military areas; censorship of the communication media (telegraph and postal service); and suppression of newspapers (usually accompanied by the arrest of editors).

While these forms of censorship were relatively new, the constitutional problems that attended them were not entirely unfamiliar. Although the nation had never experienced broad wartime censorship and no court had ruled on such wartime issues as the right of habeas corpus, and freedom of speech and press, the men who wrote the Constitution had contemplated the fate of the document's proscriptions during wartime. James Madison wrote Thomas Jefferson in 1788, questioning the ability of the Bill of Rights to stand up in extraordinary times:

The restrictions however strongly marked on paper will never be regarded when opposed to the decided sense of the public, and after repeated violations in extraordinary circumstances they will lose even their ordinary efficacy. Should a Rebellion or insurrection alarm the people as well as the Government, and a suspension of the Hab. Corp. be dictated by the alarm, no written prohibitions on earth would prevent the measure.[5]

Jefferson reminded Madison there would always be the legal check of the judiciary whose members would not be impressed or influenced by the passion of the population.[6] The Civil War would indeed test Jefferson's confidence in the system.

Harper's Weekly summed up the problems Lincoln was faced with in trying to balance the necessities of war against the requirements of constitutional government. The constitution, explained the editor, requires the president to be accountable to the Congress, his cabinet, his military advisers, and the people. While this system works in peacetime, "it remains to be seen whether [it is] compatible with a great civil war."[7]

The press represents the people and must always be given the maximum of freedom, said the editor. The question was "whether newspapers, working for private ends or in the interest of unpatriotic malcontents, should be suffered to weaken the hands of Government, during war-time, by malevolent opposition."

The answer to that question often depended on one's politics. Copperheads and Peace Democrats, who were generally anti-abolition, anti-war, and pro-Union, contended that the Constitution remained steadfast during the war as the only instrument of continuity. It symbolized all that was being fought for; to lay it aside during the war meant a victory for despotism. This position was reflected in a satirical rewrite of the Protestant catechism:

> What is the Constitution?
>   A compact with hell—now obsolete
> What is the meaning of the word "traitor"?
>   One who is a stickler for the Constitution and laws
> What did the Constitution mean by Freedom of Press?
>   Throwing Democratic papers out of the mail. [8]

Radical Democrat and Philadelphia lawyer Edward Ingersoll wrote the following eloquent defense of freedom of speech and press in wartime:

Liberty of speech, liberty of the press, liberty of the person. . . . They are as essential to the safe conduct of the government in this hour of peril, as they are to the happiness of the people; and it is as great administrative madness in the emergency to attempt to throw them aside, as it is indicative of popular madness, to be willing to relinquish them.[9]

Radical Republicans, who supported the war administration and wanted slaveowners brought to their knees, held that the Constitution must be suspended for the safety of the country and in order to bring the war to a speedy and victorious end. Wendell Phillips, now a prominent abolitionist, was a spokesman for the radical viewpoint. In one speech he noted that the habeas corpus, the rights of free meeting and of free press—"the three elements which distinguish liberty of despotism"—had been annihilated. However, he vowed that it was necessary to do anything to save the ship. "It is necessary to throw everything overboard that we may float. It is a mere question of whether you prefer the despotism of Washington or that of Richmond."[10]

However, a large majority of pro-war, anti-slavery Republicans who wished to see a speedy end to the war and a peaceful reconstruction of the Union, opted for a middle ground between Ingersoll and Phillips. They reasoned that the Constitution could remain viable during wartime. However, there might be circumstances of real danger that would require the temporary suspension of the Constitution. Archbishop John Hughes of Boston, a strong supporter of the administration, explained this moderate view in a letter to Bishop Patrick Lynch of Charleston, South Carolina:

You know that free speech and free press are essential constituents of the first notions of Anglo-Saxon liberty. But the Anglo-Saxon, whether of the South or of the North, would see the whole world set in a blaze rather than put limits to the freedom of the press or the unbridled license of the tongue, except when the laws interpose of the protection of public authority or individual rights of character and property.[11]

This middle ground was subscribed to by most Northern editors who understood all too well the necessity of maintaining the widest freedom in order that they could serve in their unique role as the eyes and ears of the public. The *Chicago Tribune* explained this special function of the press: "[L]eading and influential journals like our own are in some sort regarded as watchmen on the walls, to look for approach of danger toward what their readers hold dear."[12]

Editor Joseph Medill described the press as "narrators of facts, exponents of policy and enemy of wrongs." In time of war, these duties are quadrupled and liabilities magnified, and the press must rise to meet them. He told his fellow editors that they must not hold their peace where incompetence or rascality is in evidence. Nothing exempts the military from criticism or denunciation. In fact, it was the duty of the press to denounce anyone inside or outside the government who stood in the way of victory.[13]

This chapter cannot begin to address all of the incidents of censorship that fueled the discussion and debate about the extent of freedom of expression during wartime. However, numerous incidents are described that represent the different types of censorship activity that took place and that elicited contemporary dialogue.

THE MILITARY CONTROL COMMUNICATIONS

When the first 75,000 volunteers were called up and ordered to fortify Washington, troops from Massachusetts marched southward through Baltimore, a hot bed of pro-Southern sentiment. A riot broke out, killing several men. Lincoln immediately ordered the remainder of the troops to march around the city. Secretary of State William H. Seward prohibited the publication of the names of the men killed or wounded, placed telegraph lines out of Washington under the control of a State Department censor and prohibited any messages regarding the Baltimore riots sent from the capital.[14] At the Baltimore end of the line, police cut down one mile of telegraph line and poles along the Baltimore to Philadelphia route. The Washington *Daily National Intelligencer*, noting the destruction of telegraph facilities and suspension of telegraph service, suggested that the government should, instead, have appointed censors to examine messages.[15]

Ben Perley Poore, editor of the Boston *Journal*, wrote in his memoirs that the telegraph was not seized to prevent news of Baltimore but to prevent messages about the interception of a steamer heading South with supplies. However, Seward admitted to Poore that to relay information about Baltimore "would only influence public sentiment and be an obstacle in the path of reconciliation."[16]

More experienced correspondents looked upon these new controls as a small inconvenience that could be circumvented with a little ingenuity. Also, few believed that government controls would last long. In fact, few expected the war to last through the end of the year.

As Confederate troops pushed toward Washington, General Winfield Scott, commanding general of the Union army, issued an order on July 8, 1861, prohibiting all telegraphic dispatches concerning military operations unless those messages were approved by himself.[17]

The *New York Times* correspondent explained the full implications of Scott's orders to his readers. He wrote that Washington reporters were prohibited from sending telegraphic messages relating to troop and munitions movement, strength of forces, supplies, and contemplated actions. According to the correspondent, the orders stopped anything "which would in the slightest degree interest the public." The result was a one-day delay of news from Washington to New York.[18]

If the purpose of the censorship was to stop the flow of news to the South, said the *Times*, the problem could be better met by a voluntary self-censorship. A warning to newspapers to refrain from publishing harmful information would have been more appropriate and would have been promptly obeyed. The newspaper argued correctly that censorship of the telegraph out of Washington was like "stopping a spigot, and allows the bunghole to remain open." The Washington newspapers were not prohibited from publishing the information, the mails were still open, and so too were the railroad lines out of the capital.[19]

Colonel John Forney, editor of the Philadelphia *Press* and close friend of Lincoln, supported Scott's measure, blaming its necessity on newspapers that leaked military secrets to the enemy. According to Forney, the war could have been over three months after the surrender of Fort Sumter had it not been for the revelations of newspapers. Therefore, General Scott had been brought to a "painful sense of the injury" and was forced to issue the order.[20] A few days later, Scott's orders were replaced by a "gentlemen's agreement" whereby newspapers would be allowed to report on battles actually occurring, but would agree not to publish troop movements, troubles among troops, or predictions of defeat or victory.[21]

As troops continued to pour into the Washington area, many Northerners saw an opportunity to end the war quickly and decisively. Against General Scott's advice, Lincoln ordered Magor General Irvin McDowell to attack Confederate positions at Manassas Junction, thirty miles from Washington. The press representatives made haste to the battle areas and covered the skirmishes with enthusiasm and delight. Headlines in Northern papers shouted predictions and declarations of a Union victory. Early on Sunday, July 21, it appeared that the outnumbered Union forces had indeed managed their first major victory, but toward the afternoon, events changed.

Henry Raymond, editor of the *New York Times*, accompanied the army and witnessed several skirmishes. He was returning to the battlefront after sending a telegram predicting a major victory when he met Federal troops, wagons and horses in full retreat toward Washington.[22]

Reporters who managed to get back to Washington that Sunday night found the doors to the telegraph office closed. When word of McDowell's defeat reached Washington, General Scott had closed the telegraph office and no word of the defeat was allowed out of the city until the next morning.[23] Consequently, Monday morning subscribers were still reading about an imminent Northern victory at Bull Run; on Tuesday, they read about the Confederate victory. Press reports do not indicate that any "great outcry went up" over the government's interference with the telegraphs.[24] Some papers were angry that their readers and correspondents had been inconvenienced, but most were too preoccupied mourning the defeat and playing armchair generals.

The *New York Times* appears to be the only major paper to lash out against Scott's orders. The Wednesday following the Battle of Bull Run, Raymond explained to his readers that it was the government, not the *Times*, that had suppressed the news of the defeat. He recognized that under certain circumstances government must suspend use of the telegraphs to prevent the dissemination of false information. "But we cannot conceive of any state of things which can justify the Government in deliberately suppressing what it knows to be true; and thus promulgating what it knows to be false." Believing that the public and the press have the right to know the truth, the paper warned that the government should henceforth exercise "the delicate function of censorship with a strict regard to justice and the public good."[25]

James Gordon Bennett, editor of the New York *Herald*, explained to his readers that the story of the defeat was delayed when the telegraph had been closed down "because the news was bad." Calling the action "foolish," Bennett warned the censors that "letting the news come as long as it was favorable, and then suddenly stopping it when the first symptoms of disaster appeared," had led readers to believe a victory had been gained.[26]

Harper's Weekly, reacting to the delay in getting news as well as to criticism of the defeat, said government should pass no law restraining freedom of expression. But, such a proscription presupposes that freedom of speech and press will not be abused to the detriment of the nation. Therefore, every newspaper editor should insure that no information useful to the enemy is needlessly communicated.[27]

Three days after the First Battle of Bull Run, Lincoln named thirty-four year-old General George B. McClellan commanding general of the Army of the Potomac. Within the week, the new commander called representatives of the capital press corps to his headquarters and in uncharacteristically diplomatic terms asked the newspapers to cooperate with him in these trying times. Correspondents, most of whom represented papers in Washington, Philadelphia, New York, Cincinnati, and Boston, made a "gentlemen's agreement" not to publish any information that would give aid and comfort to the enemy. In exchange, the government was requested to provide transmission facilities for stories.[28]

But the agreement was short-lived. A week later Secretary of War Simon Cameron, under the auspices of the 57th Article of War, issued General Order No. 67, prohibiting all communications about troop movements, camps, arsenals, troops, entrenchments, or military affairs, which might be directly or indirectly given to the enemy, unless the release was authorized by the major general in command. To disobey this order could result in the death penalty.[29]

This order was transmitted to the office of the American Telegraph Co. in Washington with the added instructions from the company president, Edward S. Sanford, that no telegram (except military communications) "relating to late, present, or contemplated movements of the Army" could be transmitted. The instructions rescinded McClellan's week-old "gentlemen's agreement" with the Washington press corps: "The former rule, permitting such army information as appeared in the Washington papers to be telegraphed, is rescinded."[30]

The Cincinnati *Daily Gazette* accused newspapers of breaking the gentlemen's agreement. "It was asking a great deal from reporters to refrain from reporting. It was requiring a renunciation of the profoundest enjoyment which journalism can afford." However, since reporters had been unable to make the sacrifice, the general "is going to take stringent measures, whatever that is. We hope he will."[31]

The *New York Times* also saw the new telegraphic censorship as a necessity and a "temporary surrender" of rights.[32] But, when it became apparent months later that the end of the war was not imminent, the *Times* became more belligerent toward the various censorship measures. On December 5, 1861, the paper published a map of gun emplacements and earthworks on the Potomac and described the number and composition of the divisions there. After seeing the "treasonable" publication, which was "clearly giving aid, comfort & information to the enemy," General McClellan wrote Secretary of War Cameron, demanding that "the interests of our arms require the suppression of the treasonable sheet." Apparently, the

General's anger was felt by Raymond, who replied that the information had been released to the paper by army headquarters.[33]

To delay news of another major defeat of Union forces at Ball's Bluff near Leesburg, Virginia on October 21, Secretary of State Seward ordered the government's telegraph censor, H. E. Thayer, to prohibit all messages from Washington which related to civil or military operations except for dispatches sent by the regular agent for the Associated Press.[34] Consequently, it was weeks before the real story of the battle was known.

The House Committee on the Judiciary conducted an investigation into telegraphic censorship of the press to determine if such censorship existed in the capital, to what extent and by whose authority. Numerous correspondents testified before the committee, detailing the chronology of censorship and the difficulty of operating under the newest orders from Seward.[35]

Newsmen complained that by allowing dispatches to be filed only by the Associated Press agent, only the "dry matter of fact and detail" would be transmitted. They also complained about the government censor H. E. Thayer, a mathematical instrument maker, who was indifferent to political matters. According to testimony, Thayer was "wholly destitute of qualifications" and practiced a wide discretion that "went far beyond the boundaries of propriety."

The committee report acknowledged that numerous dispatches of political, personal, and general nature had been suppressed by the telegraphic censors, and correspondents had been forced to find other means of relaying their stories. The report stated that because of the importance of the telegraph to the press and the country, it "should be left as free from government interference as may be consistent with the necessities of the government in time of war." The House adopted the committee's resolution, which prohibited interference unless the message contained information that could aid the enemy.

The congressional report changed nothing, for Congress had already passed a law in January authorizing the president to take control of the railroads and telegraph facilities. Under this law, all telegraph lines and offices were placed under the military supervision of the War Department, where they remained for the duration of the war.[36]

Before the end of February, the new Secretary of War, Edwin M. Stanton, had taken full charge of the telegraph, issuing orders that any newspaper publishing military news not approved by the War Department or the commanding general would be denied all access to the wires or the rails. He also named Sanford, president of the American Telegraph Company, as military censor of all telegraphic messages; and Anson Stager, general manager of Western Union Telegraph Co., as military supervisor of all telegraph facilities.[37]

Prompted by detailed revelations in some newspapers about the build up of forces in the Washington area, Stanton sent a message on February 25, to all editors and publishers that "public safety requires all newspapers to abstain for the present from publishing intelligence in respect to military operations by the U.S. forces." Another message to chiefs of police in the larger cities ordered the seizure of any newspaper that "tomorrow" published military information received by telegraph "or otherwise."[38]

This second order resulted in editors being roused out of their beds in the early hours of Wednesday, February 26. According to stories in the Chicago *Tribune*, police entered that city's newspaper offices around 3 A.M., stopped presses, and seized copies of Wednesday's papers. Officials took the papers to headquarters where a representative from each newspaper was required to answer for the content of his publication. According to the *Tribune*, "censorship did occur" that morning.[39]

Despite the inconvenience and the delay in getting the newspaper to subscribers later that morning, the editor of the *Tribune* conceded that the order was not only proper but should have been issued months earlier. "Rights must sometimes give way before the pressure of a great public necessity," said the editor, but warned that military information not dangerous to the Union cause or old news should not be touched by the censors. He also was concerned that the censorship be conducted by "men of fairness and sense" who will not use this new power for annoyance and petty revenge.

The *Tribune* noted that ever since Bull Run a "rigid, unnecessary and frivolous" censorship had been exercised, but so far had not effectively denied information to the readers. Therefore, the editor was willing to go along with this new order because "something great" was about to happen that would end the war quickly.[40]

The *Weekly Tribune* of the same date appeared less generous, calling the order arbitrary and "an Austrian censorship on the American press" that was no longer necessary because the rebellion was broken.[41] The Chicago *Times*, an avowed anti-war newspaper, agreed to obey the order but believed it would result either in the suspension of newspapers or the establishment of military censorship in every town where a newspaper was published.[42]

The New York *Times* called to the government's attention the role of the press as the eyes and ears of the public. Newspapers earn their reputation by promptness and accuracy; such censorship could be fatal to newspapers because the public would lose all respect for them. The mere fact that penalties could be assessed for printing the truth destroyed public confidence in what little information the readers did receive, argued the editor. The blanks left by censorship are being filled with rumor and imagination. "So profoundly has the Government erred in meddling with the Press."[43]

Although the order was modified three days later to allow publication of past events, its effect was still felt by a number of publications. The editors of the Washington *Chronicle*, the Boston *Journal*, and the New York *Journal of Commerce* were arrested and threatened with court martial for publishing contraband information.

However, other editors were getting away with defying the order. The Chicago *Tribune* complained when a small paper in Vermont printed prohibited information but was not suppressed. "The order is a farce," said the *Tribune* editor. When the war is over, threatened the editor, "there are several official reputations that will suffer by the light of future history" for this order.[44]

The *New York Times* alleged that the New York *Herald* had broken Stanton's order when it published information on General Nathaniel Banks's advance into Virginia. While other newspapers had similar information, most had refused to publish it. The *Times* called on Stanton to withdraw the order or punish the *Herald*. If he did neither, other newspapers would break the order that had so far served only to cripple loyal journals and aid disloyal ones.[45]

The Philadelphia *Inquirer* called Stanton's order "simple and rational" but motivated by "ill-concealed impatience." Although expected to be only temporary, the order should have been issued earlier because it had the effect of making newspapers more cautious, keeping military plans from the enemy and suppressing speculation.[46]

The New York *Herald's* reaction to the order was that of a loyal subject, willing to bow to military necessity. For James Gordon Bennett, the "most just and most necessary" order would only affect the New York abolitionist journals like the *Tribune*, *Times*, and *World* who helped the enemy by "unrestricted, treasonable and premeditated revelations." The order would ensure that "a good newspaper, like a good citizen or a good soldier will do its utmost to assist the government." Bennett hoped that Stanton would rigidly enforce the order and not allow it to become a dead letter.[47]

Two days later, the *Herald* published a lengthy editorial on the relation of the press and government during wartime. Bennett's views, probably printed for the benefit of the abolitionist *Tribune*, hardly paralleled the ideal of the "watchmen on the walls." The press's duty in wartime is to "be a mediator between government and the people." To do this, the press must necessarily assume the position of "a voluntary department of government," morally bound to sustain the government and to refrain from publishing "dangerous and ill-timed criticism." But there must be some trade off; the government should keep the press well-informed and under control.

The "independent" press had no problems with the government. Through its "ability, talent, skill, energy, wisdom and statesmanship," the loyal press had become an "efficient aid to the executive and the chosen guardian of the liberties of the press." Stanton's order, concluded Bennett, "can't be regarded as any infringement upon those rights of the press."[48] Bennett, however, would soon tire of the censorship and call for its repeal.

The Cincinnati *Commercial*, angered over the inefficacy of the order, called it an "abominable farce" with a "flavor of humbuggery" about it. The paper said that it was time for the people and the press to make themselves heard in definite terms about the order.[49]

The New York *Tribune* complained about the everyday effects of Stanton's order, explaining that correspondents could not send reports from Cairo, Louisville, or St. Louis. Assuming that other newspapers were having similar problems, Horace Greeley urged their editors to insist that the Secretary of War "employ few natural fools in the management of the telegraph, or the nuisance of supervision and suppression will annoy the public quite as much as the journals." But, if it is necessary "to temporarily kill the Press in order to save the Nation, so be it," said Greeley in a show of patriotism aimed at his arch enemy Bennett.[50]

When it became evident that McClellan's Army of the Potomac was not going to move toward Richmond, Stanton amended his order to permit information about past military activities.[51] William H. Russell, correspondent for the London *Times* and a thorn in the side of the administration, wrote several weeks after Stanton's amended order went into effect that "the press is bound in rigid censorship, which, indeed is submitted to by the people of the North with very good grace." He explained that neither telegraph messages nor correspondence referring to military movements "can be published with safety."[52]

When the Army of the Potomac began gathering by the tens of thousands in the Washington area during March 1862 for McClellan's Peninsula campaign, Stanton reminded reporters of his February order and restricted them from communicating anything about the movement of the army. On March 25, Stanton also restricted the mails. Postmasters were instructed to notify publishers in their area not to publish information that had been omitted from the telegraph. Refusal to obey the order would result in suspension of mailing privileges.[53]

The Chicago *Tribune*'s Washington correspondent complained to the First Assistant Postmaster General about the order's ambiguity, stating that "it could be productive only of mischief, and in all probability would fail to secure the object for which it was intended." The correspondent contended that the order was unlawful because it substituted "an arbitrary and capricious will" in the place of due process.[54]

On April 2, as more and more reporters amassed around Fortress Monroe, the staging area for McClellan's campaign, Stanton added more fuel to the fires of complaint when he revoked all press passes and ordered all correspondents to leave Fortress Monroe. The Cincinnati *Daily Gazette* ridiculed Stanton's "vigorous measures" to suppress army correspondence and news as an indication of a "determination that the military plans and movements shall be known only to the Government and the enemy."[55]

However, this "severe turn" in military censorship was quickly revoked. According to confidential dispatches to major newspapers, Stanton promised that restrictions would be "materially modified" and that reporters would be allowed back into Fortress Monroe to report full descriptions of battles. Apparently, the order revoking press passes was aimed at Russell of the London *Times*.[56] In fact, Russell was ordered off the boat he was taking to Fortress Monroe.

But censorship remained tight at Fortress Monroe. Several reporters were arrested, and the Philadelphia *Inquirer* was temporarily denied telegraph privileges when it was thought that a report about a skirmish near Yorktown had not been approved. When Stanton learned that the report had been approved by the department commander, telegraph privileges were restored.[57]

According to the Cincinnati *Daily Gazette*, it was the "plain duty" of the military "to adopt the most effectual measures practicable to prevent the enemy from receiving knowledge.... In a time of war, the press must concede a portion of its rights and interests to the common good."[58]

But, Sanford, the military supervisor of the telegraph, found the censorship at Fortress Monroe uneven and sloppy. He convinced Stanton to issue an order April 12, abolishing local censorship and replacing it with "a simple, uniform and equitable system" of individual responsibility.[59] Under the new system, each reporter would be issued a pass to enter lines after promising not to reveal the location of troops or headquarters; names of generals or fighting units; descriptions or pictures of union fortifications or lines; numbers of troops, transports, or artillery; or movement of troops.[60] The official-looking two-page promissory, or parole, was used as a press pass by many reporters throughout the war and on various fronts.

Some newspapers rejoiced at the new and relaxed rules. The Chicago *Tribune* noted that wiser men and a better understanding of the press had prevailed. By lifting the censorship, the loyal press would be able to keep a check on commanders and "furnish a medium through which they will be made strictly responsible for their acts without the power to gloss over blunders."[61]

The new parole system was enforced during the early weeks, but soon became a logistical nightmare. Nevertheless, some publishers were caught revealing sensitive information. Soon after the parole system went into effect, Stanton prohibited the sale of *Harper's Weekly* in the Fortress Monroe area. The newspaper had printed detailed engravings that revealed the number and location of headquarters, troops, and weaponry during the siege of Yorktown. According to Gen. McClellan, the publication of the engraving was in violation of orders and against "all rules of common sense."[62]

John Bonner, editor of the illustrated weekly, fumed over the brief suspension. He wrote that the newspaper would not allow its business to be interfered with at the "whim of any military officer whomsoever." And any general who undertook to stop sales or circulation of *Harper's Weekly*, "does so at his peril. We shall hold him responsible for damages before a jury of his country."[63] Several weeks later, Fletcher Harper, publisher of *Harper's Weekly* and *Harper's Monthly*, was summoned to Washington to answer for the indiscretion.

Two months into the Peninsula campaign, McClellan made getting news from the front line difficult by forbidding correspondents from accompanying any of the advanced divisions on the march or from going beyond general headquarters, which at that time was located at Roper's Church, Virginia.[64] But enterprising correspondents were known to don uniforms to get to the lines or to smuggle out Richmond newspapers, which carried some details of battles.[65]

When McClellan found that official reports by his commanders after the Battle of Williamsburg were being sent to newspapers, he asked Stanton to issue an order prohibiting the publication of these reports.[66] McClellan had warned his officers that letter writing "deserves grave censure" if not the full penalties allowed under the 57th Article of War.

This strong censure did not succeed in plugging the leaks at the battlefront, and McClellan continued to seek help from Stanton. He wrote the secretary that several newspaper correspondents were in violation of the February 25 order. He urged Stanton to hold all newspaper editors responsible for the publication of vital information.[67] Stanton never complied with the requests. On June 5, McClellan informed Stanton that the full orders of the march from the Chickahominy River appeared in the Baltimore *American*. To McClellan, nothing could have been more damaging.[68]

McClellan was fighting another battle on the peninsula—the one against General Robert E. Lee. When it became evident to McClellan that he would not be reinforced with supplies and men in time to capture Richmond, he was forced to move back down the peninsula beginning June 25. Details of the Seven Day's Battles—the last five battles fought as the army marched toward the mouth of the James River—were sketchy. Correspondents followed McClellan's orders not to accompany troops to the front and hurried back to Fortress Monroe. But they were not allowed to telegraph what little information they had. It was a week before most Northern newspapers had any details of the retreat and the losses during the final week of the Peninsula campaign.

One journalist, however, did leave the area with an exclusive, although inaccurate, story of McClellan's activities. Charles C. Fulton, editor of the loyal Baltimore *American* and an Associated Press agent, offered an exclusive report about the Peninsula battles and about a conversation he had with Lincoln. However, permission to telegraph the story was denied and Fulton was arrested for "flagrant and outrageous breach of confidence." Apparently, the arrest orders came directly from Lincoln who felt Fulton had taken advantage of their private conversation. Some congressmen, like Morton Wilkins of Minnesota, were so concerned about the arrest of the only loyal editor in Baltimore that a resolution was introduced in the Senate demanding an explanation for the editor's arrest. However, the resolution never came to a vote.[69]

Once again, tight censorship had delayed bad news. And once again, Congress took note of the excessive censorship. Massachusetts Senator Henry Wilson, chairman of the Senate Military Affairs Committee, called the censorship "the most disastrous to the interests of the country, and so it has been always." He argued that it would have been better to allow the press its freedom and let the public be its censor. "It appears to me that we have an organized system of lying in this country that is calculated to degrade and deceive and delude the American people."[70]

After the Peninsula campaign, Stanton's office was able to maintain control over the Washington telegraph, but as the war spread west and south, telegraphic censorship was left to local commanders. Censors in the more remote arenas of war were either very lax, allowing great detail to go over the wire, or they were very strict. Newspaper editors complained throughout the war about the lack of consistency, the untrained censors, and the stupidity of some of the information that was censored.

When the Philadelphia *Inquirer* again printed contraband information, Stanton ordered the arrest of all editors who had reprinted the article. The New York *Herald* blamed the problem on the lack of censors with common sense. It would make more sense, said Bennett, to arrest the censors who allowed prohibited information to be sent. He suggested that the whole problem of incompetent censors could be solved by getting rid of them and requiring correspondents to wear identification badges and to place their names on all dispatches. The government could then place then legal responsibility for publishing contraband directly onto the newspaper.[71]

Stanton never entertained these suggestions and continued to the end of the war censoring the telegraph whenever he was close enough to do so. In March 1864, as General Ulysses S. Grant, newly appointed general in chief of all Union armies, began his Virginia campaign against Lee, Stanton proposed to tighten telegraphic censorship between Grant's headquarters at Culpepper Court House, Virginia and Washington. Grant agreed: "I have no objection to prohibiting the use of telegraph lines here by newspaper correspondents, on the contrary I think it very strongly advisable."[72]

THE MILITARY AND THE CORRESPONDENT

Closely akin to the wartime regulation of telegraphic and postal messages was the prerogative of military commanders either to suspend press credentials or to arrest correspondents and banish them from the front lines. Both of these measures of "military necessity" were practiced with regularity by most generals. Often, however, the practice was based on a double standard. The correspondent who praised his general would be accepted with open arms into the most intimate of military circles. But the reporter who criticized either the personal traits or military skills of officers could find himself relegated to the rear lines.

The *New York Times*, which had a large force of correspondents scattered throughout the Northern departments, took the lead in criticizing generals who acted arbitrarily against individual reporters. On one occasion, after General William T. Sherman had rescinded orders directing reporters to leave his district, the *Times* suggested that the general could alleviate a lot of problems if he would simply recognize the necessity of correspondents and establish better relations with them. "If men in public positions will regard journalists as simply gentlemen," and treat them accordingly, pleaded the *Times*, there would be no problems.[73]

The *Times* also wanted a consistent information policy. Reporters needed to know the rules and penalties under which they were expected to operate. "Whatever can be properly communicated to the people should be allowed to be sent; what cannot, should be entirely withheld or given with directions against its publication." While officers had a perfect right to limit the number of reporters and to require that they be men "of character, of education and of responsibility," said the *Times,* the job of balancing the necessities of war with the public's right to know should not be left to "the caprice, the resentments, or the fancied self-interest of individual officers." The *Times* continued: "It is very rarely that a military man can be found who is capable of understanding what public opinion is, or who can be made to comprehend that the Press has any other rights than those which he may be pleased to confer upon it."[74]

The disagreement over how best to balance military necessity and the First Amendment on the battlefront led to numerous expulsions or arrests of correspondents. Some of the more notable anti-press generals included Henry W. Halleck, Grant, and Sherman.

Following General Grant's bloody Union victory at Shiloh in April 1862, Halleck, then commander of the Department of Missouri, assumed command of Grant's Army of the Tennessee. He began a slow push with over 125,000 troops toward Corinth, Mississippi, twenty-three miles from Shiloh. The movement was much too slow for the dozens of correspondents accompanying the army. This impatience often led to inaccurate reports and speculation. To stop misleading reports and to rid the camps of spies, Halleck issued an order April 27, revoking all press passes that had not been renewed or countersigned. When it came to Halleck's attention that his order had been ignored not only by the newspaper representatives but also by his own officers, he issued Field Order No. 57 on May 13, expelling all "unauthorized hangers on."[75] To support his general, Stanton issued a bulletin from Washington prohibiting the publication of any information about the army's move toward Corinth until it had been authorized by the War Department.[76] At least one correspondent, Walter Isham of the Chicago *Times*, was arrested under the Field Order and placed in jail until reprimanded and released by

Halleck.[77] Other reporters were offered nominal military positions by field officers in order to evade the order.[78]

When it became apparent that "hangers on" included credentialed newspapermen, the press corps signed a protest. But Halleck was firm, claiming that the only way to rid the camps of spies was to expel all civilians. The reporters suggested that Halleck adopt a parole system similar to the one McClellan was using in his Peninsula campaign. The general refused. He also refused to acknowledge any passes issued by the War Department and ordered all correspondents to the rear. Defeated in their attempts to remain with Halleck's army, all but three of the regular correspondents returned to headquarters at Cairo, Illinois.[79]

The New York *Herald* called Stanton's news embargo an "experiment" but vowed that the paper would get the story out using any conveyance "from balloon to an army wagon." A couple of days later, Editor Bennett blamed Halleck's order on correspondents and editors in the Midwestern press who persisted in publishing important military information. He vowed that the *Herald's* reporters would remain with the army. If any of his correspondents remained in camp, it was not evident from the news columns. During the next three weeks, the *Herald* published either brief reports filed at Cairo by the Associated Press or reprinted stories from Confederate papers.[80]

Soon afterwards, Halleck was called to Washington to take over as commander of all Union armies. But this did not end the expulsion or arrests of reporters in the western departments. General Sherman and General Grant, who had resumed command of the Army of the Tennessee, filled the censorship void left by Halleck's departure.

In August 1862, Isham of the Chicago *Times* once again ran afoul of the military after his paper published a false story about new Confederate ironclads that had run the blockade off Mobile, Alabama. The report of thirteen new gunboats for the Confederacy created a stir in Washington. Probably at the instigation of Stanton and Gideon Wells of the Navy Department, Grant ordered Sherman to arrest Isham for the story "which is both false in fact and mischievous in character." Isham was arrested and sent to Alton, Illinois where he remained in prison without trial for three months. Sherman took great delight in making the arrest. He wrote Grant, "I regard all these newspaper harpies as spies and think they could be punished as such."[81]

Back in the East, Halleck resurrected one of McClellan's original plans to strike at Richmond directly from the north. He brought in General John Pope from the West and placed him in command of the Army of Virginia. He ordered McClellan, recuperating at Harrison's Landing from his flight down the York River Peninsula, to join Pope between Washington and the Rappahannock River.

The New York *Tribune* apparently intercepted telegrams ordering McClellan's evacuation of Harrison's Landing and published the details before the army had even packed up.[82] Halleck was angry. He telegraphed Pope on August 20: "I think your staff is decidedly leaky. The substance of my telegram to you is immediately telegraphed back here to the press. ... Clean out all such characters from your headquarters."[83]

Halleck also ordered Pope to expel all newspaper correspondents from the Army of Virginia, which Pope did on August 22.[84] The Philadelphia *Inquirer* noted the next day that correspondents had begun returning to Washington from Pope's camps; "their departure thence was involuntary."[85] The paper blamed the "stringent renewal of censorship" on the New York *Tribune's* indiscrete revelations.[86] The New York *Herald*, convinced the order affected only reporters from other papers, said it "serves them right." But when it became clear that *Herald* reporters were among those expelled, the paper "deplored the order" and explained that it harmed the people more than it did the newspapers or the enemy.[87]

The *Herald* again chastised the government's censorship: "Never did the government commit a greater blunder than in permitting interference with the newspaper reporters in the legitimate exercise of their profession." Taking his editorial from John Milton, Bennett argued that the people had the right to know; to conceal even disasters was against sound policy. "Let the reporters alone" and truth will be set right by the competition. "The people are sovereign, and they have a right to information; and no man, be he high or low in office ought to conceal it from them."[88]

Many editors were concerned that since Halleck's press expulsions in Mississippi and in Virginia had been so successful, the War Department might make expulsion a permanent wartime policy. According to the Philadelphia *Inquirer's* Washington correspondent, Lincoln and Stanton were taking just such a recommendation under advisement. Although the decision would probably rest with Stanton, the writer informed readers that Lincoln believed family and friends needed to know what was happening on the battlefront. Also, he did not believe that the press had made disclosures that were valuable to the enemy.[89]

Halleck, on the other hand, believed that reporters were as much out of place in an army as lawyers, judges, or dry goods merchants. War should be carried out by soldiers without interference and with a secrecy that can only be accomplished by excluding all civilians. The writer conceded that he did not know Stanton's present state of mind on the subject, but did know his position "a short time ago." Stanton felt that some indiscretions had occurred among the press, but felt that it was unjust to expel all correspondents because of the faults of a few. The writer concluded that no general exclusion of reporters would occur, but the rules of conduct would be much stricter.

Before McClellan could work his way back toward Washington, Stonewall Jackson marched his troops to Manassas Junction and stood between Pope and Washington. Pope, his attention drawn from Richmond, turned his troops around and marched toward Jackson, meeting him in defeat at the Second Battle of Bull Run. It was not until after the defeat that correspondents were allowed back into the army lines, just in time to describe Pope's retreat into Washington—a replay of the 1861 debacle.

Back in the West, General Sherman became the bane of correspondents who he believed were spies. From the earliest days of the war, Sherman had been a target of the press. The New York *Herald* called him "eccentric" and the Cincinnati *Daily Gazette* called him a "monomaniac." The Cincinnati *Commercial* let the world know that Sherman was "insane" and thanked God the army had not been damaged "through the loss of the mind of a general."[90]

But Sherman remained in the army, earning high praise for his heroism at the Battle of Shiloh in April 1862, amid criticism of Union leadership. Sherman wrote often to his family about the press and vowed "to get even with the miserable class of corrupt editors yet."[91] The general got his chance to get even when he was made military governor of Memphis. He warned that any reporter who came within his command would be arrested as a spy, court martialed, and hung.

In December 1862, Sherman was ordered by General Grant to command part of what would turn out to be a failed assault on Vicksburg, Mississippi. Before beginning his expedition, Sherman issued General Orders No. 8, prohibiting under the penalty of treason the publication of any information about his movements which might reach the enemy, and forbidding any civilians from accompanying the troops. Violation of the latter would result in either conscription as a soldier or deck hand. Sherman's orders were ignored for the most part by reporters, several of whom had passes issued by the War Department or by General Grant.

Sherman was ordered to attack Vicksburg from the north while Generals Grant and Banks supported him from the south and east. But the lines of the latter had been cut in half, leaving Sherman alone to wage a futile assault against well-entrenched Confederate lines. Sherman's attack was repulsed. It was a humiliating disaster for the Union, and Sherman was blamed. The St. Louis *Democrat* called it a "stupid blunder."[92] Once again, he was fair game.

ne of the reporters who accompanied the river transports and blamed Sherman for the defeat was Thomas W. Knox of the New York *Herald*. Knox accused Sherman of mismanagement and of expending more energy against reporters than against the Confederates. He also alluded to the earlier reports of insanity, calling for Sherman to be replaced.

Sherman, "willing no longer to tamely bear their misrepresentations and infamies," struck back at the Northern press by arresting Knox. "I am now determined to test the question. Do they [reporters] rule or the commanding general? If they rule I quit. . . . I will never again command an army in America if we must carry along paid spies."[93]

162   The Course of Tolerance

The court-martial took place at Young's Point, Louisiana, headquarters
of the Department of the Tennessee, in February 1863. Knox was charged
with three counts: giving intelligence to the enemy, being a spy and disobeying orders.[94] The charges were based on Knox's presence on the transport
Continental during the operation and his account of the battle published
January 18, two weeks afterwards. The original account for the *Herald* had
been taken from the mails under Sherman's orders. But Knox rewrote his
story and took it to Cairo, Illinois, himself to place in the mails. Two weeks
latter, after the published story reached Sherman's camp, Knox was arrested.[95]

During the protracted trial, Knox argued that his articles, published after
the defeat and after most Northern newspapers had published the same
information, could not have aided the enemy; that he had a pass from
General Grant; and that Secretary of War Stanton had approved publication
of reports after fighting was over.

Knox was found not guilty of giving intelligence to the enemy or of being
a spy. He was, however, found guilty of disobeying Sherman's orders prohibiting civilians from accompanying the troops. But the court could find
no criminal intent. Knox was banished from the Army of the Tennessee.[96]

Irate at the outcome, Sherman requested that the case be reviewed by the
president. He charged that the verdict usurped all of the power of a commanding officer. He believed that newspaper articles had "lost us millions
of money, thousands of lives, and will continue to defeat us to the end of
time, unless some remedy be devised."[97]

While Sherman fumed, Lincoln did review the case at the request of several
of Knox's friends. But he did not interfere; Lincoln instructed that Knox
return to Grant's headquarters and remain there only if General Grant
agreed. After accusing Knox of violating orders, breaking down Sherman's
influence and blasting his reputation, telling lies and making insinuations
against the general's sanity, Grant placed the decision over Knox's future
in Sherman's hands.

Sherman's answer:

Come with a sword or musket in your hand, prepared to share with us our fate in
sunshine and storm, in prosperity and adversity, in plenty and scarcity, and I will
welcome you as a brother and associate; but come as you now do...as the representative of the press, which you yourself say makes so slight a difference between
truth and falsehood, and my answer is, Never.[98]

Sherman warned that "if the press be allowed to run riot, and write up and
write down at their pleasure, there is an end to a constitutional government
in America, and anarchy must result."

Other generals had banned reporters from their commands, but the significance of the Knox case is that the military's action received the blessing of the president, thus establishing a precedent for a commander's discretion in relation to the press that continued into the twentieth century.

Four months after Sherman's failed assault on Vicksburg, Grant and his Army of the Tennessee were once again preparing to take the impregnable Gibraltar of the Mississippi. Emotions ran high, and information leaks were dealt with summarily. One such leak was a dispatch sent by the Associated Press (AP) correspondent at Cairo. The telegram, sent April 3, revealed that federal troops, working at night, had built a gun emplacement behind levees directly across from Vicksburg. The next day, another dispatch said the federal guns had silenced the rebel battery on the opposite shore.[99]

In fact, the battery was not complete and the army was building it at night to avoid detection. Grant ordered the AP correspondent L. W. Myers arrested and jailed in Memphis. According to Myers, the dispatch had been approved by an aide de camp. Grant's disposition of Myers is unknown.[100]

While Grant was besieging Vicksburg, General Joseph Hooker, 2,000 miles to the east, was moving his Army of the Potomac into Pennsylvania to stop Lee's northward advance. Although Hooker would soon be replaced by General George G. Meade, he remained in command long enough to give the press some grief. He complained to Halleck of a report in the New York *Herald* detailing the location of his troops. "Is there no way of stopping it?" Halleck replied that leaks could not be prevented as long as reporters were allowed to accompany the army. "I expelled them all from all our lines in Mississippi. Every general must decide for himself what persons he will permit in his camps."[101]

Hooker had already sent a dispatch to all editors, "requesting" that they publish neither the location of troops or of his headquarters nor any official reports that had not been sanctioned for publication. "After any fight the reporters can open their fire as loudly as they please." If this request was obeyed, he would give the press every facility for gathering and transmitting news, "including the license to abuse or criticize me to their hearts' content."[102] However, he found it necessary to arrest and banish a New York *Tribune* correspondent for writing a letter revealing contraband information.[103] The editor of the Washington *Star* was arrested for treason several days later by the War Department for publishing the same information.

When Sherman began his march to Atlanta in May 1864, he excluded correspondents from the transports. His order encouraged soldiers to continue corresponding with family and friends, but discouraged reporters who "will not take a musket and fight, but follow an army to pick up news for sale, speculating upon species of information dangerous to the army and to our cause."[104] Although a few reporters managed to evade the orders, news-gathering was difficult and information about the march through Georgia was limited. Sherman congratulated himself on the "paucity of news from the army," and the inability of the "busy and mischievous scribblers for newspapers" to carry out their work.[105]

When Sherman marched into Atlanta on September 1, 1864, he was praised as a national hero even by those newspapers that had long been his greatest critics. But as he was preparing for his next assault toward the Atlantic, his news embargo sprung a leak. In November 1864, the Indianapolis *Journal* predicted that the general was preparing to march on Charleston. Sherman demanded that the editor be arrested. Grant, who had replaced Halleck as general-in-chief of all Union armies in March, supported Sherman. He wrote the War Department that the dangerous leaks had compromised this final assault on the coast. But Stanton was unimpressed with the pleas and blamed Sherman for being too loose-tongued around personnel.[106] Nevertheless, Sherman managed to keep important information about his next move out of the newspapers.

Earlier in the summer, during the Wilderness campaign, several generals sought Grant's help in dealing with two New York correspondents. The New York *Tribune* printed a report from William Kent that accused General Winfield Hancock of failing to support an assault on Petersburg, Virginia, a major stumbling block in reaching Richmond. His pride injured, Hancock asked to have Kent arrested. Meade forwarded the request to Grant, asking that Kent either be arrested or ordered out of the army camps. "His article is full of malicious falsehoods; and he should be severely punished for it." After some reflection and not wanting to attach more importance to Kent than he deserved, Meade suggested that Grant merely expel Kent from the army. However, Kent had since left the army. Grant, nevertheless, revoked the reporter's pass.[107]

At the end of September, Kent appealed his expulsion to Lincoln. The president, much as he had done a year and a half earlier in the Knox case, left the decision to the army. Grant denied Kent's pass and explained to the president that although accommodations were made for the correspondents, "they cannot be permitted to misrepresent facts to the injury of the service. When they so offend, their pass to accompany the army is withdrawn and they are excluded from its lines."[108]

At about the same time, William Swinton wrote a letter to the *New York Times*, criticizing General Ambrose Burnside's 9th Corps at the Battle of Bethesda Church. Grant ordered Swinton arrested. But like Kent, Swinton had already returned to Washington. He was notified that his pass had been revoked and he would not be permitted to return to the army.[109] Incensed that one of his reporters had been summarily dismissed for having sent "incorrect statements," editor Raymond suggested that Swinton's real fault was being "too accurate."[110]

Arrests of reporters continued up to the last months of the war. Bradley Osbon, who had covered the war since the first bombardment of Ft. Sumter, was arrested in January 1865 for revealing details of the naval assault on Wilmington, Delaware. He was tried by court martial after the war was over and found not guilty on June 5, 1865.[111]

SUPPRESSION OF NEWSPAPERS

To complete the circle of censorship, the government suppressed newspapers, ordered the arrest of editors, and denied newspapers postal privileges. Closer to the front, commanders prohibited the distribution of "treasonous" newspapers in their camps.

Instances of mob violence against pro-slavery or anti-war newspapers, legitimized by official suppression, also occurred sporatically during the war. One contemporary source reported twenty-nine newspapers destroyed by mobs during the duration of the war and over two dozen officially suppressed by military or civil authorities.[112] For example, the Bangor, Maine, *Democrat* was burned out and the editor placed in jail for his own safety; the offices of the Westchester, Pennsylvania, *Jeffersonian* and the *Starke County Democrat* (Ohio) were wrecked; the offices of the *Palmetto Flag* of Philadelphia were attacked; and the editor of the Essex County *Democrat* (Massachusetts) was tarred and feathered and ridden out of town on a rail.[113]

And as had occurred during the 1830s, many of these mob activities were encouraged by local newspaper editors. The Philadelphia *Inquirer* condoned the wrecking of the Westchester *Jeffersonian*, saying that the "traitorous expressions of the sheet have long been annoying to the residents of this place." About the attack on the Essex City *Democrat*, the *Inquirer* noted that the editor had eventually promised to "keep his pen dry in aid of rebellion" and had promised never again to publish an article against the North or in favor of secession.[114]

Newspapers also praised official suppression. The case of the *Christian Observer*, a Presbyterian newspaper published in Philadelphia, illustrates newspaper reaction to the seizure of disloyal papers. Amasa Converse, a long-time defender of slavery and the South, published the *Christian Observer* in Richmond and Philadelphia. On June 1, 1861, Converse was prohibited from sending any mail to the South, a successful attempt by the government to frustrate his Richmond operation.[115] However, Converse did not tone down his newspaper. On August 22, he published a letter that described federal troops killing Southern women and pillaging homes. That afternoon, Converse was arrested and his newspaper confiscated. Locally, there was a general sigh of relief that the treasonous publication had been put to rest. The Philadelphia *Inquirer* said that the *Observer* "teemed with villainous articles" and the marshal had taken a "wise and judicious step" in suppressing the paper. The *Inquirer* noted that the *Observer* "had dwindled down from sleekness and prosperity to want and neglect, and the sudden process of the law barely outstripped the natural order of things."[116]

The Philadelphia *Evening Bulletin*, which had earlier called Converse an enemy of the United States, warned readers that treason was not made more acceptable by being garbed in religious cloth; in fact, it was far worse because it was more concealed.[117] Converse was never prosecuted. He moved to Richmond, where he resumed publishing his paper on September 19. In that first Southern edition he explained that it was necessary for him to leave the North because Lincoln had no respect for freedom of the press and, as editor, he would allow no one to tell him what he could print.[118]

Like censorship of the telegraph, newspaper suppression did not go unnoticed by Congress. In July 1861, a joint resolution was presented to the Senate asking approval and confirmation of those actions taken by Lincoln to suppress the rebellion. Among those actions were the blockading of Southern ports, unlawful searches and seizures, and the suspension of the writ of habeas corpus.

When debate on the joint resolution reached the floor of the Senate, the most outspoken opponent was border Senator John C. Breckenridge of Kentucky. In his lengthy speech decrying the actions of Lincoln, Breckenridge warned that the nation was "rushing...from a constitutional government to a military despotism." To prove this point, the senator described how 400 soldiers entered the offices of a St. Louis paper, destroyed type, and suppressed the paper because it was "fabricating reports injurious to the U.S. soldiers in Missouri."[119]

But Senator Lane of Indiana countered that where traitorous newspapers were concerned, "the Administration have shown a forbearance beyond all parallel in history. No government on earth would tolerate treason of these papers....I not only approve of the destruction of that St. Louis paper, but I rejoice at it as an evidence of returning common sense."

A friend of Breckenridge's, Anna Ella Carroll of Baltimore, also responded to the senator's speech and defended the closing of newspapers. In her mind the St. Louis newspaper was in the service of the South and engaged in destruction of the Constitution and the government. Anyone aiding the rebellion "by treasonable utterance, whether spoken or written, is as amenable to martial law as though enrolled in the Confederate army." And if the rebellion were to grow to override both judicial and legislative powers, the president, "instead of suppressing one press, he may extend it to all presses engaging in exciting and stimulating treason."[120]

And that is exactly what Lincoln's administration did. Most of the newspapers that were suppressed were edited by conservative Democrats who considered themselves loyal Americans wanting to end the war quickly even if it meant promising the South not to interfere with slavery. They favored an "honorable compromise." During the first year of the war, these peace organs received moral support from lingering anti-abolition sentiment, Union defeats such as Bull Run, and economic hard times. But as the war continued without promise of end or compromise, moderate "Peace Democrats" became "War Democrats," leaving the more radical anti-abolition elements of the party to continue their bitter attacks against the "wholly unconstitutional" war. Soon, these radical Democrats, more prominent in the Midwest, became known as Copperheads, named after the deadly snake.

During the second week of August 1861, several pro-secession, pro-Southern newspapers in New York published lists of newspapers that opposed the war, demonstrating how many well-meaning citizens rejected the "unholy war" that had been perpetrated by ill-meaning persons in Washington. However, this show of Southern sympathy was not appreciated. Placards appeared around the city warning readers to beware of opposition organs.[121] Also, a federal grand jury issued a hastily prepared presentment asking the U.S. Circuit Court whether five local pro-Southern newspapers could be subject to indictment. The grand jury accused the *Daily News, Journal of Commerce, Day Book, Freeman's Journal,* and the Brooklyn *Eagle* of "expressing sympathy and agreement with the rebels and dissatisfaction with the employment of force" against the enemy.[122]

The grand jury acknowledged that "free governments allow liberty of speech and of the press to their utmost limit, but there is nevertheless a limit." The conduct of these disloyal papers is condemned by all, concluded the presentment, but "the grand jury will be glad to learn from the court that it is also subject to indictment and condign punishment."[123]

The Brooklyn *Eagle*, which had accused abolitionists and Negroes of maneuvering the country into war, flouted the grand jury's request. The editor vowed to vindicate and maintain the principle of free speech and free press.[124]

Although none of the editors was indicted, the presentment was forwarded to Postmaster General Montgomery Blair, who issued an order on August 22, prohibiting the postal transmission of all newspapers listed in the presentment. Blair, relying on precedent set by Amos Kendall in 1835 and other instances of postal censorship, argued that the crime of treason needed to be stopped by "prompt and direct interference" rather than "by slow judicial prosecution."[125]

The *Journal of Commerce* suspended for one day, but resumed publication for local buyers. Editor Gerard Hallock wrote that no newspaper could survive long without the privilege of using the postal system. An order preventing newspapers from using mails was just as effective a tool for destruction as would be an order for their suppression.[126]

Prompted by the grand jury's presentment, as well as by the suppression of papers in other states, *Harper's Weekly* said the New York journals had gone beyond a fair opposition and were "pernicious, mischievous, and calculated to do great public injury."[127]

The Chicago *Times*, a pro-slavery, anti-abolitionist organ, was uncertain whether the government's actions were lawful. It was much better to tolerate the newspapers until legal means could be found to deal with their incendiary nature.[128]

James Wall, a correspondent for the *Daily News*, asked Blair for an explanation of the mail censorship. Blair replied that he did not seize the newspapers because they were dangerous but because the "objects of the writers were traiterous" and the demands of the people for help from the government could not be overlooked, "although I do not myself apprehend any serious effect of such writings."[129]

However, when Blair defended his actions in a letter to the House Committee on the Judiciary in January 1863, he claimed that he had acted in the belief that the Postmaster General had the power to prevent hostile matter from reaching the enemy and from instigating others to cooperate with the enemy.[130] While the Post Office has no authority to suppress publication, Blair said, it does have the authority to prevent circulation. The First Amendment is not a license to "aim blows at the existence of the government, the Constitution, and the Union."

Although Blair cited numerous examples of postal censorship by his predecessors, he rejected the idea that local postmasters had the discretion to determine what could or could not pass through the mails. He also dissented from the view that in times of peace and in absence of criminal activity, anyone could exclude materials "obnoxious to some special interest, but not aimed against government, law, or the public safety." Even in time of war, continued Blair, the power to confiscate should be used with "great care and delicacy."

The House Committee on the Judiciary found that the Postmaster General had the right and duty during wartime to deny the use of the mails to treasonable publications. "The act of the Postmaster General was not only within the scope of his powers, but induced solely by considerations of the public good."[131]

Suspension of postal privileges also meant the seizure of any proscribed newspapers already in transit. The U.S. marshal in Philadelphia seized 2,000–3,000 copies of the New York *Daily News* from a steam packet and examined all newspapers passing south via an express coach. "A general satisfaction was expressed by those around at the proceedings," reported the Philadelphia *Inquirer*.[132]

A correspondent from Baltimore wrote that if editors destroy the very institutions which give them protection, "I see no reason why they should be exempt from punishment more than private individuals."[133] The Chicago *Tribune* supported the activites in New York, saying that "no nation can allow its existence to be thus trifled with."[134] When a man takes sides with the enemies of his country, said the editor, he is as dangerous as any traitor. "And whenever a newspaper becomes a danger to the existence of the Government, it should be punished by fine and suspension."

The New York *Times* took a balanced approach. Freedom of the press and other "minor rights and duties" may have to be curtailed in the presence of "overwhelming public necessity," said the editor. "The temporary surrender of these rights is a small price to pay for their permanent and perpetual enjoyment."[135]

The New York *Herald* called for the government to detail an armed force to carry out the suppression. Bennett, believing the action of the Post Office to be incomplete, recommended that the New York *Tribune*, New York *Independent*, and the *Liberator* "be squelched" as well as "the whole of the anti-slavery leaders, beginning with Wendell Phillips" who ought to be arrested and sent to Fort Lafayette military prison.[136] The Chicago *Times* joined with the *Herald* in calling for the suppression of these other "abolition-republican" journals that favored emancipation—"a measure as revolutionary as the rebellion itself."[137]

The Post Office's actions against the New York newspapers also brought out the mobs. Bennett wrote that such action was not surprising, but "there can be no justification for the suppression of liberty of speech or of the press by the dangerous interposition of mob law." He counseled citizens to leave it to the law to deal with treason.[138] The Philadelphia *Inquirer* also warned against mob rule, predicting that such newspapers will either die of neglect or be silenced by the law, but not by mobs.[139] Indeed, on September 15, The New York *Herald* was "grateful to announce" that the *Daily News* was suspended.[140]

On September 11, editor Benjamin Wood and correspondent James Wall, "a brawling, noisy secessionist" who "read his secession paper at all the corners" and "exulted in our defeat at Bull Run," were arrested by order of the Secretary of War.[141] Wood posted a notice on the door of the office stating that the *Daily News* was suspended until freedom of the press was restored.[142]

Also arrested was a crippled newsboy who had been apprehended in New Haven, Connecticut for selling the "damnable secession sheet," on the Naugatuck Rail Road.[143] James McMaster, editor of *Freeman's Journal*, was arrested three days later. All were charged with treason under the 57th Article of War.

Correspondent Wall, an inveterate letter writer, left a good accounting of his arrest in the record books of the State Department. On the day of his arrest, he wrote Secretary of State Cameron denying that he had ever committed a treasonous act and was "more loyal to-day to the Government than many a loud-mouthed pretender whose loyalty can only be measured by his interests."[144]

Wall was released on September 24, after signing an oath of allegiance to the United States.[145] Despite more than a half-dozen letters sent during and after his imprisonment to the Secretary of War and Secretary of State,

Wall was never informed of the specific charges against him. James McMaster of the *Freeman's Journal* was released a month later after signing his oath of allegiance under protest.[146]

Taking their cue from New York, grand juries in Westchester County and Trenton, New Jersey, also issued presentments against local newspapers. The Westchester grand jury asked for the suppression of the Yonkers *Herald*, Highland *Democrat* and the *Eastern State Journal*. It also asked that two New York German-language papers, the *Staats-Zeitung* and *National Zeitung*, be prevented from circulating in the county.[147]

Horace Greeley's New York *Tribune* endorsed the action of the Westchester grand jury, saying that "the legal right to suppress is as unquestionable as the right to suppress obscene publications." It was not a question of liberty of press, but of license, which requires "wholesome restraint."[148] Bennett's *Herald* also agreed, noting that in times of peace the rights of the press are determined by the Constitution and the laws, but in times of war, "the laws of war prevail."[149]

Official action was taken against only the German-language papers. On September 9, the New York Postmaster denied mailing privileges to the *National Zeitung* and *Staats-Zeitung*.[150] Oswald Ottendorfer, editor of the *Staats-Zeitung*, explained that incriminating stories forwarded to Washington were actually clipped from his competitor, the *National Zeitung*. Ottendorfer pointed out that among the government's warmest adherents was the *Staats-Zeitung*.[151]

The *National Zeitung* had indeed become quite rabid. Its boldness came, in part, from the fact that it was managed by a committee of German Democrats who provided the direction for Editor O. Bengue. Kennedy forwarded several copies of the newspaper to Washington, stating that his department stood ready to execute any order against the paper.

Months passed without action. Finally, the Department of State asked a federal judge for legal advice on the culpability of the papers. Although the judge's "fingers itch to write yes," he said it would be difficult to punish them. "Besides, unlimited abuse of public men has always been the first resource of papers of small circulation edited by hot-brained partisans with more zeal than discretion."[152] No action was taken against the *National Zeitung*.[153]

The Trenton, New Jersey grand jury issued its presentment against the Newark *Evening Journal*, Warren *Journal*, Hunterdon *Democrat*, New Brunswick *Times*, Plainfield *Gazette*, and the Hackettstown *Gazette*. The grand jury, acknowledging a due regard for freedom of speech, did not seek official action. Instead, it urged all citizens to withold their patronage from the named publications, and left it "to the wholesome action of public opinion" to put these newspapers out of business.[154]

No action was taken against the newspapers mentioned in the New Jersey presentment until March 1863, when E. N. Fuller, editor of the Newark *Evening Journal*, was arrested by civil authorities for inciting to insurrection and for discouraging enlistments. Fuller was convicted and sentenced to pay a small fine.

New York was not the only center of newspaper suspensions and arrests of editors. Baltimore, a hotbed of pro-Southern sympathy, witnessed the permanent suppression of eight newspapers and the temporary suspension of four during the war.[155] Arrests of pro-Southerners were made easier when Lincoln suspended the writ of habeas corpus in Maryland immediately after the riots in April 1861.

Three of the newspapers subject to repression were the *South*, *Daily Exchange*, and the *Daily Republican*. But when an order to suppress the three newspapers was issued, a group of loyal citizens protested, fearing that such a move would only encourage Southern sympathies and lead to riot.[156]

Nevertheless, Postmaster General Blair endorsed a request from the Baltimore postmaster to suppress the three offending publications. Major John Dix, commanding officer of Baltimore under General McClellan's command, refused to carry out the suppression unless it was authorized by McClellan. He also cautioned Blair that although Union sympathizers would like these newspapers suppressed, there were many who thought differently. "The city is now very quiet and under control." Haste in this matter could result in "a political Bull Run disaster in this State."[157]

McClellan did not support Dix's assessment. Within two weeks, the local postmaster denied mailing privileges to the three newspapers.[158] The *Exchange* continued to circulate locally for several days until its editor Frank Key Howard and an associate, S. Teackle Wallis, were arrested. Thomas Hall, editor of the *South*, also was arrested as part of a general round-up of more than a dozen disloyal persons including members of the Maryland legislature.[159]

The day after Howard, Wallis, and Hall were arrested, the *Exchange* printed a bitter editorial about the "brutal conduct and disgraceful ruffianism" of the police in arresting the editors.[160] Publisher and interim editor of the *Exchange*, W. Wilkins Glenn, was arrested, and the paper suspended. Since Glenn's primary interest in the paper was financial rather than editorial, he was released six weeks later after promising not to "edit the *Exchange* nor republish it nor contribute to any paper so long as the censorship of the press is exercised in Baltimore." [161] Editor Howard remained in prison until the end of November 1862, when he and Thomas Hall of the *South* were released as part of a general amnesty for all prisoners from Maryland.[162]

Incidents of suppression increased in 1862 after the Post Office was placed under the War Department, thus opening up an avenue for military officers to censor newspapers. Commanders could now order postmasters within their districts to seize suspected newspapers from the mails. This occurred with great frequency in Illinois, Missouri, Kansas, Ohio, West Virginia, California, Oregon, and Kentucky.

When Postmaster General Montgomery Blair was asked by the Senate by what authority military commanders suppressed the circulation of newspapers, he answered: "the law of public safety." He added that postmasters were required to obey the orders of the military, thus taking all responsibility for mail censorship out of the hands of the Post Office.[163]

Military commanders not only suspended mailing privileges but also had the prerogative to suppress the distribution of newspapers within their camps. Such action was usually taken to prevent exposure of troops to anti-war journals or to prevent Confederates remaining in captured areas from learning that there was much pro-Southern sympathy in the North. In the Midwest, the opposition newspapers were often blamed for desertions and draft riots.

General Grant, who never hesitated to banish correspondents from his camps, appears to have been alone in his belief that military commanders did not have the power to suppress the publication or distribution of papers in his army. In February 1863, three of his district commanders in Tennessee prohibited circulation of the anti-administration Chicago *Times* in Memphis, Jackson, and Humbolt.[164]

The *Illinois State Journal* praised the orders as "a just and necessary rebuke."[165] But when Grant learned of the orders, he revoked them. Since the paper had not been suppressed "by authority from Washington," he doubted whether any field commander could legally issue such an order. Grant was not oblivious to the damage such opposition newspapers could do. He wrote his daughter that he was concerned about desertion, and accused Northern secessionists of protecting the soldiers. He hoped the administration would act on this problem by suppressing disloyal papers.[166]

Beginning in mid-1862, suppression of newspapers on the homefront moved out of the Northeast and into the more politically volatile military districts of the Midwest. This new locus of activity was a direct result of Lincoln's announcement in September 1862 that he intended to issue the Emancipation Proclamation and the simultaneous order denying the writ of habeas corpus.

The Democratic Party as well as radical Copperheads saw Lincoln's actions as further evidence that this was a war of abolitionists aimed at subverting the very Constitution it was meant to preserve. Consequently, Copperheads quickly gained strength in border states such as Ohio, West Virginia, and Missouri as well as the southern counties of Illinois and Indiana.

The most prominent Copperhead was Clement L. Vallandigham, a rabid pro-secessionist who served as a congressman from Ohio until his defeat in the 1862 elections. Vallandigham's return to Ohio in March 1863 after Congress adjourned coincided with the assignment of General Ambrose E. Burnside to the command of the Department of the Ohio.

When Burnside arrived in Ohio, he walked into a nest of Copperheads guarded by a strong press. But there also remained in the state a strong Republican organization that dared to brand Copperheads as treasonous. In one March incident, the office of the Columbus, Ohio, *Crisis*, a strong Democratic paper edited by Samuel Medary, was wrecked by soldiers and civilians. The editor of the Dayton *Empire* retalliated by calling for the seizure of Republican property for security against further violence against Democrats. "For every Democratic printing office destroyed by a mob, let an abolition one be destroyed in turn."[167] Threats were met by counter-threats until Burnside was forced to declare martial law in Columbus.

Vallandigham's return to Dayton from Washington was greeted with a parade and numerous anti-Lincoln speeches. Burnside, who had little tolerance for anti-administration rhetoric, reacted to the celebration by issuing General Order No. 38 on April 13. The order stated that the "habit of declaring sympathy for the enemy" would no longer be tolerated. At the first opportunity, Vallandigham defied the order. At a mass meeting in Mt. Vernon, he spewed forth the typical Copperhead castigations against the war, abolitionists, Lincoln, and Republicans. He insisted that "General Order No. 1"—the Constitution—guaranteed his right to criticize the administration.

Vallandigham was arrested in Dayton several days later. When word of his arrest spread through Dayton the next morning, a crowd of about 200 people gathered outside the offices of the friendly Dayton *Empire*. But soon the gathering turned into a mob against the nearby Dayton *Journal*, a Republican organ. By the end of the day, half a city block was burned to the ground.

In Cincinnati, Vallandigham went on trial despite arguments that civilians could not be tried by the military as long as the civil courts were still in operation. When that argument failed, Vallandigham's lawyer tried to convince the military tribunal that his client had not said all that he was accused of saying. The military court found Vallandigham guilty and sentenced him to prison for the duration of the war. Lincoln interceded and changed the sentence to banishment to the South.

The treatment of Vallandigham by General Burnside was met with a tremendous outpouring of resentment. Much of this sentiment came from Wilbur F. Storey, editor of the Chicago *Times*. During the first two years of the war, Storey's reaction to various censorship activities, including Stanton's telegraphic censorship of 1862 and the suppression of newspapers elsewhere, had been fairly mild for an aggressive Copperhead. But following the Emancipation Proclamation, Storey became violent, attacking Lincoln, the war, and abolitionists and detailing the horror that would come should Negroes be freed.

Storey's anger was quickly turned against General Burnside when he learned of Vallandigham's arrest and trial. Storey wrote, "If a terrible retribution does not fall upon the perpetrators of this foul wrong, then is not

God just."[168] After weeks of lamenting the death of civil liberties, the *Times* culminated its hatred with an issue on May 30 in which Burnside was called the "Butcher of Fredericksburg." The *Times* compared the general's actions to the hated Alien and Sedition Acts.[169]

On June 1, General Burnside issued General Orders No. 84, suppressing the Chicago *Times* and banning the New York *World* from the district. General Burnside gave as his reason "the repeated expression of disloyal and incendiary sentiments" by the paper. He ordered the military to take possession of the *Time's* office. Burnside's order of June 1 was received in Washington the same day, and Lincoln and Stanton reacted immediately urging the general "to take an early occasion to revoke that order." According to a letter from Stanton, "the irritation produced by such acts is in [Lincoln's] opinion likely to do more harm than the publication would do." Although the president approved of Burnside's motives, he wished to be consulted before civilians were arrested and newspapers suppressed. Stanton's letter was sent through the mails, an indication that the secretary and president were in no rush to have the order suspended.

Burnside probably did not receive Stanton's letter until a week later. Meanwhile, Storey applied to the U.S. circuit court for a temporary injunction, which he received. Judge Thomas Drummond ordered the commander of Fort Douglas to delay any action against the *Times* until the motion for a permanent injunction could be heard. Meanwhile, Storey rushed to publish the last edition of the *Times* for June 3 before troops entered the offices at 5 A.M.

Later that morning, Judge Drummond declined to hold hearings on the injunction. However, he did issue a statement supporting the administration but denouncing Burnside's action: "I personally have contended and shall always contend, for the right of free discussion and the right of commenting, under the law and the Constitution, upon the acts of the officers of the government."[170]

That same morning a bipartisan group of city leaders and politicians, including U.S. Representative Isaac Arnold and Senator Lyman Trumbull, met at the courthouse and passed a resolution requesting Lincoln to revoke the order. The resolution was telegraphed to the president as was a similar message from U.S. Supreme Court Justice David Davis.[171] The next day, June 4, Lincoln wrote Stanton that the Burnside order should be revoked. "If you concur in opinion, please have it done." Burnside revoked the order against the Chicago *Times* and the New York *World*.[172]

A year later, Lincoln wrote Arnold that it was the "dispatch of Senator Trumbull and yourself and proceedings of the meeting which it brought me" that induced him to revoke the order. But he also acknowledged, "I am far from certain to-day that the revocation was right."[173] The uncertainty was probably the consequence of a second telegram that Arnold sent in the early hours of July 4 denying his endorsement of the earlier resolution.

At least one scholar believes this second telegraph from Arnold convinced Lincoln to send another message the evening of the 4th, directing that if Burnside had not acted upon the earlier order, "you need not do so but may let the matter stand as it is until you receive a letter by mail forwarded yesterday."[174] Had Burnside not acted quickly to rescind his order after receiving the first telegraph, the Chicago *Times* might have been silenced for almost two weeks.

The Illinois House of Representatives, a predominantly Democratic group, passed a resolution (forty-seven to eighteen) calling Burnside's suspension order "revolutionary and despotic." The legislators denounced Burnside's order as a violation of both the federal and state constitutions and destructive of all those God-given principles that had been recognized by civilized societies for centuries.[175]

No paper was more outspoken against the Chicago *Times* than its crosstown rival, the Chicago *Tribune*, which said the suppression had been deferred too long, and that the "dragons teeth" had already been sown by the "malignant and unpatriotic" supporters of the *Times*.[176] The *Tribune* commended Burnside for acting in good faith: "Burnside did right; and no man who believes that martial law is ever necessary or proper can deny it." But the paper criticized Lincoln's revocation as "a most unfortunate blunder," saying that Lincoln should have waited for the court to hand down a decision. "As the matter stands it is a triumph of treason."[177]

Almost two weeks after the suppression, Joseph Medill, editor of the *Tribune* began analyzing the events in an attempt to justify the *Times*'s fate. In a lengthy editorial, Medill vowed that he had no sympathy for those who asserted an absolute freedom of speech because in society, speech is always limited by the prevailing conditions. Freedom of speech can be restrained by civil law in time of peace, but in war time, "the greater the danger, the narrower the limitations." Until the war is over "we must be content to accept whatever the altered conditions of the times and the country may demand as a requisite of national salvation."[178]

On another occasion Medill compared martial law to a judge's power of contempt. Both powers are necessary to accomplish broader inherent goals—maintenance of judicial authority on the one hand, maintenance of military authority on the other.[179] Another argument supporting Burnside that was used by the *Tribune* as well as by Lincoln himself was Andrew Jackson's use of martial law in New Orleans in 1815. Jackson may have been harsh, said the *Tribune*, but he was right.[180]

President Lincoln, responding to a letter written by citizens protesting the arbitrary treatment of Vallandigham, also justified the use of martial law by citing the Jackson affair. "No one denies that [the safeguards of the rights of citizens] have so stood the test up to the beginnings of the present rebellion if we except a certain matter at New Orleans." After reviewing the history of the earlier affair, Lincoln noted that the conditions were the same in 1815 as they were 1863. However, "the permanent right of the people to public discussion, the liberty of speech and the press, the trial by jury, the law of evidence, and the Habeas Corpus, suffered no detriment whatever by that conduct of Gen. Jackson, or it's[sic] subsequent approval by the American congress."[181]

Many newspapers criticized Burnside for declaring martial law so far from the battlefront. However, Lincoln argued that military arrests can be made whenever and "*wherever* the public safety does require them." Cognizant of the effect opposition journals had on desertion, Lincoln asked: "Must I shoot a simple-minded soldier boy who deserts, while I must not touch a hair of a wiley agitator who induces him to desert?... To silence the agitator, and save the boy, is not only constitutional, but withal, a great mercy."[182]

The Chicago *Times* suspension resulted in an unusual unity of sentiment among both loyal and opposition journals across the North. In New York, representatives of twelve of that city's newspapers met following the supression of the *Times* to discuss the "nature and extent and rightful limitation (if any) of the liberty of public journalists to criticize the acts of those charged with the conduct of the Government in time of war and civil convulsions." In a set of resolutions sent to Lincoln and his cabinet, the editors asserted the right of the press to criticize freely the acts of civil and military authorities. Although they did not want to claim any special treatment or exemptions, the editors resolved that any limit of rights should be confined to areas where hostilities actually existed or were threatened. However, the editors did agree that the suppression of newspapers "palpably treasonable" was proper.[183] Conspicuously absent from the editor's meeting was a representative of the *New York Times*. Raymond explained that he did not attend because "we regard this whole matter as one upon which each individual editor must exercise his own judgment and act accordingly." The press's utility, said the paper, depends on its independence—"The complete freedom of each individual editor to express, without dictation from Government, or from any class or profession, even his own" views on public affairs.[184]

However, the *New York Times* did agree with the editors on the subject of military arrests. While the press's freedom is not unlimited, the claim by Burnside that the press was amenable to military power "is simply absurd," said the *Times*, and shows how little military men know about the nature of democracy. "For a military officer to march a company of soldiers into a man's house or office and suppress him of his business, because he deems him guilty of a violation of law, is simply a piece of madness." The *New York Times* called Lincoln's revocation of Burnside's order a "just and timely act."[185]

Greeley in the New York *Tribune* called the president's action the "wiser and safer course." However, Lincoln was not being consistent if one compared this revocation to his action in the case of Vallandigham whose words were no worse than those of the Chicago *Times*. "Yet it is better to be inconsistently right than consistently wrong—better to be right to-day, though wrong yesterday, than to be wrong both days alike," said Greeley.[186] Bennett at the *Herald* joined with his long-time political adversary, the *Tribune*, saying that as bad as the papers were, the people would not permit them to be put down by military despotism. The *Herald* argued that the "tyrannical military edicts" had not originated with Burnside but with abolitionists like Stanton and Secretary of Treasury Salmon P. Chase, a "pair of third-rate politicians."[187]

The Washington *Daily National Intelligencer* accused Burnside of substituting the will of a commander for the established law of the land when there was no necessity to do so. Such zeal, said the editor, was more dangerous to democracy than all its enemies.[188]

The New York *Evening Post* was baffled that papers in New York, containing much worse material, had gone untouched. "Have we different systems, different rules of government, different ethics, different notions of propriety, in the thousand different localities of our broad land?"[189]

The Washington *Daily Chronicle*, a favorite of Lincoln's, praised Burnside for acting with the highest motives in suppressing the Chicago *Times*. The paper also praised Lincoln's quick action in revoking the order, stating that Lincoln operated from a better vantage point than Burnside and could see the larger picture and "enlarged principles" that had to be considered over military necessity. Comparing Lincoln and Burnside, the editor said, "the one acted as a soldier and the other as a statesman."[190]

The "statesman" Lincoln must have been gun-shy about military suppressions following the *Times* affair. Four months later, he wrote General John Schofield in St. Louis that he was only to suppress newspapers "when they may be working palpable injury ... and, in no other case will you interfere with the expression of opinion in any form or allow it to be interfered with violently by others." He urged Schofield to exercise "caution, calmness and forbearance," a warning he probably wished he had issued Burnside.[191]

But a year later, Lincoln had set aside any qualms about suspending newspapers. This time the victims were two anti-administration organs, the New York *World* and *Journal of Commerce*. The journals, however, were not suppressed solely because of their political stance, but because of a trick played on them by two Wall Street speculators.

After Congress passed the first draft bill in March 1863, the North not only witnessed numerous bloody draft riots, but Wall Street saw the price of gold and silver rise with every draft call. To take advantage of the rising price of precious metals, two reporters for the Brooklyn *Daily Eagle* (the same paper mentioned in the 1861 grand jury presentment) forged a draft proclamation with the signatures of Stanton and Lincoln. The notice was disguised as an Associated Press dispatch and delivered by messenger to almost all of New York's newspapers.[192] The proclamation arrived in the

early hours of May 18, in time for some newspapers to question the order
and learn that it was a forgery. But by the time the *World* and *Journal of
Commerce* received the dispatch, the editors had left the offices and the
decision to remake the front page with the late bulletin was made by the
foremen of the respective press rooms.[193]

When the forged proclamation appeared on the streets that morning,
many were surprised that the two papers had scooped the *New York Times*
or the New York *Herald*. Just as the perpetrators predicted, the price of
gold began to rise. But when it became apparent that the draft order for
400,000 men was a fake, the price plummeted along with the reputations
of the newspapers. Although General John Dix informed Washington almost
immediately that the editors had been the hapless victims of a clever forgery,
Lincoln ordered the arrest of the publishers and editors and the seizure of
the newspaper offices.[194]

Dix, as reluctant to carry out the arrests as he had been when in command
of Baltimore in 1862, did arrest editor Gerard Hallock at the *Journal of
Commerce* office. But Lincoln rescinded the arrest before Dix's troops could
locate the other three men involved. But while the editors were free, their
papers remained under armed guard for two more days. Also seized by
order of the War Department were the offices of the Independent Telegraph
Company in New York, Baltimore, Philadelphia, Harrisburg, and Pittsburgh. The telegraph company was originally suspected of being a party to
the forgery.

The real forgers, Francis Mallison and Joseph Howard, were arrested
within two days. After Dix informed Stanton of the arrests, the newspaper
offices were returned to their proprietors before noon on May 21.[195]

Again, the Northern press spoke with a united voice in defense of the
newspapers. The New York *Tribune*, expressing the general sentiment,
wrote that "no journal should be punished for a mistake which might have
very innocently been committed by the most loyal paper in the land."[196]
The New York *Daily News*, which had also been listed in the 1861 grand
jury presentment, said it was "preposterous" to believe that the papers had
anything to do with the forgery.[197]

The *New York Times*, again demonstrating a conservative independence
from its bretheren, was less tolerant of the *World* and *Journal of Commerce*,
accusing the papers of the "grossest carelessness." But the papers were
certainly not guilty of treason, the *Times* said.[198]

Manton Marble, editor of the *World*, knew that underlying the arrest
and suspension was a political motive that could not be overlooked. In an
editorial, he queried Lincoln: "Had the Tribune and the Times published
the forgery...would you, Sir, have suppressed [them] as you suppressed
The World and the Journal of Commerce? You know you would not. Is
there a different law for your opponents and for your supporters?"[199] These

last suppressions are significant because they were the only ones known to have been ordered by Lincoln, himself.

CONCLUSION

Censorship of the Northern press during the Civil War has been described by numerous scholars, and the conclusion has always been the same—that a censorship of the press did exist. Orders were promulgated by the War Department and by military commanders from coast to coast mandating censorship of telegraphic dispatches, the suspension of postal services, the denial of distribution privileges, the arrest or expulsion of correspondents, the military seizure of newspaper offices, and the arrest of editors. All of these actions occurred outside of the civil law in the name of military necessity.

However, this is not to say that freedom of press was entirely crushed. In fact, freedom of speech and press thrived in an atmosphere charged with discord, confrontation, and diversity of opinion. Despite mob violence and official suppression, the vast majority of opposition journals remained untouched throughout the war. Despite telegraphic censorship and the arrest and expulsion of correspondents, details of almost every skirmish and battle eventually reached readers.

The Northern press generally was at liberty to condemn the war, denounce the president and his cabinet, vilify the military, malign the troops, and disclose vital information. Even in the border states, most newspapers remained free to applaud Jefferson Davis, salute Confederate generals, espouse secession, and exalt slavery.

However, the very existence of censorship indicates that there was a line, albeit fuzzy and smudged, over which the majority of newspapers—both loyal and opposition—dared not step. Censorship was imposed to stop or punish the flow of information immediately useful to the enemy, to suppress information that directly interfered with enlistment, or to halt newspapers in occupied areas that sympathized with the Confederacy. However, it was also used to suppress political opinion in states where there was no military activity.

Secretary of War Stanton, the driving force behind wartime censorship, summarized the administration's philosophy in a report he issued after the arrest of a New York *Herald* reporter: "Newspapers are valuable organs of public intelligence and instruction. . . . But no matter how useful or powerful the press may be, like everything else, it is subordinate to the national safety."[200]

Although Lincoln spent many hours in the telegraph offices and knew what was being censored, there is no evidence that he had a habit of interfering. Instead, he deferred to his military officers and to Stanton. He also deferred to others on the issue of newspaper suppression except when he believed a newspaper had overtly subverted the draft or encouraged desertion. This would explain his silence in the early Baltimore and New York suppressions, his uncertainty about revoking Burnside's orders against the Chicago *Times*, and his order to suspend the New York *Journal of Commerce* and *World* for publishing the fake draft notice.

Both Stanton and Lincoln allowed their commanders to decide when newspapers endangered a particular military department. And few generals demurred when it came to arresting or banishing reporters from their camps or suspending newspapers.

Lincoln said very little about freedom of expression during his political life. But his acquiescence to blatant denial of those freedoms tends to speak louder than any rhetoric. Much of the newspaper suppression took place in states where there was no military activity. The New York newspapers were closed down not because they gave information that might endanger public safety, but because they expressed political opinions that diverged from those of loyal unionists. In New York, Chicago, Philadelphia, throughout the Northeast, and even in occupied states, suppression of newspapers because of disloyal sentiment went on without the protection of the civil courts and with Lincoln's full knowledge. He had the authority to curtail such censorship, but chose not to. Instead, he used Jefferson's argument that too strict an adherence to the law could result in the destruction of all law.

In truth, Lincoln had no political reason to rein in his officers. Congress supported his actions and with the exception of Chief Justice Roger Taney's 1861 opinion that suspending the writ of habeas corpus was unconstitutional, the Union was united behind Lincoln's activities. He was given an open mandate to conduct the war as he saw fit. There was no strong Republican voice of opposition to Lincoln's unconstitutional actions.

Newspaper editors, presumed to be the victims in this battle over censorship, often were the persecutors as well. With few exceptions, editors wailed as loudly against the censorship of their telegraphic dispatches as they railed against government's refusal to suppress opposition journals. The same editors who eloquently defined the values and role of the press during war time, also readily particularized a wide variety of speech that was beyond protection. When it came to supporting freedom of press for themselves, editors were defiant. As for the opposition's right to enjoy the same freedom, many passively stepped aside and let the authorities deal with the problems. Others actively supported official suppression and even baited crowds to mob action. It was not until Burnside's closing of the Chicago *Times* in June 1863 that newspapers began to speak with any united voice against arbitrary military censorship.

The Civil War years added a great deal to the debate over the boundaries of freedom of press and even increased people's understanding of the vital role the press could play in times of upheaval. But that national experience also demonstrated that a war at home can stress the Constitution beyond its own strength, forcing government to temporarily suspend cherished guarantees. Military necessity had become an acceptable exception to the guarantees of the First Amendment—an exception that was carried into the twentieth century, blessed by the U.S. Supreme Court,[201] and subscribed to by every wartime administration since.

NOTES

1. William Jay, *Miscellaneous Writings on Slavery* (New York, 1853), pp. 534-35.

2. Henry Ward Beecher, "On Which Side is Peace?" in *Patriotic Addresses* (New York: Fords, Howard, & Hulbert, 1891), pp. 196-202.

3. J. Cutler Andrews, *The North Reports the War* (Pittsburgh: University of Pittsburgh Press, 1985).

4. Senate Bill 33, calling for the suppression of insurrection and sedition was postponed indefinitely at the recommendation of the Committee of the Judiciary; *Congressional Globe*, 37th Cong., 2nd. sess., pt. 4, p. 3245.

5. Gaillard Hunt, ed., *The Writings of James Madison* 9 vols. (New York: G. P. Putnam's Sons, 1900–1910) 5: 271-73.

6. Paul Leicester Ford, ed., *The Works of Thomas Jefferson* 12 vols. (New York: G. P. Putnam's Sons, 1905) 5: 80-83.

7. *Harper's Weekly*, August 3, 1861.

8. Frank Freidel, ed., *Union Pamphlets of the Civil War* 2 vols. (Cambridge: Belknap Press, 1967) 2: 981.

9. Ibid., 1: 256.

10. Ibid., 1: 301-302.

11. Ibid., 1: 120.

12. Chicago *Tribune*, October 3, 1861.

13. Ibid.

14. House Report 67, 37th Cong., 2nd sess. (1862).

15. Washington *Daily National Intelligencer*, April 23, 1861.

16. Benjamin Perley Poore, *Perley's Reminiscences of 60 Years in the National Metropolis* 2 vols. (Philadelphia: Hubbard Bros., Publishers, 1886) 3: 78–79.

17. *War of the Rebellion: A Compilation of the Official Records of the Union and Confederate Armies* (Washington, D.C.) Ser. III, 1: 324, [hereinafter referred to as O.R. (Army)].

18. *New York Times*, July 13, 1861.

19. Ibid.

20. Baltimore *American*, July 12, 1861.

21. Cincinnati *Daily Gazette*, July 17, 1861.

22. Andrews, *The North Reports the Civil War*, pp. 91-92.

23. *New York Times*, July 24, 1861.

24. *Contra*, Andrews, *The North Reports the Civil War*, p. 95.

25. Ibid.

26. New York *Herald*, July 24, 1861.

27. *Harper's Weekly*, August 17, 1861.

28. House Report 64, 37th Cong., 2nd sess. (1862).

29. O.R. (Army), ser. III, 1: 390.

30. Ibid., pp. 394-95.

31. *Daily Cincinnati Gazette*, August 12, 1861.

32. *New York Times*, Sept. 8, 1861.

33. Stephen W. Sears, ed., *The Civil War Papers of George B. McClellan, Selected Correspondence, 1860–65* (New York: Ticknor & Fields, 1989), p. 142.

34. House Report 64, 37th Cong., 2nd sess., p. 3. (1862).

35. Ibid.

36. O.R. (Army), Ser. III, 1: 879, 899.

37. O.R. (Army), Ser. III, 1: 899.

38. Ibid.

39. Chicago *Daily Tribune*, February 27, 1862.

40. Chicago *Daily Tribune*, February 27, 1862.

41. Chicago *Weekly Tribune*, February 27, 1862.

42. Chicago *Times*, February 27, 1862.

43. *New York Times*, February 28 and March 4, 1862.

44. Chicago *Daily Tribune*, April 10, 1862.

45. *New York Times*, March 3, 1862.

46. Philadelphia *Inquirer*, February 27 and 28, 1862

47. New York *Herald*, February 28, 1862.

48. New York *Herald*, March 3, 1862.

49. Cincinnati *Commercial*, April 3, 1862.

50. New York *Tribune*, February 27, 1862.

51. Andrews, *The North Reports the Civil War*, p. 193.

52. Cincinnati *Daily Gazette*, April 3, 1862.

53. Chicago *Tribune*, March 25, 1862.

54. Ibid., March 29, 1862.

55. Cincinnati *Daily Gazette*, April 4, 1862.

56. *Ibid.*

57. Andrews, *The North Reports the Civil War*, p. 195.

58. Cincinnati *Daily Gazette*, April 17, 1862.

59. Ibid.

60. Ibid., April 25, 1862.

61. Chicago Daily *Tribune*, April 21, 1862.

62. Merl M. Moore, Jr., "More About the Events Surrounding Suppression of *Harper's Weekly*, April 26, 1862," 12 *The American Art Journal* 82–85 (Winter 1980).

63. *Harper's Weekly*, May 3, 1862.

64. O.R. (Army), Ser. I, 9: pt. 3, 167.

65. Andrews, *The North Reports the Civil War*, pp. 201-202.

66. O.R. (Army), Ser. I, 9: pt. 3 , p. 175.

67. Ibid. p. 194.

68. Ibid., p. 214.

69. O.R. (Army), ser. II, 4: p. 108-109; Nicolay and Hay, eds. *Complete Works of Abraham Lincoln* 12 vols. (New York: Century Co., 1907) 7: 243–44; *New*

York Times, June 30, 1862; *Congressional Globe*, 37th Cong., 2nd sess., p. 3050 (1862).

70. *Congressional Globe*, 37th Cong., 2nd sess., p. 3202 (1862).

71. New York *Herald*, June 16 and 24, 1863.

72. John Y. Simon, *The Papers of Ulysses S. Grant* 16 vols. (Carbondale: Southern Illinois University Press, 1973) 10: 221n.

73. *New York Times*, December 25, 1861.

74. Ibid., August 26, and December 25, 1862; June 3, 1863.

75. Philadelphia *Inquirer*, May 28, 1862.

76. New York *Herald*, May 16, 1862.

77. Chicago *Times*, May 29, 1862.

78. Philadelphia *Inquirer*, May 28, 1862.

79. Ibid.

80. New York *Herald*, May 16, 17, 23, 1862. Apparently one *Herald* correspondent remained in camp, too sick to leave with the rest of the press corps; Andrews, *The North Reports the Civil War*, p. 186.

81. Simon, *Papers of Ulysses S. Grant*, 5: 274–276; also O.R. (Army) Ser. I, 17: pt. 2, pp. 178-79.

82. Philadelphia *Inquirer*, August. 21, 1862.

83. O.R. (Army) Ser. I, 12: pt. 3, p. 602.

84. Chicago *Tribune*, August 28, 1862.

85. Philadelphia *Inquirer*, August 23, 1862.

86. Ibid., August 21, 1862.

87. New York *Herald*, August 27 and 29, 1862.

88. Ibid., August 31, 1862.

89. Philadelphia *Inquirer*, August 24, 1862. The correspondent was probably editor William W. Harding's brother, George, who had a personal relationship with Lincoln and Stanton.

90. New York *Herald*, December 19, 1861; Cincinnati *Gazette*, December 12, 1861; Cincinnati *Commercial*, December 11, 1861.

91. William T. Sherman, *Memoirs of William Tecumseh Sherman, by Himself* (Bloomington: Indiana University Press, 1957), p. 227.

92. St. Louis *Democrat*, January 15, 1863.

93. O.R. (Army) Ser. I, 17: pt. 2, pp. 587-88; p. 238.

94. Ibid., pp. 889-92.

95. Ibid.; Thomas W. Knox, *Camp-fire and Cotton-field: Southern Adventure in Time of War* (New York, 1865; reprint ed., New York: Da Capo Press, 1969), pp. 250-63.

96. O.R. (Army), Ser. I, 17: pt. 2, pp. 587-88.

97. Ibid., p. 893.

98. Ibid., p. 895.

99. *Illinois State Journal*, April 5 and 6, 1863.

100. Simon, *The Papers of Ulysses S. Grant*, 8: 37–38n.

101. O.R. (Army) Ser. I, 27: pt. 1, p. 52.

102. Ibid., Ser. I, 27: pt. 3, p. 192.

103. New York *Tribune*, June 18, 1863.

104. O.R. (Army), Ser. I, 38: pt. 4, p. 272.

105. Sherman, *Home Letters*, p. 295.

106. *O.R.* (Army), Ser. I, 39: pt. 3, p. 740.

107. Ibid., Ser. I, 40: pt. 2, 567, 583, 593; Simon, *The Papers of Ulysses S. Grant*, 11: 158–160n.

108. Simon, *The Papers of Ulysses S. Grant*, 11: 161n.

109. Ibid.

110. *New York Times*, July 14, 1864.

111. Andrews, *The North Reports the Civil War*, pp. 618-19.

112. *The American Annual Cyclopaedia and Register of Important Events, 1862–1865*, 4 vols. (New York: D. Appelton, 1862–1875).

113. Ibid.

114. Philadelphia *Inquirer*, August 21, 1861.

115. A full account of Converse's career as a newspaperman can be found in Arnold Shankman, "Converse, *The Christian Observer* and Civil War Censorship," 52 *Journal of Presbyterian History* 227–44 (1974).

116. Philadelphia *Inquirer*, August 23, 1861.

117. Philadelphia *Evening Bulletin*, August 24, 1861.

118. Shankman, "Converse, The Christian Observer and Civil War Censorship," p. 236.

119. *Congressional Globe*, 37th Cong., 1st sess. pp. 137-144 (1862); John C. Fremont suppressed a number of newspapers immediately after proclaiming martial law in Missouri. Union soldiers ransacked the *Shelby County Weekly Union*; in Macon, Missouri, the First Iowa Volunteers took over the *Missouri Register*, renamed it *The Whole Union*, but had to close down after the first issue.

120. Anna Ella Carroll, *Reply to Speech of Hon. J. C. Breckenridge delivered in the U.S. Senate, July 16th, 1861 & In Defense of the President's War Measures* (Washington: Henry Polkinhorn, 1861), pp. 14-15.

121. New York *Daily News*, August 12, 1861.

122. A copy of the presentment can be found in House Report 16, 37th Cong., 3rd sess., pp. 3-4; also, *Daily Cincinnati Gazette*, August 19, 1861.

123. Ibid.

124. Brooklyn *Eagle*, August 18, 1861.

125. House Report 16, 37th Cong., 3rd sess., p. 2 (1862).

126. *Journal of Commerce*, August 29, 1861. The *Day Book* also suspended publication and was succeeded by the *Caucasian*, which advocated the subordination of the Negro. The *Caucasian* was excluded from the mails in January 1862; Richmond *Dispatch*, January 13, 1862.

127. *Harper's Weekly*, August 31, 1861.

128. Chicago *Times*, August 27, 1861.

129. Philadelphia *Inquirer*, September 11, 1861.

130. House Report 16, 37th Cong., 3rd sess., p. 2 (1862).

131. Ibid., pp. 10-15.

132. Philadelphia *Inquirer*, August 23 and 24, 1861.

133. Ibid.

134. Chicago Daily *Tribune*, August 20 and 29, 1861.

135. *New York Times*, September 8, 1861.

136. New York *Herald*, August 25, 1861.

137. Chicago *Times*, August 27 and 28, 1861.

138. Ibid., August 24, 1861.

139. Philadelphia *Inquirer*, August 27, 1861.

140. New York *Herald*, September 15, 1861.

141. O.R. (Army), Ser. II, 2: 772, 774.

142. New York *World*, September 16, 1861.

143. O.R. (Army), Ser. III, 3: 54.

144. Ibid., p. 772.

145. Ibid., pp. 775-77.

146. Ibid., p. 804.

147. New York *Herald*, September 10, 1861.

148. New York *Tribune*, September 9, 1861.

149. New York *Herald*, September 10, 1861.

150. O.R. (Army), Ser. II, 2: 494.

151. Ibid., pp. 494-495.

152. Ibid., p. 504.

153. Ibid.

154. Philadelphia *Inquirer*, September 26, 1861.

155. A detailed account of this censorship can be found in Sidney T. Matthews, "Control of the Baltimore Press During the Civil War" , 36 *Maryland Historical Magazine* 150 (June 1941).

156. O.R. (Army), Ser. II, 1: 590.

157. Ibid., pp. 590-91.

158. Ibid., p. 591; *Daily Exchange*, September 11, 1861.

159. O.R. (Army), Ser. II, 2: 778–779, 793; Ser. I, 5: 193–196.

160. *Daily Exchange*, September 14, 1861.

161. O.R. (Army), Ser. II, 2: 780–81.

162. Ibid., p. 786.

163. Senate Executive Doc. 19, 37th Cong., 3rd sess (1862).

164. O.R. (Army), Ser. I, 24: pt. 3, pp. 40-41; *Illinois State Journal*, February 9, 13 and 14, 1863.

165. Ibid., February 14, 1863.

166. Simon, *The Papers of Ulysses S. Grant*, 7: 325.

167. Dayton *Empire*, March 14, 1863.

168. Chicago *Times*, May 27, 1863.

169. Chicago *Times*, May 30, 1863.

170. Chicago *Tribune*, June 4, 1863.

171. O.R. (Army), Ser. I, 23: pt. 2, p. 385.

172. *Ibid.* Ser. III, 3: 252; Ser. I, 23: pt. 2, p. 386; Ser. II, 5: 741.

173. Nicolay and Hay, *Complete Works of Abraham Lincoln*, 10: 108. Craig Tenney in his article "To Suppress or not to Suppress: Abraham Lincoln and the Chicago *Times*," 27 *Civil War History* 248 (1981) concludes that: "This uncertainty, or ambivalence—taken with his tacit acceptance of press suppression early in the war, his implicit support of Burnside in the Vallandigham proceedings, and his willingness to delay lifting of the suppression order... does not argue in favor of characterizing Lincoln as a friend of the press. The evidence... suggests he was much more ready to accommodate political cronies than opposition editors"; p. 259.

174. Tenney, "To Suppress or Not to Suppress," p. 257.

175. *The American Annual Cyclopaedia*, 3: 424.

176. Chicago *Tribune*, June 4, 1863.

177. Ibid., June 5, 6 and 13, 1863.

178. Ibid., June 17, 1863.

179. Ibid., June 22, 1863.

180. Ibid., June 5, 1863.

181. Roy Basler, ed., *The Collected Works of Abraham Lincoln* 9 vols. (New Brunswick, N.J.: Rutgers University Press, 1959) 6: 262, 268–69.

182. Ibid., p. 262-69.

183. *New York Times*, June 9, 1863.

184. Ibid., June 12, 1863.

185. Ibid., May 5, June 3, 12 and 13, 1863.

186. New York *Tribune*, June 6, 1863.

187. New York *Herald*, June 7 and 9, 1863.

188. Washington *Daily National Intelligencer*, June 6, 1863.

189. New York *Evening Post*, June 6, 1863.

190. Washington *Daily Chronicle*, June 6, 1863.

191. Basler, *Collected Works of Abraham Lincoln*, 6: 492–93.

192. *The American Annual Cyclopaedia*, 4: 389.

193. Ibid.

194. Ibid., p. 390.

195. Ibid.

196. New York *Tribune*, May 19, 1864.

197. Ibid., May 20, 1864.

198. *New York Times*, May 19, 21, 23 and 24, 1864.

199. New York *World*, May 23, 1864.

200. Robert S. Harper, *Lincoln and the Press* (New York: McGraw-Hill, 1955), p. 133.

201. *Near v. Minnesota*, 283 U.S. 697 (1931).

Chapter 7

"The Rule of Reticence": War and Reconstruction in the South

For Southerners, the election of Lincoln in November 1860 meant the South would continue to be exploited economically by Northern trade monopolies and by tariffs that favored Northern manufacturers. It also meant that the South's cultural makeup would be tipped off balance, eventually leading to the amalgamation of races. And, of course, Lincoln's election meant that the South's slave-based economy, particularly in the deep South, would die, leaving the Southern aristocracy destitute. For the South, these were sufficient reasons to call for secession. Among those leading the secession movement were newspaper editors such as John Daniel of the Richmond *Examiner*, Roger Pryor of the Richmond *Enquirer*, and John Forsyth of the Mobile *Advertiser and Register*.

But not everyone in the South was a secessionist. Just as in the North, there were groups of "submissionists" and "cooperationists" who opposed secession or, at least, wanted to delay it in hopes that some compromise could be reached. But when the Confederate government demanded the surrender of Federal forts throughout the South, including Fort Sumter, the final delicate thread of national unity was broken and a new nation was formed.

The new republic was not radically different from the one abandoned. The Confederate Constitution replicated the federal constitution of 1787, with further clarification on the right of property in slaves and on states rights. It also outlawed bounties and legislative monies for internal improvements. The new constitution did have its anti-democratic elements such as restrictions on suffrage and a short ballot that allowed many offices to be filled by legislative rather than popular vote. Yet, the Confederate

Constitution did retain the basic civil guarantees of religion, assembly, petition, freedom of speech and press, and fair trial.

When Jefferson Davis was inaugurated in February 1862, he noted with pride that the Confederacy had preserved all of the people's inherited liberties while Lincoln had suppressed them in the North. "There has been no act on our part to impair personal liberty or the freedom of speech of thought or of the press."[1]

Davis's pride was not false. Many champions of an unhampered press rose during these years despite the widespread dissatisfaction with the Davis presidency and the conduct of the war. However, it must be remembered that the South had also boasted a dedication to freedom of speech and press in the 1830s when it accepted mail censorship and laws against speaking against slavery.

Thomas C. DeLeon, a newspaper correspondent, wrote after the war that nowhere on the globe was the freedom of the press more thoroughly vindicated than in the South. "Criticism of men and measures were constant and outspoken," but as long as their origin was in honest conviction, the critics were left alone.

However, DeLeon also noted that the Southern press had not been that lever which it had elsewhere become. "It was rather a local machine than a great engine for shaping and manufacturing public opinion." In fact, most Southerners depended on Northern newspapers for information other than local affairs.[2]

Representative Gholson of Virginia did not necessarily agree with DeLeon's description of the Southern press. As defeat appeared imminent in the early months of 1865, Gholson praised the newspapers for the immeasurable part they had played in the struggle. He contended that the press had been a powerful auxiliary in the war, furnishing "the great arguments of the justice and right of our cause." It had cheered the people in their hour of despair, it had convinced deserters to return to the army, and it had kept the fears of subjugation before the people.[3] And earlier in the war, Rep. Ethelbert Barksdale, a Mississippi editor, claimed that the press had "accomplished more than any other agency in arousing the people of the South to a sense of their wrongs and the necessity of separation from the old government."[4]

Whatever its influence, the Southern press suffered greatly during the four-years rebellion. Unlike its Northern counterpart, which prospered during the war, the Southern press was reduced by shortages of paper, type and ink; by lack of telegraphic or postal services; by enlistment or conscription of employees; and by enemy invasion. Some newspapers resorted to printing on half sheets of wrapping paper, wall paper, writing paper, or colored paper. Many printed off only one copy and posted it in a central location. Others, like the Memphis *Appeal*, refused to surrender in the face of invasion and moved their presses on wagons from place to place. There is no accurate pre- and postwar census of Southern newspapers, only piece-meal figures for certain states. For example, in Mississippi only sixteen papers out of seventy-five survived the war. In Virginia, forty newspapers were suspended during the first year of the war.[5] In Texas, fifty out of sixty newspapers were suspended.[6]

WARTIME CENSORSHIP

For those newspapers that did survive, one of the biggest problems was getting news. After the war broke out, the Southern bureau of the Associated Press closed, and newspapers found themselves either without war news or with inaccurate news. To solve this problem, editors formed a cooperative news agency called the Press Association of the Confederate States of America. Under the management of John S. Thrasher, the association placed correspondents with all of the armies and in all of the major cities, arranged for telegraphic services, and secured cooperation from most of the generals. Each member of the association received weekly news summaries and in turn provided the association with local news. The association proved to be an invaluable source of information throughout the war.

Censorship in the South was double-edged, wielded by both the Confederacy and the invading Union armies. The Confederacy imposed similar types of censorship on the Southern press as Washington imposed on the Northern press. Southern newspapers experienced telegraphic censorship, exclusion of reporters from the battlefront, and occasional suppression. However, suppression was more likely to be the work of the enemy than of mobs or Southern generals.

Most Southern editors willingly censored themselves to confuse Union generals, to allay local fears, or to boost morale. For example, when Sherman's news embargo proved successful as he moved from Atlanta and through the Carolinas, the Northern press was forced to rely solely on Southern newspapers. To stop such news from reaching Northern readers, newspapers in Mobile and Richmond stopped publishing what they knew of Sherman's march and began publishing unreliable conjectures.

On another occasion, the Richmond *Enquirer* refused to continue discussion of General Braxton Bragg's humiliating defeat at Chattanooga in November 1863, because the assaults would injure and impair Bragg's ability to serve the cause.[7]

From the Beginning

As Bradley Osbon of the New York *World* was reporting the shelling of Fort Sumter from the U.S. cutter *Harriet Lane*, a reporter for the Charleston *Mercury* was covering the event from the Confederate steamer *Seabrook*. And on shore in Charleston, reporters from every part of the country mingled with thousands of spectators gathered at the city's wharves. It was reporters for the Charleston *Courier* and the Macon *Telegraph* who gave the nation its first description of Major Robert Anderson consoling his men amid the burned out fortifications.[8]

The Southern press was probably better prepared spiritually for the war than was the Northern press. Many editors had been preaching secession for months, if not years, and the vast majority were loyal Confederates. Even editors like Aaron Willington of the Charleston *Courier*, who had been a strong Unionist, was fully behind the Confederacy after Fort Sumter. A few, like Robert Ridgway of the Richmond *Whig*, were more reluctant to embrace the new era. Ridgway, a strong Unionist, was replaced by a secessionist immediately after Lincoln sent out his first call for volunteers. The South also had its dissident anti-administration papers like the Charleston *Mercury* or *Brownlow's Knoxville Whig*, which was eventually suspended and the editor given a military escort out of the South.

With such a high spirit of loyalty, there would seem to be little use for sedition laws, martial law, or suspension of the writ of habeas corpus. However, the Confederate Congress did deal with these issues. In January 1862, they debated a bill identical to the U.S. Secretary of War Cameron's General Order No. 67 that would penalize any newspaper that published information about the number, disposition, and movement of troops; the cargo of vessels; and descriptions of military fortifications and armaments. The Richmond *Daily Whig* supported the bill, believing that the proscribed information was of no use to anyone except to "Yankees and persons of morbid curiosity." The editor claimed that since the *Whig* never published such damaging information, such a bill would not interfere with their operation "as long as it is confined to designated information. But it is better, both for government and people, to let the press alone—subject only to public opinion."[9]

The Richmond *Examiner* was not concerned about the bill except to say that it did not go far enough. The editor felt it was strange that congress had not provided a way to deal with Yankee spies and other communications such as the post office and railroads.[10]

More outspoken against the bill was the Richmond *Dispatch*, which warned against the South's propensity for imitating Northern actions, particularly when it came to censorship. The editor contended that the bill was really a measure to hide corruption and abuse in the military at a time when all power and authority was with the military. It was better, said the editor, that the enemy know all the South's military plans than to stifle the public press. As for the argument that the bill would stop the press from giving out vital information, the *Dispatch* editor concluded that the press was being made a scapegoat. The North had numerous spies, there was unhampered travel between the sections, and the Northern newspapers had greater access to the Confederate army than did the Southern press.[11] The bill was never passed.

In September 1862, Senator Landon Haynes of Tennessee introduced a resolution asking the judiciary committee to inquire into the expediency of having a sedition law. Senator T. J. Semmes of Louisiana, in traditional Southern rhetoric, decried the resolution stating that Congress had no right to interfere with freedom of the press. He noted that the senate might just as well inquire into the expediency of abolishing slavery. The bill died quickly after Senator Louis Wigfall of Texas compared it to the Sedition Act of 1798.[12]

The first draft law had exempted all newspaper editors from service, but in the next session, there was an attempt to exempt a wide variety of newspaper employees including mail clerks and stenographers. In opposing the move, Senator Brown of Mississippi accused the senate of favoring newspapers over other businesses. He noted that "a newspaper was a private enterprise conducted for individual interest and emolument; and there was no reason why its employees should be exempted any more than the clerks of any merchant."

Senator Herschel Johnson of Georgia said "a free press was a great tower of strength in the country, and should be protected." He noted two ways to break down the power and usefulness of the press. One way was to suppress newspapers and jail their editors, as was being done in the North. The other way was to deprive editors of their employees.[13]

The Richmond *Examiner* protested attempts to draft newspaper employees. On the pragmatic side, argued the editor, the newspaper is a complicated machine that one cannot stop and start at will nor operate with only a handful of employees. Also, a newspaper's very survival depends upon its continuity. On the philosophical side, he argued that the exemption of employees was necessary because "an unfettered press independent of government favor or control, should continue to exist in a country that pretends to be free ... and such a press cannot exist unless this immunity is afforded it."[14] In the end, the exemptions for newspaper employees were rejected.

In late 1864, President Davis, desperate to find new men for the army, proposed that the exemption for editors be lifted. However, the proposal was defeated.[15]

Despite much heated debate and opportunities to legislate against freedom of the press, the Confederate Congress never passed any laws curtailing the press. However there was censorship by the military, which was more inconsistent and erratic than military censorship in the North. The military, less concerned about a free press than Confederate legislators, recognized the need for military secrecy. In May 1861, the military took over telegraph lines throughout the South.

In late June 1861, General P.G.T. Beauregard, camped at Manassas

Junction, clipped two articles from the Charleston *Mercury* that he claimed prejudiced the future operations of the army. One article he termed "positively treasonable." Noting the lack of any military regulations forbidding publication of dangerous material, the general requested Secretary of War Leroy Walker to correct the deficiency and to prevent newspaper reporters from coming within several miles of the front lines.[16] Walker's response was a letter to all newspapers urging them to let patriotism act as a restraint on publication. He reminded editors of what had happened to editors in the North who had published damaging information. "Derive profit from [the North's] example" by being more judicious, Walker urged, while at the same time promising his steadfast support of an uncompromised press.[17]

But the offending Charleston *Mercury* was not convinced that Southern newspapers were used by the Federal army to develop military strategy. Editor Robert Barnwell Rhett insisted that the public had a right to know everything possible about the war, and if the press had a fault it was in withholding too much information from the Southern people.[18]

Southern newspapers were constantly being warned throughout the war not to publish harmful information. In May 1862, the Advisory Council of Virginia, responding to a request from General Robert E. Lee, advised Richmond editors to abstain from publishing sensational information as well as "everything that in military operations it would be essential to keep from the enemy." The Council warned that the "public safety imperatively demands a compliance with this request."[19]

After General McClellan withdrew to Harrison's Landing after the Battles of the Seven Days in July 1862, General Lee called the attention of the new Secretary of War, George Randolph, to a story in the Richmond *Daily Dispatch* that described the number and movement of Confederate forces around Richmond. He asked Randolph to take all necessary steps to prevent further publicity of troop strength and movement. But the Secretary, like his predecessor, had no immediate remedy. The Confederate Congress had passed no legislation to prevent such publications and if an editor were arrested, he would be immediately freed on a writ of habeas corpus unless there were evidence of treason. Randolph's only recourse was to send a copy of General Lee's letter to all newspapers in Richmond, threatening "a more rigid censorship" if the newspapers did not correct their wrongs. "It is the ardent wish of the department that this revolution may be successfully closed without the suppression of one single newspaper in the Confederate States," wrote Randolph.[20] After receiving the letter, the editor of the Richmond *Examiner* ensured Randolph that, as always, his newspaper would "be studious to observe that rule of reticence."[21]

Apparently, not all of Richmond's newspapers felt threatened by Randolph's warning. In late September, the Richmond *Enquirer* gave General Lee's strength at 60,000. For this indiscretion, the *Enquirer* was "respectfully" requested to refrain from giving statements even about the approximate strength of Confederate forces.[22]

In October 1862, the Secretary of War censored an Associated Press dispatch about General Jeb Stuart's forays into Pennsylvania. The secretary ordered that any reported movement of Confederate troops, from whatever source, must be approved by the adjutant general. The Charleston *Daily Courier* relayed this information to its readers so that they would "appreciate the extent of the restrictions upon the privilege of using the telegraph."[23]

The Charleston *Daily Courier* established its own list of "dos and don'ts:" (1) never allude to the number or position of our forces; (2) never describe points likely to be occupied by the enemy or utter doubts as to their strength; (3) never refer to the arrival or departure of troops; (4) never discuss the future or hint at actions to be undertaken; and (5) avoid details of strength and confine narration to things already done.[24]

A Confederate officer wrote a letter to the Atlanta *Intelligencer*, asking that newspaper to refrain from publishing anything that the North could use against the South "even at the risk of making them dull."[25]

Even in the last months of the war, as Sherman's army marched into the Carolinas, Southern newspapers continued to honor requests to keep silent about the activities of Union troops. Newspapers in Virginia received a request from General Lee in February 1865 "to take no notice, for the present, of military affairs in the Carolinas." The Richmond *Examiner* agreed to comply, knowing that "our readers will readily appreciate the motives of this reticence."[26]

The Memphis *Appeal* was more skeptical of the "rule of military reticence," and complained that oftentimes a request not to publish "is not adopted ordinarily so much from a regard for the public service, as it is from some motive personal to those in authority."[27]

John Daniel, editor of the Richmond *Examiner*, wrote in 1862 about the role of a free press during wartime. He noted that abuses and corruptions are endemic to war because all power is in the hands of the military and all authority is in civil government. Unless the press is free to denounce those abuses they will lead to a rottenness in government. Even if the revelations of the press should give aid and comfort to the enemy, it was better than silence. Daniel was unable to find a single disaster or injury traceable to the press. He condemned those officials who tried to stifle exposure of the corruption in the name of national security.[28]

At the Front

Southern reporters had a more difficult time trying to cover battlefront activities than did their Northern counterparts. From the very beginning, generals willingly excluded reporters from their camps, particularly if the commander's heroism had not been sufficiently aggrandized in the news copy.

In the days before the Battle of Bull Run in July 1861, General Beauregard issued an order expelling all civilians from the Confederate camps. The same day, the general seized all telegraph facilities and the railroad, making it next to impossible for reporters to file timely stories with their newspapers.[29] While Northern newspapers complained about the censorship in Washington that delayed news of the July 21 defeat at Bull Run, Southern newspapers were also late in printing the story of their victory. But the delay in the South was caused by the slowness of the telegraph, not censorship.

Meanwhile, Colonel D. H. Hill, commanding the First Regiment of North Carolina Volunteers at Yorktown, issued a general order forbidding "newspaper scribblers" from giving information to the enemy about the number and movement of troops and the results of battles. The order, duplicating a similar one from army headquarters, directed field commanders to use their best efforts to prevent this "foolish and pernicious itching for newspaper notoriety." The Memphis *Daily Appeal* correspondent asked, "Why will our government encourage a system, the only result of which is to keep the public mind in a state of continual suspense?" Withholding information only encouraged rumors and false stories. The writer suggested that if the press would not be allowed access to timely information, then the government should publish its own news bulletins, a suggestion similar to that made by James Gordon Bennett of the New York *Herald* a year later when Union General John Pope expelled reporters from Virginia.[30]

In January 1862, General Joseph Johnston expelled all reporters from his army. The apparent motive was the publication in the Richmond *Dispatch* of an article written by William G. Shepardson. The article revealed the winter headquarters of various army units around Richmond. Johnston immediately complained to Secretary of War Judah Benjamin and asked that legal action be brought against Shepardson. But Benjamin had no statutory authority under which to make such an arrest. Richmond was not under military law nor had the Confederate Congress suspended the writ of habeas corpus. He wrote Johnston that the best remedy for such mischief was "a stricter and less lenient application of military law." And that is just what Johnston did when he issued General Order No. 98, excluding the reporters.[31]

The Southern press protested that Johnston's order punished everyone because of the indiscretions of one correspondent. Newspapers also warned that such censorship was being used to hide incompetence and the shortcomings of the army.[32] To fill in the gaps left by such battlefront censorship, Southern newspapers clipped stories from the Northern press or published letters from various members of the army.

During the summer months of the Peninsula campaign, reporters again were excluded from Confederate lines. The Richmond *Examiner* sent two reporters to the York River rail line where the first pickets were stationed. The reporters were ordered to stop and turn back. The editor complained of this treatment, noting that Northern correspondents were free to gather details of both the Union and Confederate lines. The editor, however, remained "content to wait for accounts from Northern papers."[33]

The Richmond *Enquirer* received numerous complaints that its casualty lists were incomplete and that the exploits of many brigades and regiments were being omitted. The editor tried to explain that since reporters were excluded from the lines on the York Peninsula, newspapers had no way of knowing the facts of battles until the official reports were issued. In the interim, the paper had to depend on stories told by returning wounded.[34]

Taking the lead from Johnston and Secretary of War Benjamin's criticism that there was much "too lenient toleration of the presence of newspaper reporters" in the camps, confederate generals began an aggressive campaign against the press. After the bloody defeat at Shiloh in April 1862, General Beauregard returned to headquarters in Corinth, Mississippi from which point he sent out raiding parties to thwart the Union advance.

When it became obvious that the Confederate army would not be able to hold Corinth, Beauregard made plans quietly to slip his army out of the town. To ensure secrecy, the general issued General Order no. 54, sending all newspaper correspondents from Corinth on the next train and prohibiting them from returning to within twenty-five miles of the front lines. The order also forbade soldiers from writing letters about the army's movements.[35]

Beauregard's orders came three days after General Halleck had issued similar orders expelling correspondents from the Union army. While Northern correspondents returned to Cairo, Illinois Southern correspondents started west toward Memphis where they awaited news from the front.[36]

Following Beauregard's withdrawal from Corinth, the Union's fleet of gunboats moved down the Mississippi, capturing Memphis in June, forcing Confederate troops out of Missouri, and joining Admiral Farragut's fleet above Vicksburg on July 1 to lay siege to that river town. General Earl Van Dorn, commanding troops at Vicksburg, declared martial law in southern Mississippi and eastern Louisiana. To carry out the intentions of martial law, Van Dorn ordered the arrest of anyone giving information to the enemy, of anyone criticizing Confederate currency, and of any editor publishing troop movements or publishing anything that would impair the public's confidence in the military or the president.[37]

Although there is no evidence that Van Dorn's order was enforced against the press, some congressmen in Richmond felt Van Dorn had exceeded his power by issuing an arbitrary proclamation of martial law and by muzzling the press. During debates over the extension of the writ of habeas corpus, Representative Foote of Tennessee denounced the order as a "tyrannous invasion of the rights of the people of Mississippi." The proclamation was an unwarranted assault upon freedom of press, and any man who would attempt to overthrow that freedom "was worse than Lincoln and his myr-midons." If any officer ever again issued such proclamation, continued the congressman, he would call upon the people to put down the tyrant who dared to invade their rights. Foote was convinced that President Davis had not countenanced such an interference of free press by one of his generals.[38]

Representative Barksdale of Mississippi rose to Van Dorn's defense, say-ing that the congress had become unduly alarmed over the order. Although Van Dorn's order was inappropriate, the general "was prompted by his zeal in the cause of this country." Throughout the South the press had "indulged in the utmost freedom of comment upon the conduct of the war" and no one had moved to restrain it. Representative Milledge Bonham of South Carolina agreed that Van Dorn had gone too far, but also countered that some restrictions on the press were necessary during wartime in order to prevent damaging information from reaching the North.

But at least one general did carry out his threats to arrest a reporter. After General Bragg evacuated Chattanooga in September 1863, many Southern newspapers criticized his indecisiveness. One critic was John Linebaugh, a correspondent for the Memphis *Appeal*, who suggested on more than one oc-casion that Bragg was afraid to meet the Federal troops. Two days before the Battle of Chickamauga, Bragg ordered Linebaugh's arrest on charges of trea-son. The correspondent was first transported to an Atlanta prison. But when habeas corpus proceedings were begun, he was quickly escorted back to north Georgia where he remained in custody until Octobor 4. The Atlanta *Daily Intelligencer* complained that "it is by such acts that the press generally is made to suffer for the thoughtless [sic] and indiscretion of correspon-dents."[39]   Throughout the rest of the war, generals censored wire stories and ordered telegraph officials not to give information to newspapers. A correspondent for the Mobile *Daily Advertiser and Register* complained that part of his story about cavalry action at Brandy Station, Virginia, was censored by the telegraph operator in Richmond. The excised portion de-scribed a rout of Jeb Stuart's cavalry after he was surprised by Union forces. The correspondent was irate that the entire story appeared in all the Rich-mond papers and was spread far and wide before his story ever reached Alabama. He likened the telegraphic censorship to trying to "chain the waves or silence the wind." Deny the people the right to criticize the conduct of those in authority, and the latter will soon come to regard themselves im-mune from accountability. "Where Silence reigns, there ignorance and Slav-ery hold their leaden sway."[40]

General Robert E. Lee, a severe critic of the newspapers, stated many years after the war that "patriotism did not seem to influence them [editors] in the least."[41] The Richmond *Examiner* agreed, criticizing correspondents from Southern newspapers that hung around the city or Lee's army and wrote everything to be seen, heard, or imagined "without any apparent regard for consequences."[42]

But the editor of the Richmond *Daily Whig* countered that withholding information from the public neither encouraged the enemy nor demoralized the public. "On the other hand, on such occasions, the public always conclude that no news means a reverse to our arms."[43]

Newspaper Suppression

The Confederate press was relatively free of military or mob suppression, intimidation or arrests of editors. One reason was the recognition by Southern editors, contrary to General Lee's impressions, that the cause of the army was also the press's cause—a cause that went beyond the pocketbook interests that drove so much of the Northern press at that time. Patriotism led to self-restraint. Self-restraint resulted in less military restraint.

But not everyone practiced this form of patriotic self-censorship. Early in the war, the editor of a Knoxville newspaper created such a stir with his pro-Northern sentiments that he was forced to abandon his newspaper and hide in the Smokey Mountains until given a military escort out of the South.

Tennessee had a large contingent of militant Unionists in the eastern part of the state. One of the most visible and vocal Unionist leaders was the intemperate and pugnacious William Gannaway "Parson" Brownlow, editor of the *Brownlow's Knoxville Whig*. Parson Brownlow, an anti-Democrat, anti-secessionist, anti-Catholic, anti-abolitionist, and anti-Presbyterian, was, if nothing else, a stout-hearted pro-Unionist. He used the *Whig* to harangue the arrogant military and the treasonous Confederates and to libel secessionist leaders.

Parson Brownlow's traitorous diatribes received wide publicity throughout the North where he became a folk hero to many. In Tennessee, secessionists called for the suppression of the *Whig*. But President Davis refused to condone the suppression of a single newspaper in the South, not even the Knoxville *Whig*. Davis said in August 1861, that "no journal should be proscribed for opinion's sake, unless for the utterance of open and avowed treasonable sentiment, tending to sedition and insurrection by force of arms." He would not condone the suppression of "the inalienable prerogatives of the press to indulge in criticism, however severe, against the administration and those in authority."[44]

However, it was not uncommon for the *Whig* to be seized at post offices, thrown off of mail trains, or burned. Parson Brownlow accused postmasters throughout Tennessee of withholding mail that contained advertising and subscription money, forcing him to cut back publication from tri-weekly to weekly and to cut the number of pages published.[45]

By the end of October 1861, the *Whig* was in financial trouble. The editor had been unable to collect subscriptions or debts; his family was being intimidated; his eldest son had been arrested for lending a pro-Union book to a neighbor; and circulation of the paper was being interrupted. He tried to cover these financial problems by publishing a spurious rumor that he was about to be arrested. In his last issue of the *Whig* on October 26, he charged that the real reason for his "arrest" was "to dry up, break down, silence and destroy the last and only Union paper" left in the South. Noting Davis's promise to leave him alone, the constitutional guarantee of a free press, and the outrage of Southerners against Lincoln's anti-press activities, Parson Brownlow had expected "the utmost liberty to be allowed to one small sheet whose errors could be combated by the entire Southern press." Instead, his paper had been denied circulation and now it would have to be discontinued or watered down to "meet the approval of a pack of scoundrels" in Knoxville. "And this is the boasted liberty of the press in the Southern Confederacy."[46]

Troops continued to harass Brownlow and his family until he was forced to leave Knoxville.[47] Meanwhile, the military, using the excuse that they needed steam power to alter outdated arms, took possession of the *Whig*'s building and press.[48]

In Washington, there was some debate about how best to launch a military campaign against Tennessee. The Union army decided to enter eastern Tennessee and cut off rail communications between Knoxville and Richmond. The east Tennessee campaign was called off at the last minute; word of the change did not reach the mountain guerrillas. On November 8, organized units of Union sympathizers burned nine railroad bridges in eastern Tennessee, stretching from the Alabama to the Virginia borders.[49]

Although little damage was done to the bridges, a general panic struck the region, and civil and military authorities arrested hundreds of suspected bridge-burners. Those who were not hung, were sent as prisoners of war to Alabama. Because Parson Brownlow was in the vicinity of some of the bridge-burning incidents, an order for his arrest was also issued based on information that he had not only made speeches condoning and provoking the bridge burnings but also knew when the incidents would occur. The district attorney also noted that the *Whig* "has been the great cause of the rebellion in this section and most of those who have been arrested have been deluded by his gross distortion of facts and incited to take up arms by his inflammatory appeals to their passions and infamous libels upon the confederate states." [50]

Parson Brownlow claimed that he knew nothing about the bridge burnings. He contended that he was astonished by the incident and condemned the act "most unqualifiedly and regard it as an ill-timed measure."[51] Parson Brownlow evaded arrest by hiding in the rough terrain of the Smokey Mountains.

Meanwhile, petitions were being sent to President Davis and Secretary of War Benjamin asking that Parson Brownlow be allowed to leave the

Confederacy lest he be killed by a mob. On November 20, the Secretary of War granted Parson Brownlow permission to leave the Confederacy under military escort. The secretary reasoned that "I would greatly prefer seeing him on the other side of our lines as an avowed enemy."[52]

Parson Brownlow returned to Knoxville where, he was told, he would be provided with a passport and an escort through the lines to the Kentucky border. But no sooner had the editor returned than he was promptly arrested by civil authorities on the outstanding warrant. The arrest warrant specified that Parson Brownlow had committed the crime of treason by having published, since June 1861, various treasonous editorials in the *Whig*.[53]

Angry that he had been duped into returning, Parson Brownlow wrote Secretary of War Benjamin: "Which is your highest authority—the Secretary of War, a major-general or a dirty little drunken attorney?" On December 27, the editor was released to the local military commander to be escorted out of the state; however, Parson Brownlow and his family remained under house arrest in Knoxville until he was well enough to be transported to Kentucky.

Brownlow traveled throughout the North, giving speeches and receiving a martyr's welcome wherever he went. When General Ambrose Burnside's Federal troops captured eastern Tennessee in the fall of 1863 and entered Knoxville, Brownlow was close behind. The Union army located a new press and type, gave him $1,500, and lent him an ambulance to bring his family from Cincinnati. On November 11, 1863, the Knoxville *Whig and Rebel Ventilator* was issued, proclaiming itself an *"unconditional* Union Journal."[54] "The Fighting Parson" would eventually be twice elected governor of Tennessee and serve a term as U.S. Senator.

Not only was eastern Tennessee strongly Unionist, but so was the mountain region of North Carolina. The North Carolina Unionists were well organized and their sentiment was reflected in the refusal of the state's voters to call a secession convention in February 1861.

One of the state's leading newspapers, the Raleigh *Standard*, was edited by William W. Holden, who had been a pro-secessionist throughout the 1850s. When the threat of separation became more real, Holden joined the peace movement. But after Ft. Sumter fell, Holden reverted to his secessionist rhetoric. After Confederate losses at Gettysburg and Vicksburg, Holden did another about-face and became an active conservative who once again supported the peace movement.[55]

In September 1863, Holden's pro-Union editorials and his encouragement of Unionist meetings enraged a regiment of Georgia infantry, who raided the *Standard* office and scattered type in the street. Peace activists reacted the next day by attacking the loyal Raleigh *State Journal*, destroying its press and type.

After the writ of habeas corpus was suspended, Holden suspended publication of the *Standard* between February and May 1864, fearing prosecution for treason. He told friends, "I felt that if I could not continue to print as a free man, I would not print at all." Holden's fear of prosecution was real. A friend once told the editor that had it not been for the intervention of a mutual friend, President Davis would have ordered Holden's arrest. Holden continued to publish his paper throughout the war with only sporadic suspensions due to shortages of paper or fear of censorship.[56]

The Enemy

The greatest threat of suppression came from the Northern invaders. The local newspaper was usually one of the first businesses shut down when Federal troops marched into a Southern town. As General Sherman moved across the South, newspapers from Memphis to Richmond were closed, destroyed, turned over to Unionists, or forced to move.

The most dramatic story of survival is that of the Memphis *Daily Appeal*. Ever since the defeat at Shiloh in April 1862, the editors of the *Appeal* had vowed not to give in to "Lincoln's hireling minions," even if it meant destroying their own press. "Sooner would we sink our type, press and establishment in the bottom of the Mississippi river, and be wanderers and exiles from our homes."[57]

On the eve of the fall of Memphis, June 5, the editors and staff moved their press 100 miles south to Grenada, Mississippi where they began republishing three days later. The editors again promised that "The Appeal will not swerve from its course, come what will, no matter how great the sacrifices we may find it necessary to make."[58] The paper remained in Grenada until after Thanksgiving when it moved another 100 miles south to Jackson, Mississippi. In May 1863, the *Appeal*'s equipment was loaded on a flat boat along with some mules, and poled across the Pearl River with Federal troops close behind. They made their way slowly toward Atlanta, where the *Appeal* was published again on June 6.

The paper's perseverance was also reflected in editorials that encouraged the South to keep up the fight even in the face of terrible defeat. "So long as there is retreating room left, there is ground for faith, hope and confidence," wrote the editors.[59]

As Sherman approached Atlanta, the staff of the *Appeal* once again packed up equipment and shipped it to Mobile, where the paper began publishing once again on September 20, 1863. The paper continued in Montgomery until mid-April 1865, when it was forced to split up its operations. Part of the equipment was sent to Columbus, Georgia, and the rest to Macon. The *Appeal* was captured and burned by federal troops in Columbus. What staff had not dispersed was paroled, and many made their way back to Memphis where the paper began a second life in November 1865.[60]

While the *Appeal* chose to leave Memphis in June 1862, the rest of the city's papers decided to stay put. The Memphis *Avalanche* continued publication for about a month when it was suspended. The *Avalanche* clashed with local authorities over an editorial which criticized the way civilians were being treated. Colonel William S. Hillyer warned the editor that "no criticism of the acts of the military authorities of the United States will be permitted in the press of Memphis.... You will not repeat the offense." If there were complaints, said Hillyer, they should be aired before the military commander, not before the public.[61]

But the *Avalanche* would not be intimidated. Two days after the warning, the paper printed an anonymous letter criticizing Confederates who turned Union informers. The next day, Hillyer wrote the *Avalanche:* "You will suspend the further publication of your paper. The spirit with which it is conducted is regarded as both incendiary and treasonable, and its issue cannot longer be tolerated. This order will be strictly observed from the time of its reception." The editors sold the newspaper to two pro-Union men who published it under the name of *Memphis Bulletin.*[62]

To crack the whip on pro-Southern editors, Colonel Hillyer prohibited the publishing of any newspaper in the district unless the editor had taken an oath of allegiance and had renounced loyalty to the Confederacy. When General Sherman became military governor of Memphis in July, one of his first acts was to rid the city of the remaining Confederate newspapers. The Memphis *Argus* was temporarily transferred to Thomas W. Knox of the New York *Herald* and Albert D. Richardson of the *New York Times.* The military took over the abandoned offices of the *Daily Appeal* and published a new paper called the *Union Appeal.*

The next spring, while General Grant was directing troops for the siege of Vicksburg, it became difficult to keep rumors of troop movement out of the newspapers. The Memphis *Bulletin* published several stories about General Grant's activities, prompting an order to arrest the paper's editor. General Grant gave the commander at Memphis permission to take over the *Bulletin* and use it to print the letter list and news from the North.[63]

While newspapers like the Memphis *Appeal*, the *Chattanooga Rebel* and the Knoxville *Daily Register* retreated to safer ground, and many like the Memphis *Bulletin* or *Argus* were transferred to friendlier editors, other newspapers were less fortunate. When the Memphis *Appeal* escaped from Jackson, Mississippi in May 1863, the presses of the local *Jackson Mississippian* were destroyed by federal troops.

In February 1865, the *Charleston Courier* was seized by order of General Quincy Gillmore and turned over to two Northern correspondents who had accompanied federal troops into Charleston. The paper was not returned to the original owners until nine months later.[64]

In March 1865, soldiers destroyed the offices of the Fayetteville, North Carolina, *Telegraph* and *Observer*. In the first week of April 1865, General Grant ordered the "arrest of all editors and proprietors of Richmond papers still remaining in the City.... Be quiet about it so none escape."[65] But when

Richmond was captured, the city was put to the torch and only one of the city's newspapers survived the fire.

RECONSTRUCTION

The South emerged from the war impoverished, devastated, and burned-out—both literally and spiritually. Plantations had to be rebuilt, industry had to be revived, and white society had to adjust to its new status among a population of freedmen. Some valiantly clung to the old ways; others submitted to Northern subjugation with an eye toward the future when the South would once again stand strong. But the road to normalcy would be pitted with a Northern reconstruction policy that demanded, among other things, that blacks be free to enjoy their new harvest of civil rights.[66]

The process of reconstruction began as early as January 1, 1863, when Lincoln signed the Emancipation Proclamation. The Proclamation declared that all slaves, except those in the loyal border states and those in states under Federal occupation, were free. This momentous decree marked the final shift in Lincoln's war policy. Unlike Northern abolitionists, Lincoln had insisted that preservation of the Union was the central issue of the war, not the abolition of slavery.

However, as the war dragged on, it was imperative that a new policy emerge to weaken the Southern spirit. The policy was emancipation. Slavery had already begun to disintegrate in the South, but the Proclamation served to hasten its demise. Fugitives flocked to enlistment centers; fugitive camps were set up near Union army camps; soldiers and well-meaning "missionaries" taughte blacks to read and write. The plantations were left in the hands of women, old men, and crippled veterans.

The demise of slavery, internal disputes between slaveowners and up-country yeomen, and lack of capital to continue the war helped undermine the Confederates' will to fight. The South was crumbling militarily, economically, and socially, and it was up to the Federal government to act as a change agent to bring about a reconstructed South.

Lincoln signed the first reconstruction act in December 1863. The Proclamation of Amnesty and Reconstruction allowed Southern states to reorganize once 10 percent of their 1860 electorate, with certain classes of rebels excluded, had taken a loyalty oath and had pledged to accept the abolition of slavery. Provisional civil governments could be organized under military supervision. After the assassination of Lincoln, Johnson continued the presidential reconstruction, vowing that the South would not be degraded or debased in the process.

By January 1866, every state except Texas had met the requirements of presidential reconstruction. However, there was one major flaw in the 1863 Amnesty Proclamation that would serve to dash the South's hopes for a quick reconstruction. One provision allowed the states to adopt temporary measures to deal with blacks, "considering their present condition as a laboring, landless and homeless class." As a result, when Southern states wrote new constitutions and passed new laws, they refused to enfranchise black voters and resurrected old slaves codes to keep blacks in their place. In addition, they allowed, according to Northern Republicans, too many former rebels to participate in the process of reconstruction, thus returning far too many Democrats to Congress.

A small contingent of radical Republicans in Congress spent the summer of 1865 spreading propaganda to denounce Johnson's liberal policy and to convince moderates that an extreme and restrictive reconstruction policy must be adopted toward the South. By early 1866, the radicals began modifying presidential reconstruction with a Civil Rights Bill and bills aimed at giving more support and Federal authority to the Freedman's Bureau. When Johnson vetoed both bills, he precipitated a war between Congress and the presidency that eventually resulted in a moderate presidential reconstruction policy being replaced with a radical congressional reconstruction policy.

With the impending threat of a new reconstruction policy and the radicals' war on Johnson, many Southern Democratic editors set aside their conciliatory attitude toward the North. But Governor David S. Walker of Florida warned newspapers about adding fuel: "The custom which has so long prevailed among our people and newspapers both South and North, with such disastrous results, of speaking evil of each other, should be desisted from." He warned that every intemperate paragraph would be reported to the North and made to play a part in the radicals' cause.[67]

In March 1867, Congress passed the Reconstruction Act of 1867, a radical reconstruction plan that once again placed the South under total military control. The South was divided into five military districts commanded by the General-in-Chief U.S. Grant, who was accountable only to the U.S. Senate—thus avoiding any possible undermining by President Johnson. The district commanders were given the primary function of overseeing the registration of all eligible black and white male voters and supervising the election of conventions to draft new constitutions. In order to be readmitted to the Union, each state had to ratify the Fourteenth and Fifteenth Amendments.[68]

Presidential Reconstruction: 1863-1867

The Richmond *Whig* quoted from the New York *Commercial Advertiser* that 800 newspapers had been published in the South before the war; and only fifty remained at the end. Noting these figures, the Unionist editor Robert Ridgway saw an important role for the Southern press: "[O]ur soldiers having overthrown the insurgents, it will now be the duty of our loyal journalists to rekindle the smouldering [sic.] fires of patriotism, infuse new ideas into the South and win back our deluded countrymen to their first love."[69] However, within a month Ridgway was on his way back North, and the *Whig's* wartime editors, who had escaped before the burning of Richmond, had returned to take up the cry against the amnesty oath, confiscation, and other acts of reconstruction.[70]

Many editors returned after the war to find their presses destroyed and buildings in disrepair. Some had the task of digging up and cleaning printing equipment they had buried in a neighboring farm. But, once their offices were put in order, they set about to put the South back in order. The majority of Southern newspapers took on a conciliatory attitude, hoping to become instruments in healing the breach. They editorialized about reviving shops, industries, and farms. They selected from a wide variety of scientific magazines to reprint the latest in agricultural technology or mechanical engineering. And, while they looked back longingly at the Old South, there was in those early months a sense that the Southern spirit had not been entirely devastated by the war.

Also, the Southern newspaper clung to its traditional role as piper for the ruling party. With very little income from advertising, the Southern newspaper was almost entirely dependent upon public printing contracts and legal advertising. Editors often found themselves straddling political fences in order to keep their presses running. In addition to the predominantly conservative white press in the South, there were several notable black Republican newspapers. The New Orleans *Tribune* was founded by Dr. Louis C. Roudanez and edited by a Belgian, Jean-Charles Houzeau. By 1866, nine black newspapers were being published in the South, most of which were patronized by Republican office holders.[71]

One of the most controversial aspects of presidential reconstruction was the amnesty oath, which all but the highest civil and military officers under the Confederacy could take in order to be enfranchised. Many Southerners, including editors, refused to take the oath. One of the earliest states to qualify for readmission under Lincoln's Amnesty Proclamation was Arkansas. In 1865, the Little Rock *Daily Gazette* and *Daily Pantagraph* carried editorials advising against taking the oath. General Joseph Reynolds, believing the editorials countenanced disloyalty, closed the *Pantagraph* when the editor refused to disclose the name of the editorial's author. The *Gazette* was not closed, but the military kept a close watch on future issues.[72]

In Georgia, Augustus P. Burr, junior editor of the Macon *Journal and Messenger* published a humorous editorial about taking the oath. He was arrested and the paper suspended. The Albany *Patriot*, reacting to Burr's arrest and the suspension several days later of the Macon *Daily Herald*, noted that newspapers no longer had any influence, so there really was no need to threaten newspapers with suspension. The next week, the *Patriot* was warned by the local military not to criticize military actions. The *Patriot* conceded: "We will say no more about military or civil government in Georgia until a mere editorial is not labeled as treason."[73]

When the Americus, Georgia, *Sumter Republican* violated an order to promote peace and national unity, the paper was suspended.[74] The *Albany News* was also suspended after being charged with disloyalty. A sentry was sent to the press room of the Augusta *Constitutionalist* after a questionable editorial was run in that paper.[75] In North Carolina, General Thomas Ruger suspended the *Daily Union Banner* in Salisbury.

The Richmond *Whig* labeled Johnson's amnesty plan "heathenist," and called Congress's Confiscation Plan a "mean, brutal and cowardly policy. The revolting absurdity of such a policy is only equalled by its atrocious injustice." The *Whig* was suspended for 10 days. When the newspaper resumed printing, its editors, W. M. Elliot and T. C. Shields, noted with sadness that it was no longer possible to have absolute freedom to discuss all issues because the newspapers were being "cribbed, cabined and confined." Nevertheless, the editors vowed to do their best under the "embarrassing and harassing circumstances."[76]

A month latter the Richmond *Commercial Bulletin* ran an article that General Alfred Terry considered insulting to Lincoln's memory and to Johnson's administration. The paper was suppressed and the editor arrested.[77]

After writing editorials critical of the military and of President Johnson, the editor of the Petersburg, Virginia, *Daily News* was arrested and jailed in Richmond. He was released three months later.[78]

In Louisiana, the editor of the Franklin *Planter's Banner* was arrested after he published an editorial about a feud between the local provost marshal and the mayor. General Edward Canby, commanding in Louisiana, eventually ordered the editor to be released.[79] The editor of the St. Martinsville *Courier de Têche* was arrested for his continuous criticism of military occupation.[80]

Most of the foregoing suspensions and detentions were motivated by editorials mildly critical of the moderate reconstruction plans of Lincoln and Johnson or highly critical of the antagonistic military presence in the community. The newspapers generally were reflecting their communities' impatience to get on with the job of restoration. That process culminated with the Fall 1865 elections when Southern states voted for delegates to their state constitutional conventions. It was only a matter of months before those conventions ratified their new constitutions and elected their civil officers and representatives.

In the meantime, the numerous newspapers displaying disloyal tendencies prompted General Grant to issue an order in February 1866 to all of his department commanders that any decision to suspend newspapers rested solely with himself. The commanders were requested to send him any copies of newspapers that contained "sentiments of disloyalty and hostility to the Government." The commanders were asked to state whether the paper was "habitual in its utterances of such sentiments." Grant let it be known that the order was issued with a view to the suppression of these hostile newspapers.[81]

Despite Grant's threat of direct supervision of the Southern press, there was only one recorded instance of newspaper suppression in the Southern states between the date of his order and March 1867, when congressional reconstruction began. That one newspaper was the *Southwestern Baptist*, which had criticized local military behavior in Selma, Alabama.

By January 1866, all of the Southern states, except Texas, had been reconstructed. Civil officers were in place at all levels of state government and the economy was recovering slowly. In April, Johnson proclaimed the war at an end and the military began pulling back its authority.

But any hope by Southerners that they would soon be restored to full participation in the political life of the nation was dashed when radical Republicans triumphed in the congressional election of November 1866. Now in control of Congress, radicals could create their own reconstruction policy over any Johnson veto.

Congressional Reconstruction: 1867–1877

Under the congressional plan for reconstruction, the five district commanders were given absolute judicial, legislative and executive power. They were authorized to remove civil officers, fill vacancies, set aside court decisions, establish military courts, and suspend the use of habeas corpus. They were also given the power to suppress any opinion destructive of Congress's plan.

Editorial reaction to the new plan, which disenfranchised large groups of white voters and enfranchised all black males, was caustic and hostile. After the Richmond *Times* carried an editorial titled "A Black Man's Party in Virginia," General John Schofield, commander of the First District of Virginia, sent a warning to the editor. While the general wished to encourage full discussion, "the efforts of your paper to foster enmity, create disorder, and lead to violence, can no longer be tolerated. It is hoped this warning will be sufficient." General Schofield was not concerned about the racist tone of the editorial, but about statements derogatory of the army. He was already on record as opposing the Fourteenth Amendment and the disenfranchisement of so many whites. He opposed Congress's attempt to allow "the most ignorant of one race to vote, and deny the right to the most intelligent of another."[82]

The first major clash between the Southern press and the military took place in General John Pope's Third Military District, which encompassed Georgia, Florida, and Alabama. The general was not unfamiliar with a recalcitrant press; this was the same General Pope who expelled reporters from the Army of the Potomac in 1862.

In May 1867, a riot broke out in Mobile when a Pennsylvania congressman tried to deliver an address to a gathering of freedmen. Taunts and jeers from whites led to gunshots and several people were killed. Pope blamed the riots on the ineffectiveness of the mayor and the chief of police, whom he promptly removed from office. Afterwards, the general ordered local commanders to keep abreast of all political meetings and to observe their conduct in order to halt any impending violence.[83]

General O. L. Shepherd, commander at Mobile, warned that "severe responsibility will attach to the publication of articles commending or exciting riot or violence."[84] But a fortnight later, the Mobile *Nationalist*, a black newspaper edited by two white Northerners and directed by a black board of advisors, carried a letter that objected to the indiscriminate firing of weapons in the air. However, the letter writer advised, if a man is attacked he has the perfect right to defend himself. Shepherd immediately ordered a guard to stand watch over the *Nationalist* offices for two days to prevent further distribution of that particular issue.[85]

The *Nationalist* accused Shepherd of taking revenge against the newspaper for not "slavering him with praise" and for criticizing his soldiers' conduct toward blacks. "It is bad enough to have a wise man for a censor, but from being judged by an ass, good Lord, deliver us!"[86]

Pope ordered the guard withdrawn and reprimanded Shepherd, whose interference was "unauthorized and extremely disproved." He prohibited any officer or soldier from interfering with newspapers or speakers on any pretext. Even if the expression was treasonous, action could only be taken with the approval of Pope himself.[87]

Pope found it increasingly difficult to carry out Congress's mandate under the opposition of both the press and civil government. Believing "it is surely better to have an incompetent but loyal man in office, than to have a rebel of whatever ability," Pope replaced many duly elected civil officers with those of Republican ilk. However, the newspapers "commenced immediately to denounce, in terms of unscrupulous and unqualified abuse," all persons who accepted such appointments. It became, according to the general, almost impossible to find men willing to carry both the burden of public office and the wrath of the public.[88]

But the general knew that extensive replacement was not feasible. Instead, he decided to deal with outspoken civil officers by placing them under a gag order. In his first general order, setting forth the basic outlines of his military policy, Pope prohibited any civil officer from using his influence and position to interfere with reconstruction. Pope hoped to stop influential authorities from using either personal or official opinion to openly denounce reconstruction policy.[89]

The first civil officer to run afoul of the order was the provisional governor of Georgia, Charles Jenkins, who denounced reconstruction policy as "palpably unconstitutional and grievously oppressive." Jenkins advised Georgians to ignore military rule in a peaceful and temperate manner and to endure until clearer minds ruled in Washington.[90]

Infuriated that the governor would so flagrantly violate his gag order, Pope threatened to have Jenkins removed from office. He wrote to General Grant, expressing his grave concern that if such influential men as Jenkins were allowed to flout his orders, then every minor officer would be able to defy the military commanders at all levels. But Pope delayed issuing a removal order for Jenkins until he learned whether the governor, who had been in Washington for some time, was aware of his gag order.[91]

Jenkins claimed that he was unaware of the order and apologized. He said that he would have never imagined that such remarks, especially from someone who held elected office, would be banned. "I supposed I was exercising such freedom in the public expression of opinion relative to public matters as seems still to be accorded to the citizens of this republic."[92]

The combination of the gag order and excessive removals from office apparently worried some in Washington. In July 1867, Pope wrote Grant an extensive explanation and justification for his action.[93] He affirmed that, except in cases of office holders, "it has been and will continue to be my course to permit and encourage the widest latitude of speech and of the press in this district." He reasoned that no policy of reconstruction could be carried out unless men were permitted to discuss the issues openly. "It would not be difficult to find in the violent speeches of such men abundant cause for silencing them, but reconstruction accomplished in this manner would be no index of the public sentiment." It is better, continued Pope, that the battle be fought openly and that reconstruction be blessed "after the fullest and freest discussion."

But Pope was not entirely confident about the future, nor did he have that much respect for Southerners. Perhaps he had been reading too much of the Northern press, which had a penchant for characterizing white Southerners as ignorant, barbarous, and lazy. He questioned whether Southerners were even fit for self-government. "Have the sluggishness of mind and body and the tendency to assail by violence the right of opinion and discussion" made democracy an impossible goal? He alluded to the Southern tendency, dating back to the 1830s, to repress freedom of speech and press. This tendency was not confined to one single party, but prevailed throughout the South, according to Pope.

But a gag on civil officers was only half a remedy. Pope also had to find a mechanism for gagging the disloyal press. Initially, he told Grant that he was contemplating issuing an order that would prohibit the publication of material that abused or denounced the government or its officers.[94] But Pope never issued the sedition order. It did not take long, however, for him to adopt a strategy that was as old as the press itself—deny disloyal newspapers the patronage of state and local printing contracts and legal advertising.

From the beginning of congressional reconstruction, moderate Republicans were intent upon maximizing Southern cooperation and ending reconstruction quickly. To promote reconciliation, public education, economic development, and equal rights, the moderate Republicans used such tools as printing patronage and the Union League, a political organization to educate blacks about their rights.

In March 1867, Congress passed an appropriations act allowing government printing contracts to be let to Southern newspapers. The decision as to which newspapers would receive these contracts was placed directly in the hands of Clerk of the House of Representatives Edward McPherson, a moderate.[95] In Texas, Mississippi, Arkansas, and South Carolina, where there were few Republican newspapers, competition for the contracts was slight. But in the larger states, competition was keen and boisterous.[96]

In Virginia, the Richmond *New Nation* and the Alexandria *Virginia State Journal* received printing contracts. But when the *New Nation's* radical editor, James Hunnicut, began editorializing for broad disenfranchisement and confiscation, McPherson withdrew the contract and the paper ceased publication. In Florida, McPherson withdrew the printing contract from the *Jacksonville Florida Times* when it began supporting a group of radicals campaigning across the state in a mule-drawn wagon.

In Georgia, where there were a half-dozen Republican newspapers, McPherson first let the contracts to the *Savannah Republican* and the Augusta *Loyal Georgian*. But when word reached McPherson that the Savannah paper was not truly a Republican paper, the contract was withdrawn and given to the Atlanta *New Era*. Even with the government printing contract, the *Loyal Georgian*, a small weekly with a predominately black readership, was barely able to stay afloat. It was bought out and merged with the Augusta *Daily Press* to become the *National Republican*, and retained the original printing contract.

It was the spoils of the conservative Democratic and moderate Republican papers that Pope hoped to remove in August 1867 when he issued General Order No. 49. Using his gag order against civil officers as a starting point, Pope prohibited officials from giving advertising to any newspaper that had opposed or obstructed reconstruction.

The general reasoned that while most local officials were abiding by the word of his original gag order, they were ignoring its spirit by supporting hostile newspapers. The civil officers, according to Pope, were using their office to obstruct and oppose reconstruction every time they let a printing contract to a disloyal newspaper. "Such use of the patronage of these offices is simply an evasion (perhaps intentional) of the provisions of the general order."[97]

The reaction of newspapers in the district was immediate and rancorous. Editors claimed that without the patronage dollar, freedom of the press would be eviscerated. Pope countered by accusing conservative newspapers of having for too long used patronage, violence, and intimidation to silence the voice of loyal newspapers. Turnabout was fair play as long as it was done under the cover of law and in the interest of the people and the maintenance of the civil government.[98]

The editor of the Jacksonville, Alabama, *Republican,* a moderate paper, complained that the "oppressive nature of Gen. Pope's despotic order" had

deprived the paper of its legitimate patronage. He considered selling the
paper, but was unable to get a fair price. The editor published a smaller
edition until the advertising was restored in June 1868. According to the
editor, the *Republican* was suffering in common with 200–300 other papers
in the district.[99] When the *Elmore Standard* of Wetumpka, Alabama, lost
the county printing contract, the editor had to lease his equipment until
advertising was restored.[100]

Once again, Governor Jenkins was among the first to react to General
Order No. 49. He protested that the order violated Georgia law, which
required legal notices such as sheriff's sales, probate proceedings, and court
citations, to be published in the local newspaper. However, Pope assured
Jenkins that official advertisements would continue to be published. "It is
likely that the names of the newspapers and their course on reconstruction
may be changed, but I think that these changes will not injuriously affect
the interests of the people."[101]

Because the records of small newspapers in Georgia, Alabama, and Mississippi are incomplete, it is difficult to say what effect the order had on the
survival of the rural county press. Indeed, the names of papers did change.
Doubtless some Democratic newspapers were forced either to sell out to
Republican editors, or change their political tone. For example, the *Moulton
Advertiser* (Alabama) was forced to suspend and was replaced by the *Moulton Union*, a Republican campaign paper.[102] Larger communities were able
to support both loyal and opposition papers.

Indicative of the lengths to which newspapers would go to ensure a flow
of legal advertising was a notice placed by Editor Burr in the Macon Journal
and Messenger. Burr, who had suspended operation for two months because
of lack of funds, announced to administrators, executors and guardians that
Pope's order applied only to public officers and did not apply to officers of
the court: "you are at liberty to select any journal you please for advertising
over your own name."[103]

General George G. Meade replaced Pope as commander of the Third
District in December 1867. In February 1868, he issued General Order No.
22, modifying the newspaper patronage order. The revised order prohibited
papers from receiving public printing contracts if their editorials had threatened officers. However, the provisions did not apply if the county only had
one newspaper. Meade reasoned that "opposition to reconstruction, when
conducted in a legitimate manner, is not to be considered an offense."[104]

But in April, Meade issued an order prohibiting the publication of "incendiary" articles. The latter order was enough to chill the Montgomery,
Alabama, *Daily Mail*'s comments about Meade's harsh style of justice. Said
the editor, "The lips of our Alabama journals are pinned together by the
bayonet and our hands are fastened in iron cuffs." Nevertheless, the editor
did not spare words when he accused Meade's administration of making

"a Hell of Heaven." The commander in Alabama wanted the paper suppressed, but Meade refused.[105]

In the Second Military District, the Charlotte, North Carolina, *Carolina Times*, edited by Captain R. P. Waring, was suppressed after the editor complained that the South was "under a more grinding despotism" than any nation had ever been. Waring was arrested in Raleigh on Christmas Day 1867. He was tried and convicted of sedition and ordered to pay a $300 fine. Waring returned to his paper but was forced to suspend publication in the fall of 1868.[106]

General E.O.C. Ord, commander of the Fourth Military District, also had his problems with the press in Arkansas and Mississippi. In August 1867, the *Constitutional Eagle*, published in Camden, Arkansas, criticized the local troops for drunkenness, indecency, profanity, and "obscene exhibitions." When the local detachment was prohibited from suppressing the paper, about thirty soldiers wrecked the newspaper office, broke the press, destroyed the next issue of the *Eagle* and dumped type into the river.[107]

When Camden's mayor asked for an explanation, Colonel Charles Gilbert replied that the "paper unnecessarily exasperated the soldiers; but... there is no reason to anticipate a repetition of the act." Colonel Gilbert reported the incident to General Ord and explained that the paper had shown a great deal of impertinence by commenting about the military, especially since the military was not the servant of the people, "but rather their masters."

General Ord replied immediately that "the military forces are the servants of the laws, and the laws are for the benefit of the people." He ordered the commander to explain why he had not tried to prevent the raid. In January 1868, the commander of the local detachment was court martialed, found guilty and sentenced to forfeiture of pay for one year, demoted, and reprimanded. In his letter of reprimand, General Ord remarked that untruthful comments do not usually provoke a reasonable man, and in this case the comments about drunkenness of soldiers were resented in proportion to their truthfulness.

General Ord, however, did not hesitate to arrest William H. McCardle, editor of the Vicksburg *Times*, who allegedly had broken a direct order against any white man advising blacks to act unlawfully. McCardle allegedly had published incendiary and libelous articles about Ord, President Johnson, and others. When the local judge issued a writ of habeas corpus, General Ord made a return, stating that McCardle had been arrested under the Reconstruction Acts, not civil law. McCardle challenged the validity of the Reconstruction Acts, taking his case to the Supreme Court. However, the high court was forced to dismiss the appeal in *Ex parte McCardle* because Congress had restricted the Court's appellate jurisdiction to ensure that the Court could not declare the Reconstruction Acts unconstitutional.[108]

That censorship was not more widespread during these early years of reconstruction was due in part to the lack of enthusiasm by the district commanders for the Reconstruction Act. With the exception of Pope in the deep South and General Philip Sheridan in Texas and Louisiana (both of whom were replaced by more moderate generals), the military tried to remain removed from the politics of reconstruction and interfered with local officials only when peace was threatened. For the most part, newspapers were able to criticize the Reconstruction Act and the way it was being operationalized in their respective states. Even editors who reflected extreme conservative and white supremacist views were tolerated by the military, who agreed that the black man's entrance into the Southern political community would be folly.

During fall 1867, delegates were elected to the first state constitutional conventions. Republicans won in every state, sending a mixed bag of delegates to the conventions. The party of Lincoln was now represented primarily by carpetbaggers and scalawags (Southern whites who had opposed secession). Blacks composed less than 25% of the overall body of elected delegates. These conventions adopted constitutions that were dramatically different from their pre-war predecessors. Aside from the guarantees of black suffrage and office holding, these constitutions contained liberal economic, education, and welfare policies that reflected the Republican party's commitment to broad principles of social equality. But those policies and principles rarely went beyond words on paper. Republicans learned that for the party to remain in power, it had to win over moderates and even conservatives and the only way to do that was to agree to interpret the constitutions in the most conservative manner. These interpretations usually left blacks unable to vote, hold office, qualify for homestead exemptions, sit on juries, enjoy equal educational opportunities, or have access to public accommodations.

But many black politicians also acquiesced in this bastardizing of "social equality." Uncomfortable with the political in-fighting, determined to keep the Republican party strong, and defiant against carpetbagger intrusion, blacks often voted for their former owners or for policies that they knew would weaken their position in Southern politics.

In 1868, the New Orleans *Tribune*, the oldest black newspaper in the South, supported a former slave-owner for governor over a carpetbagger and former Union officer. The idea of English-speaking Northerners dictating the future of the state was reprehensible to many French-speaking blacks in Louisiana. The Republican party, however, quickly punished the *Tribune* by having its printing patronage transferred to the white-owned New Orleans *Republican*.[109]

Printing patronage became the primary means of maintaining party loyalty, just as it had been in the early years of the century. Southern newspapers were not profit centers, and their existence depended on some form of patronage, whether from the local, state, or Federal government. This was particularly true of the Republican papers, which found it difficult to entice the Democratic-dominated merchant class to buy advertising space. However, the patronage dollar was very fickle. Republican newspapers had to toe the correct Republican line or they could lose their contracts to another Republican paper. Often, if there was no Republican newspaper in the county, the local printing contract for legal notices would be let to a newspaper in a neighboring county. It was not uncommon for one Republican newspaper to have the printing patronage of several counties. Also, Republicans contracted to have resolutions, laws, and speeches printed for many months after they continued to be of any interest. For example, Georgia Governor Rufus Bullock paid out over $98,000 in three years to have his proclamations printed.[110]

By ensuring itself a loyal press and by enfranchising former Confederate sympathizers, Republicans gained domination in the South in 1867–1868. But the Northern wing of the party was suffering defeats. Radical Republicans were weakened by their failure to remove Johnson from office in 1868, assuring the nomination of the more moderate Republican Grant. By the time the fall 1868 campaign approached, the Republicans had agreed on a platform that supported a moderate reconstruction plan and a willingness to forge ahead in a conciliatory manner.

In the South, the campaign quickly turned to violence as Republicans and blacks were harassed, terrorized, and murdered by white mobs and members of white supremacist organizations like the Ku Klux Klan. Violence was particularly ugly in rural areas dominated by Democrats, such as in St. Landry parish in south central Louisiana. St. Landry parish hosted two Democratic papers, the *Opelousas Courier* and the *Opelousas Journal*, and the black Republican newspaper, the St. Landry *Progress*. Under the direction of a black board of directors, the *Progress* was edited by Emerson Bentley, a carpetbagger and, according to the New Orleans *Picayune*, a "social firebrand."[111]

To increase their margin of success in the fall election, Democrats had to entice more white voters into the party, and they used violence and intimidation to keep black voters from the polls. The *Progress* criticized the Democrats' activities, and the leader of the St. Landry Democrats retaliated by beating Bentley with a cane. Word of the beating spread throughout the black community, which armed itself and marched toward town. Whites also armed themselves and pursued armed blacks through the woods and fields, finally capturing 29 blacks and putting them in jail.

The next night, without protest from the deputy sheriff or jailkeeper, whites removed all but two of the prisoners from the jail and shot them to death. These murders began two weeks of killings. When it was all over, five whites were killed. Democrats stated that 25-30 blacks were killed; radicals reported from 200-300 blacks were murdered.[112]

Although Grant did carry the South, the radicalism of reconstruction and Republicanism was on the wane. To maintain a hold on state government, moderate Republican governors and legislatures handed out patronage to Democrats as well as Republicans, increasing party rifts. Republicans, always seen as foreigners—carpetbaggers, scalawags, and blacks—never managed to construct a cohesive and stable political party in the South. Factionalism came from every direction—black versus white; carpetbagger versus native; upcountry yeoman versus coastal planter. Between 1868 and 1870, Democrats began regaining strength in the South. Increasing numbers of Democrats tried to put the war and reconstruction in the background and to accept the realities of black suffrage. However, as governorships and legislatures returned to the Democratic fold, reconstruction began to fall apart. Democrats began undermining all the gains blacks had made since congressional reconstruction began. Black schools were closed, homestead exemptions were nullified, property qualifications for office holding were reinstated, segregation was legalized, the poll tax was inaugurated, and elected offices became appointive. When legal means of subordinating the blacks were not enough, violence and intimidation were used.

While violence by both white gangs and "upright" citizens had been a factor in Southern life since the end of the war, it became more predominant after 1869. The story of violence by the Ku Klux Klan, the Knights of the White Camelia, and other paramilitary supremacist organizations has been told by numerous historians. Blacks, scalawags, Republicans and anyone sympathetic to the blacks were all targets of Klan violence. But no one was willing to stop it by legal means; and the victims were unable to fight the superior military force that the Klan had become.

Through violence and intimidation, the Republican party was being weakened. Congress tried to turn the tide by passing several anti-violence laws in 1870 and 1871. The Enforcement Acts prohibited racial discrimination at the polls and sent Federal election supervisors into the South. But few convictions were forthcoming. The Ku Klux Klan Act of 1871 allowed the president to suspend the writ of habeas corpus and make it a crime to conspire to deprive citizens of their rights. Violence became so bad in South Carolina, that President Grant authorized federal troops to occupy nine counties and suspend the writ of habeas corpus. Although the number of convictions relative to the number of arrests and indictments was small, the Federal intervention and coercion had some effect in lessening the amount of violence by the time the 1872 election came around.

Grant was reelected and the Republican party experienced a brief comeback despite the strengthening of the Democratic party in the North and South. But the Depression of 1873 dealt the final blow to Republicans as voters turned against the party. In the elections of 1874 and 1875, Democratic landslides in the South assured that reconstruction had come to an end.

By 1877, all former Confederate states had reentered the Union, Federal interference had ceased, black political power had been diffused, radical Republicans had all but disappeared, and the Fourteenth and Fifthteenth Amendments were only latent images on the New South. States repudiated wartime and reconstruction debts, redistricted states to dilute the black vote, passed laws favoring land owners over tenant farmers, and closed public schools.

Southern states also reintroduced many of the Jim Crow laws of presidential reconstruction. Vagrancy laws were used to arrest unemployed blacks, nighttime (black market) sales of farm products were criminalized, penalties for minor infractions were increased to ensure a population of convict labor for white planters, protections for tenants' wages were removed, and public accommodations were segregated.

Reconstruction had failed to bring either social or economic equality to the South's black population. By 1880, blacks were no better off than they were the day after President Lincoln signed the Emancipation Proclamation in 1863.

CONCLUSION

Frank Luther Mott, in *American Journalism*, refers to the reconstruction years as a time of suffering for the Southern press that did not end until the "reign of terror" brought by carpetbaggers was over.[113] Mott was not referring to the arrests and suppressions that occurred under military rule, but instead to the subsidizing of papers by political patronage. However, without a broad base of patronage support from both parties, the Southern newspaper would have barely existed. And, thanks to the fact that printing contracts were spread widely throughout the countryside and in the cities, newspapers were readily available to anyone who could read. Also, the dramatic growth in the number of newspapers in the South after the war can be attributed in part to printing patronage. According to the 1870 and 1880 U.S. Censuses, there were 70 daily newspapers published in the South in 1860; by 1880 that number had grown to 128.[114]

The party press was still a predominate feature of American journalism. In the South, parties and newspapers were inseparable; and often the politician and editor were one in the same. Many newspapers were established to promote political identity and party organization particularly at a critical time when the future of the South was so uncertain. While some newspapers could be bought and sold on the political auction block, most remained steadfast to their party alliances even through suspensions and imprisonment. The party nature of the Southern press was not an evil, but a function of the nineteenth-century political system.

For the Southern press, suppression by military force during the early years of reconstruction was a continuation of the censorship experienced during the war years. As in wartime, only one political voice was right; the

rest were tolerated only as long as they did not overtly obstruct the reconstruction efforts. Unlike the pre-war abolitionist press, which often stood
outside the mainstream political parties, the Southern papers that suffered
suppression stood squarely in the middle of the stream, but usually the
wrong one. In such situations, the party organizations helped legitimize
opposing views, thus defusing censorship threats and enhancing the concept
of freedom of discussion.

Although the suppression and arrests of editors were noteworthy, they
were not widespread. The majority of newspapers enjoyed full freedom to
discuss all aspects of reconstruction policy, whether conservative or radical,
carpetbagger or white supremacist. It is significant that the black press in
the South seldom fell victim to violence.

The rhetoric surrounding the political issues of reconstruction was vitriolic, malicious, and defamatory. But once the military was removed from
a supervisory role, tolerance for increasingly divergent views grew. The few
incidents of violence against the press in the latter period were more a raw
response to the fear of a black hegemony rather than a practical reaction
to a press that was being too democratic. Another reason for the limited
violence against the press was the nature of the violent element, itself. Unlike
the citizen mobs of Baltimore in 1812 or of the anti-abolitionist riots, the
Klan was not out to seek redress for immediate grievances. Instead, it was
a well organized paramilitary group whose legitimacy as a sanctioning authority was widely recognized and whose grievances went far beyond any
single event. Newspapers were not needed to ignite these inflamed spirits;
the Klan provided its own fuel.

NOTES

1. James D. Richardson, ed., *A Compilation of the Messages and Papers of the
Confederacy* 2 vols. (Nashville: United States Pub. Co., 1905) 1: 383.

2. Thomas C. DeLeon, *Four Years in Rebel Capitals* (Mobile, Ala.: The Gossip
Printing Co., 1890), pp. 288-89.

3. Proceedings of the Confederate Congress, *Southern Historical Society Papers*,
52: 277–78. [Hereinafter referred to as "Proceedings"].

4. Ibid., 45: 246–47.

5. Charleston *Mercury*, January 8, 1862.

6. J. Cutler Andrews, *The South Reports the Civil War* (Princeton: Princeton
University Press, 1970), p. 44. However, the Ninth Census reported 89 newspapers
published in Texas in 1860, *Compendium of the Ninth Census* (Washington: Government Printing Office, 1872), pp. 510-11.

7. Richmond *Enquirer*, December 23, 1862.

8. Andrews, *The South Reports the Civil War*, pp. 1-23.

9. Richmond *Daily Whig*, January 18 and February 4, 1862.

10. Richmond *Daily Examiner*, January 11, 1862.

11. Richmond *Dispatch*, January 13 and 14, 1862.

12. William M. Robinson, *Justice in Grey: A History of the Judicial System of the Confederate States of America* (New York: Russell & Russell, 1968), pp. 452-3; "Proceedings," 46: 87–88, 98–99, 187.

13. "Proceedings," 48: 181–83.

14. Richmond *Daily Examiner*, March 14, 1862.

15. "Proceedings," 51: 284–288.

16. *War of the Rebellion: A Compilation of the Official Records of the Union and Confederate Armies* (Washington, D.C.); [hereinafter referred to as O.R. (Army) or O.R. (Conf.)]; Ser. I, 51: pt. 1, p. 152.

17. Baltimore *American*, July 15, 1861; Columbus *Daily Enquirer*, July 8, 1861.

18. Charleston *Mercury*, July 6, 1861.

19. O.R. (Conf.) Ser. I, 51: pt. 2, p. 115.

20. O.R. (Conf.), Ser. I, 11: pt. 3, pp. 635-66.

21. Andrews, *The South Reports the Civil War*, p. 193.

22. O.R. (Conf.) Ser. I, 51: pt. 2, p. 626.

23. Charleston *Daily Courier*, October 20, 1862.

24. Charleston *Daily Courier*, July 18, 1863.

25. Ibid., October 14, 1863.

26. Richmond *Examiner*, February 24, 1865.

27. Memphis *Appeal*, December 2, 1863.

28. Richmond *Examiner*, February 2, 1862.

29. Ibid., Ser. I, 51: pt. 2, p. 152.

30. Memphis *Daily Appeal*, July 16, 1861; New York *Herald*, August 31, 1862.

31. O.R. (Conf.), Ser. I, 5: 1021; Ser. II, 51: pt. 2, p. 428; Andrews, *The South Reports the Civil War*, pp. 161-63; Richmond *Examiner*, January 10, 1862.

32. Andrews, *The South Reports the Civil War*, p. 163.

33. Richmond *Examiner*, June 27, 1862.

34. Richmond *Enquirer*, July 12, 1862.

35. O.R. (Conf.) Ser. I, 10: pt. 2, p. 543.

36. New York *Herald*, May 16, 1862.

37. O.R. (Conf.) Ser. I, 15: 771-2.

38. "Proceedings," 45: 243–47.

39. Atlanta *Daily Intelligencer*, November 21, 1863.

40. Mobile *Daily Advertiser and Register*, June 19, 1863.

41. Robert E. Lee, *Recollections and Letters of General Robert E. Lee* (New York: Doubleday, Page & Co., 1924), p. 416.

42. Richmond *Examiner*, July 7, 1864.

43. Richmond *Daily Whig*, June 17, 1864.

44. Baltimore *American*, August 31, 1861.

45. *Brownlow's Knoxville Whig*, July 6, August 3 and September 28, 1861.

46. Ibid., October 26, 1861.

47. O.R. (Army) Ser. I, 1: 902, 920.

48. Ibid.; Atlanta *Daily Intelligencer*, November 21, 1863.

49. A contemporary account of the bridge-burning appears in Oliver P. Temple, *East Tennessee and the Civil War* (1899; reprint ed., Freeport, N.Y.: Books for Libraries Press, 1971), pp. 366-413.

50. O.R. (Army) Ser. I, 1: 907, 922.

51. Ibid., p. 902-903.

52. Ibid., pp. 904-907.

53. Ibid., pp. 908-909, 922.

54. Ellis Merton Coulter, *William G. Brownlow: Fighting Parson of the Southern Highlands* (Chapel Hill: University of North Carolina Press, 1937), p. 250-51.

55. Clement Eaton, *A History of the Southern Confederacy* (New York: The Macmillan Co., 1954), p. 33.

56. Horace W. Raper, "William H. Holden and the Peace Movement in North Carolina," 31 *North Dakota Hist. Rev.* 503 (Oct. 1954); Horace W. Raper, *William Holden, North Carolina's Political Enigma* (Chapel Hill: North Carolina University Press, 1985); William A. Graham, *The Papers of William Alexander Graham* 7 vols. (Raleigh: North Carolina Dept. of Cultural Resources, 1976) 6: 32n.

57. Memphis *Daily Appeal*, April 29, 1862.

58. Memphis *Daily Appeal*, June 9, 1862. .

59. Ibid., July 31, 1863.

60. See, Thomas H. Baker, "Refugee Newspaper: The Memphis *Daily Appeal*, 1862–1865," 29 *Journal of Southern History* 326 (August 1863); O.R. (Army), Ser. I, 49: pt. 1, p. 494.

61. *The Papers of Ulysses S. Grant*, 5: 181–82.

62. Ibid., p. 182.

63. Ibid., Ser. I, 24: pt. 3, p. 226.

64. William L. King, *The Newspaper Press of Charleston, South Carolina* (Charleston: Edward Perry, 1872; reprint ed., New York: Arno Press), pp. 123-25.

65. Simon, *Papers of Ulysses S. Grant*, 14: 345.

66. See, Eric Foner, *Reconstruction: America's Unfinished Revolution* (New York: Harper & Row, 1988).

67. Robert Selph Henry, *The Story of Reconstruction* (Gloucester, Mass.: Peter Smith, 1963), pp. 125-26.

68. 14 *U.S. Stats.* 428, 485; 15 *U.S. Stats.* 2.

69. Richmond *Whig*, June 9, 1865.

70. Ibid., July 11, 1865.

71. Henry L. Suggs, ed. *The Black Press in the South 1865–1979* (Westport, Conn.: Greenwood Press, 1983), pp. 3-23.

72. James Sefton, *The United States Army and Reconstruction, 1865–1877* (Baton Rouge: Louisiana State University Press, 1967), p. 55; Little Rock *Daily Gazette*, September 7, 1865.

73. Albany *Patriot*, July 29, August 5 and 15, 1865.

74. Ibid., Aug. 16, 1865.

75. Louis Turner Griffith and John E. Talmadge, *Georgia Journalism 1763-1950* (Athens: University of Georgia Press, 1951), pp. 91-93.

76. Richmond *Whig*, July 11 and 24, 1865.

77. Sefton, *The United States Army and Reconstruction*, pp. 55-56.

78. Petersburg *Daily News*, June 22, 1865.

79. Sefton, *The United States Army and Reconstruction*, p. 55 .

80. Joe Gray Taylor, *Louisiana Reconstructed, 1863–1877* (Baton Rouge: Louisiana State University Press, 1974), p. 66.

81. Edward McPherson, *The Political History of the United States of America*

During the Period of Reconstruction (1875, reprint ed.: New York: Negro University Press, 1969), p. 122.

82. James Sefton, "Aristotle in Blue and Braid: General John M. Schofield's Essays on Reconstruction," 17 *Civil War History* 45 (March 1971).

83. House Executive Doc. 1, *Report of the Secretary of War*, 40th Cong., 2nd sess., pp. 330-31 (1868) [hereinafter referred to as *Report of the Secretary of War, 1866–67*].

84. Ibid., p. 326-27.

85. Mobile *Nationalist*, May 30 and June 6, 1867.

86. Ibid., June 6, 1867.

87. *Report of the Secretary of War, 1866–67*, pp. 326–27; 329-31.

88. Ibid., p. 327, 351.

89. Ibid., p. 325.

90. Senate Executive Doc. 13, 40th Cong., 1st sess., pp. 98-99 (1868).

91. Ibid., p. 101.

92. Ibid., p. 101-102.

93. *Report of the Secretary of War, 1866–67*, pp. 349-54.

94. Senate Executive Doc. 14, 40th Cong. 1st sess., pp. 100-101 (1868).

95. *Statutes at Large*, ch. 167 (1867).

96. Richard H. Abbott, *The Republican Party and the South, 1855–1877* (Chapel Hill: University of North Carolina Press, 1986), pp. 133-136.

97. Ibid., pp. 325-26.

98. Ibid., p. 327.

99. Rhoda Coleman Ellison, *History and Bibliography of Alabama Newspapers in the 19th Century* (Birmingham: University of Alabama Press, 1954), pp. 90-91.

100. Ibid., p. 198.

101. Senate Executive Doc. 14, 40th Cong., 1st. sess., pp. 328-29 (1868).

102. Ellison, *Alabama Newspapers*, p. 144.

103. Macon *Journal and Messenger*, September 11, 1867.

104. House Executive Doc. 342, 40th Cong., 2nd sess., p. 131 (1868).

105. Montgomery *Daily Mail*, May 6, 1868; Sefton, *United States Army and Reconstruction*, p. 173.

106. Jack Claiborne, *The Charlotte Observer: Its Time and Place, 1869-1986* (Chapel Hill: University of North Carolina Press, 1986), pp. 12-13.

107. The details of this incident can be found in Sefton, *The United States Army and Reconstruction*, p. 152; Margaret Ross, "Retaliation Against Arkansas Newspaper Editors During Reconstruction," 31 *Arkansas Historical Qtly.* 150 (1972).

108. Ex parte McCardle, 7 Wallace 507 (1869) .

109. Carolyn E. DeLatte, "The St. Landry Riot: A Forgotten Incident of Reconstruction Violence," 17 *Louisiana History* 41 (Winter 1976); Jean-Charles Houzeau, *My Passage at the New Orleans Tribune* (Baton Rouge: Louisiana State University Press, 1984).

110. E. Merton Coulter, *The South During Reconstruction, 1865–1877* (Baton Rouge: Louisiana State University Press, 1947), p. 287.

111. New Orleans *Picayune*, October 6, 1868.

112. DeLatte, "The St. Landry Riot," pp. 41-49.

113. Frank Luther Mott, *American Journalism* (New York: The Macmillan Co., 1950), p. 368 .

114. *Compendium of the Ninth Census* (Washington: Government Printing Office, 1872), pp. 508-13; *Compendium of the Tenth Census*, pt. II (Washington: Government Printing Office, 1883), pp. 1628-31. The 1860 figures do not include newspapers in Arkansas or Florida.

Chapter 8

The Gathering Clouds: Labor Unrest and the Spanish-American War

THE INDUSTRIAL REVOLUTION BRINGS FRUSTRATIONS

In January 1865, a young German radical living in the slums of London wrote President Lincoln, congratulating him on his reelection. Karl Marx, president of the Central Council of the International Workingmen's Association, praised Lincoln for his efforts to free all Americans from the grips of the slaveholder. He declared that the Civil War "was to sound the tocsin for a general holy crusade of property against labor." And just as the American Revolution had marked "a new era of ascendancy for the middle class, so the American anti-slavery war will do for the working class."[1] Ten years later, as the nation stood mired in the depression following the Panic of 1873, Marx's prediction was, in the minds of many men of capital, uncomfortably close to realization.

The war years in the North were marked by a rapid growth in the economy that shortened the depression of 1857 and lengthened the period of prosperity. The war demand for food, clothing, weapons, and transportation produced an industrial mobilization that would eventually transform the country's economy from one based on agriculture to one based on industrial growth.

The growth could be seen in every facet of American life. The need to produce greater quantities of food moved farmers away from subsistence farming to mechanized agriculture. The Homestead Act, which offered settlers new land, also encouraged an increase in agricultural production. Federal land grant colleges were established to teach agricultural sciences and engineering. Transportation systems, which were placed under Federal control during the war, became concentrated in the hands of a few investors.

The Transcontinental Railroad, completed in 1869, opened up new land, new towns, and extended the farmers' reach to markets.

In the cities, cottage industries gave way to large factories. Increased tariffs provided the needed protection against foreign competition. Wealthy entrepreneurs, bankers, and investors bought government securities and internal improvement bonds which were payable in gold rather than the rapidly depreciating paper currency.

Workers streaming into the new factories brought with them unions, with whom management grudgingly entered into bargaining agreements for better wages and shorter work weeks. Generally, the American population was quite homogeneous in the 1870s. Ethnically, the nation was still predominantly white, Anglo-Saxon, Protestant. There was very little of the abject poverty that would emerge in the 1880s, nor were there the multimillionaires that would feed off the poor. However, the class system was still intact with social distances much greater than the geographical distances between wealth and labor.[2] Everywhere the nation was glorifying the triumph of capitalism and industry as proof that the Great Experiment really worked. Yet, all this economic activity would soon build toward rapid inflation. Inflation, overspeculation in railroads, and a general loss of faith in the economy brought on the Panic of 1873, and the nation spiraled downward into a depression that would last until 1878. But those who had prospered during the boom years hardly felt the effects of the depression; instead, they found ways to shift their economic losses to those least capable of withstanding further loss—the workers and farmers.

Farmers had borrowed heavily to mechanize production. As production rose, prices dropped, and the farmer had to buy more land and more machinery. Not only were farmers in debt, but they were being held by the throats by the exorbitant rates set by railroad and steamboat monopolies. The Western farmer was not alone in his economic problems. Eastern merchants, small manufacturers, shippers, and importers were beginning to feel the ill effects of the government's policies of protective tariffs and tight money. The city laborer shared the same foes. Just as increased production on the farm had brought lower prices, so too did increased productivity in the factories. Wages were cut, debts increased, and unions became more militant. But when workers went out on strike, they were ignored. There were plenty of men out of work who could fill the work benches, or contract laborers could be brought in from Europe to work for next to nothing.

For example, in 1877, Whitelaw Reid, owner of the New York *Tribune*, decided to initiate a third pay cut for his printers. Knowing the typographical union would not accept the cuts, Reid began assembling a new work force. The printers struck and within hours a new staff of printers was handling the *Tribune* operations. In another effort to take advantage of depression-level wages, Reid decided to build a new *Tribune* building. But several months into the project, the unskilled laborers refused to continue working and Reid hired Italian contract laborers to finish the job.[3]

The shared frustration of farmers, manufacturers, and city workers resulted in the formation during the 1870s and 1880s of a variety of anti-monopoly and free-trade organizations that extended from the trans-Mississippi farms to the Eastern shipping docks. One source has noted that these radical democratic groups were a revised version of the abolitionists, locofocos and Benton Democrats of the pre-war years that had struggled against banks, special privileges, and slavery.[4]

This radical heritage, which was revived in the trans-Allegheny after the Civil War, took on a variety of faces. The Free Trade League, which was supported by such independents as William Cullen Bryant's *New York Evening Post* and Horace White's Chicago *Tribune*, wanted an end to special legislation, particularly the war tariffs that were hurting importers, shippers, and manufacturer's agents. The Free Traders appealed to a broad spectrum of Western farmers and Eastern wage earners. But the movement died even before the Panic of 1873. The Free Traders were to be followed by the Greenback movement, Kellogism, Single Tax Party, and the Free-Silver Party plus a variety of other currency reform movements, all aimed at destroying monopolies and instituting more flexible currency policies.

The radical democratic reform movements of the 1870s and early 1880s worked within the democratic system. They established political parties, sponsored newspapers, held conventions, and hoisted their advocates onto the ballot; they even won elections. Although these reform parties would eventually die out, they would be reborn in the late 1880s in the great Populist movement that swept across the agrarian South, West and Midwest. Populism, which was primarily an economic reform movement, had a large agenda. Populists argued for government control of banks, railroads, warehouses, and communication. They believed government intervention would strengthen the small farmer and merchant to give them a fair chance at America's wealth. Populists encouraged government subsidies to farmers and taught farmers the value of joining into cooperatives. Populists also called for monetary reform by having the government loosen up the amount of money in the marketplace. All of these measures were aimed at strengthening the free enterprise system by getting rid of monopolies and the middlemen.

To speed the spread of the Populist message, newspapers throughout the South and Midwest picked up the movement's cause. The Populist press was so large that in 1891, the National Reform Press Association was created with over 1,000 member newspapers.[5] Although the Populist movement provoked strong reaction among conservatives, the willingness of the movement to work within the system, spared it from any overt attempts at censorship.

Labor Radicals and Violence

While the American farmer turned to the Populist party for representation and relief from the burden of monopolies, low wages, and tight money, the city worker was also looking for a sympathetic ear. However, with labor leadership coming predominately from the European immigrant class, the labor reform movements were less apt to "work within the system." Yet, the aims of labor's organizers, whether democratically controlled unions or socialist organizations, were similar. The basic demands were for a shorter work day, better wages, better working conditions, monetary reform, and women's rights.

While the union had traditionally been a place for American laborers to turn in bad times, the American labor union was never strong enough to outlast the numerous depressions that hit the American economy in the nineteenth century. After the Panic of 1873, many unions were unable to win concessions against employers who imported contract laborers from Europe or swept the streets for able-bodied men.

In January 1874, a mass labor meeting at New York City's Tompkins Square turned into a riot when mounted policemen charged into the crowd, clubbing and trampling workers. In 1875, the Molly Maguires led a deadly riot of Irish coal miners in Pennsylvania that resulted in 20 miners being hanged by the law. In July 1877, when railroad wages were cut, machinists from Pittsburgh to San Francisco struck and resorted to property violence. They stopped trains, pulled up track, burned stations, and destroyed cargo. Federal and state troops, police as well as private troops, were called out to quell rioters. In the end, over 100 persons were dead.

The American press reacted by calling strikers hooligans and criminals, and urged businesses to arm themselves. After the railroad strike, there were a few years of relative peace, as laborers witnessed the strengthening of defenses around industry and the popular outcry against their tactics. But as the poverty of workers increased, the time was ripe for the European-influenced reform movements to enter the scene. Bakhunin Anarchists, Marxists, revolutionary socialists, and Knights of Labor all vied for the laborer's loyalty. While these organizations did attract some immigrant workers, they found it difficult to cajole the American laborer to join. Nevertheless, the radical labor organizations grew although attempts to unite them into one single revolutionary organization had failed several times.

Anarchists were the most vocal and best organized of the European radical groups. While anarchism had existed in America since the early 1800s, its form had been philosophical and peaceful. Anarchists believed that government in all its forms was an evil and should be abolished. In its place, the people should organize themselves into loose, informal, and voluntary cooperatives. The philosophical anarchists believed that education of the people on the evils of government would eventually result in a bloodless demise of government. They demonstrated the viability of communal living by establishing cooperatives as alternatives to government.

But in Europe the philosophers were being challenged by a revolutionary form of anarchism led by Mikhail Bakhunin, an aristocrat turned revolutionary, who was thrown out of the International Workingmen's Association. These revolutionary anarchists had no patience with the philosophical branch. Instead they taught that violent overthrow of government was the only realistic solution. This violent strain of anarchism was imported into the United States in the 1880s by Johann Most, a German follower of Bakhunin. Most and his followers believed that all peaceful means of reforming capital had failed and dedicated themselves to the destruction of class rule by force. Most's New York newspaper, *Freiheit*, as well as other anarchist newspapers, instructed readers to arm themselves, told workmen where to buy guns, and how to use explosives.[6]

Because of their open avowal of violence—"propaganda of the deed"—anarchists were immediately linked to the violent labor protests of the 1880s and 1890s, including the Haymarket Riot of 1886, the 1892 Homestead strike in Pittsburgh's steel mills, the Pullman strike in Chicago in 1894, and the Cripple Creek mine strike in Colorado in 1894.

The Haymarket Riot

A major goal that united many of the labor organizations in the 1880s was the eight-hour workday. But attempts to convince industry, the public, and Washington that an eight-hour day was a humane answer to labor's many problems were thwarted at every turn. By the early 1880s many states had passed eight-hour laws, but they had many exceptions and exemptions and provided no means of enforcement. In 1877, the Supreme Court took the wind out of a Federal eight-hour law by holding the law was not a contract, but only a directive. Federal agencies were free to make agreements for longer or shorter workdays as they needed.[7]

The big push for the eight-hour day came from the Federation of Organized Trade and Labor Unions and the Knights of Labor. In 1884 the Federation declared that on May 1, 1886, an eight-hour day be adopted by all unions. A strike would become the weapon of enforcement. While many organizations favored the eight-hour proposal, most hesitated to endorse a strike. The revolutionary anarchists thought the movement was futile, calling it a compromise with capital. Unless the movement was ready to arm itself and meet resistance with violence, the movement would collapse.[8]

But as May 1, 1886 approached, the anarchist's International Working People's Association (I.W.P.A.) became more supportive of the movement as it gained strength in New York and Chicago. In February 1886, workers at the McCormick Harvester plant in Chicago were locked out in a dispute over unionization. Two days later, a strike was called. In March the plant was reopened with 300 scabs protected by an army of policemen and Pinkerton agents. A meeting of strikers was called on the day of the reopening. Two I.W.P.A. leaders were asked to speak. After Michael Schwab and Albert Parsons, editor of the English language anarchist paper *The Alarm*, spoke, the crowd was dispersed by police.[9]

On Saturday, May 1, 30,000 workers in Chicago demonstrated for shorter hours, but the day passed peacefully. On Monday, May 3, 6,000 McCormick Harvester strikers once again took up positions outside the plant where they were addressed by Augustus Spies, editor of the anarchist *Arbeiter-Zeitung*. Before Spies had finished addressing the crowd, the work bell rang at the plant and many of the strikers headed toward the workers leaving for the day. Strikers threw stones, broke windows, and fired guns at the strike breakers. Police were called in to disperse the riot. When it was over, one striker was dead and several strikers and policemen had been injured. Meanwhile, Spies had left the scene and returned to the *Arbeiter-Zeitung* where he wrote a first-hand, but inaccurate account of the day's events. His erroneous report that six men had been killed was picked up by the Chicago *Daily News* and panic spread through the city.

In a separate circular written the same day, Spies called for "Revenge! Workingmen! To Arms!" He wrote: "If you are men, if you are the sons of your grandsires, who have shed their blood to free you, then you will rise in your might Hercules, and destroy the hideous monster that seeks to destroy you. To arms, we call you, to arms!"[10] Twelve hundred copies of the circular were distributed that night. The police force was strengthened and several companies of army troops were on alert. The next day, a half-dozen skirmishes occurred throughout the city but were quickly put down by police.

On Tuesday, May 4, a demonstration was planned in Haymarket Square to protest police action. Spies again agreed to address the crowd. Circulars announcing the gathering called for: "Workmen Arm Yourselves and Appear in Full Force." When Spies saw the leaflets, he demanded that they be reprinted without the call to arms. Only several hundred of the 20,000 circulars distributed had the militant phrase.

Although a crowd of over ten thousand was expected, the organizers were disappointed when fewer than two thousand showed up. In fact, the number was so small that the gathering was moved out of Haymarket Square to a smaller gathering area. Spies, Parsons, and an associate, Samuel Fielden, addressed the crowd. But before Fielden concluded his speech, rain set in and the crowd began to break up. Twenty minutes later, a large contingent of 180 police arrived and headed toward the speakers. The police captain ordered listeners to go home. Without provocation from either police or the crowd, someone threw a bomb and it landed near a phalanx of police, killing one. Police then began firing into the crowd. Eight policemen and ten workers were killed or later died from wounds. Over fifty people were wounded. No one ever learned who threw the bomb.

The reaction across the country was one of revenge against the "anarchists of Chicago," "the offscourings of Europe," the "ungrateful hyenas," and "cowardly savages."[11] The *Arbeiter-Zeitung* was closed down and the entire staff was detained for several days. Nine men, including Spies, Parsons, Fielden, and Schwab, were arrested and charged with the murder of the policeman killed by the bomb blast. Legally, the men were not charged with actually throwing the bomb, but of having advised workers through their speeches, circulars, and newspapers to commit murder.

Judge Joseph Gary stated that the defendants' utterances had been their crime: "They incited, advised and encouraged the throwing of the bomb that killed the policemen, not by addressing the bomb-thrower specially . . . but by general addresses to readers and hearers; by every argument which they could frame; by every appeal to passion which they could make."[12]

When the trial was over, one defendant had left the country, and eight were found guilty. Of the eight, one committed suicide in prison. Spies and Parsons and two others were hung on November 11, 1887 after the U.S. Supreme Court denied their petition for a writ of error. In 1893, Illinois Governor John Peter Altgeld granted a full pardon to Fielden, Schwab, and one other who had not even been at the scene of the bombing. Altgeld believed that the men had not been tried for their involvement, however remotely, in the murders, but for their views about American society.

Although most of the men arrested were associated with the *Arbeiter-Zeitung* or *The Alarm*, and articles from the papers were introduced as evidence against them, the First Amendment right of free press was never raised as a major argument on behalf of the defendants. During the trial Parsons spoke in his own defense, arguing that the defendants had merely exercised their lawful rights to free speech, press, and public assembly. But when Judge Gary pronounced sentence, he countered Parson's free speech argument:

Each man has the full right to entertain and advance, by speech and print, such opinions as suit himself; and the great body of the people will usually care little what he says. But if he proposes murder as a means of enforcing them he puts his own life at stake. And no clamor about free speech or the evils to be cured or the wrongs to be redressed will shield him from the consequences of his crime. His liberty is not a license to destroy.[13]

According to the *Workmen's Advocate*, defense attorney Moses Salomon listed the denial of free speech, peaceable assembly, and the right of free belief among the federal questions that would be part of the defense appeal to the U.S. Supreme Court.[14] However, the actual petition submitted to the Court omitted all reference to the First Amendment, and the Court's opinion made no mention of the First Amendment.[15]

Although the immediate reaction to the Haymarket bombing was a nationwide call for the execution of all anarchists, there was no general pogrom against anarchists. In fact, the mayor of Chicago allowed the *Arbeiter-Zeitung* to begin republishing several days after the bombing—although no firm would print it.[16] It finally appeared on May 8, with the understanding that if it published any inflammatory articles it would be suspended by police. The new editor urged workers to support the paper, explaining that "a workingman's movement without a workingman's paper is an impossibility." The new staff assured readers that "should further arrests take place, there will others step into our places." The paper vowed to continue its "fight for liberty and rights."[17]

A few other newspapers were not as fortunate. Two Bohemian anarchist sheets, *The Budouenost* and the *Lampicka*, were shut down by police the day after the Haymarket Riot.[18] In New York, Johann Most was arrested for giving an incendiary speech and waving a rifle in front of a crowd twelve days before the Haymarket Riot. He allegedly stated to the crowd, "Buy these, steal revolvers, make bombs and when you have enough, rise and seize what is yours.... Shoot or be shot."[19] Police wanted to charge Most with murder, but since the murders occurred in Chicago, the best they could do was charge him with breach of peace. He was sentenced to one year in prison. The *New York Times* said of Most's impending conviction that it "will have a good effect in clearing the minds of a good many violent agitators of the notion that liberty of speech and press in the country mean liberty to incite ignorant foolish men to commit violence."[20]

Most was released in April 1887, but was rearrested on November 16 after making another incendiary speech following the executions of the Haymarket offenders. He was arrested for illegal assembly and inciting to riot and sentenced to one year in prison. Most did not go to jail until June 1891, when all of his appeals had been exhausted.

Anarchists and the Early Free Expression Debate

There was a great deal of discussion about the anarchists, their trial and execution, but little of it dealt directly with the question of freedom of speech or press. Immediately after the bombing, the *Albany Law Journal* dubbed the anarchists "long-haired, wild-eyed, bad-smelling, atheistic, fanatical, reckless, foreign wretches," and called for some law "to enable society to crush such snakes when they raise their heads before they have time to bite."[21]

After the executions, the editor of the *Albany Law Journal* published an editorial answering charges made in the Chicago Bar's *Legal Advisor* that the Illinois Supreme Court had demolished freedom of speech. The editor answered that the Illinois court had not abolished liberty of speech, but had "abolished the right to counsel murder, arson, and robbery in excited and inflammatory language." The police have the full authority to break up "seditious counsels" before they occur. The editor also called for new laws that would punish those who advocate the commission of a crime and that would bar peaceful assembly that obstructed the streets.[22]

The Illinois legislature did just that a year later when it passed the Conspiracy Law which punished anyone who advised, encouraged, aided, abetted, or incited anyone to do violence against the laws of the country. However, it was not necessary that the communication had been read or communicated to the persons who actually committed the violence. The law was never enforced and was repealed in 1891.[23]

The Haymarket Affair did not produce the quantity of contemporaneous writing about freedom of speech and press that might have been expected. However, what did appear were the first hints that the traditional interpretations of the First Amendment were about to change. These changes, which would see maturity during the early twentieth century, were a direct response to the activities of radical political groups, particularly the anarchists. The change that was discussed in these few writings was the constitutionality of censoring political speech when it threatened to disrupt the system or overthrow the government.

Never before had the nation been concerned about those who would attempt to change the basic form of government. In the first half of the century, expression that created the most serious threat was criminal libel. And when commentators wrote about the necessity of punishing licentious expression, they generally were referring to a press that "pandered to a depraved appetite for scandal" or obscenity. By subsequent actions for criminal libel, the courts were hoping they could instill a modicum of "truth, good morals and common decency" into the public press.[24] The only breaches of peace they were familiar with were those to an individual's private peace and enjoyment of good reputation.

Even when Justice Joseph Story wrote during the tumultuous abolition period about the right of state governments to punish libels that "stir up resistance to its laws, to urge on conspiracies to destroy it, to create odium and indignation against virtuous citizens, to compel them to yield up their rights, or to make them the objects of popular vengeance," he was referring only to the subsequent punishment in the form of criminal libel or sedition.[25] No court had condoned the use of prior restraint even for the most odious forms of expression. The prevailing rule of law that had developed since the Sedition Acts of 1798 was that abuses of freedom of press could be punished only in subsequent proceedings.

Thomas Cooley, writing after the Civil War, argued that prior restraint was not allowed at all and that subsequent punishment could only be used when injuries occurred to public morals or private reputation. Neither criticism nor condemnation of government was punishable at common law or by legislation.[26] In fact, in the 1903 edition of Cooley's *Treatise*, editor Victor Lane specifically addressed the issue of violent speech:

They must be left at liberty to speak with the freedom which the magnitude of the supposed wrongs appear in their minds to demand and if they exceed all the proper bounds of moderation, the consolation must be that the evil likely to spring from the violent discussion will probably be less; and its correction by public sentiment more speedy, than if the terrors of the law were brought to bear to prevent the discussion.[27]

Yet, during the century's last quarter, legal scholars found it increasingly difficult to sustain the old views against prior restraint, especially when the expression advocated violence. Many rejected Cooley's liberal stance against the power of the police to protect the public welfare.

Henry C. Adams, writing immediately after the Haymarket Affair in the brand new *Forum*, recognized that the traditional concepts of liberty of speech and press were in jeopardy as the country underwent major social and political upheavals. However, he warned against new repressive measures, fearful that they would do more harm than good. But he hinted that existing criminal laws (i.e., breach of peace, trespass, disorderly conduct, etc.) could be used to control anarchists. Unlike Cooley, Adams believed that the evil that came from violent discussion was worse than the terrors of the law.[28]

Adams posed several questions: What were the traditional values of liberty of expression? Have new forces been introduced into modern life which should lead to the modification of old liberties of freedom of speech? Do these new elements require police to be repressive?

Adams based his answer to the first question on John Stuart Mill's *On Liberty*. He quoted Mill's defense of freedom of speech as necessary to preserve "the freshness of truth in men's minds," to encourage individuality, and to allow people the freedom to develop and expand. However, Adams concluded that Mill was addressing a different sort of expression and would not have sanctioned the free use of language which becomes the first step to crime. The language of anarchists did not in any way enhance the type of debate Mill had in mind.

As to the elements that had been introduced into modern society, Adams named the "foreign element" that was unschooled and quick to "frenzy," and the invention of dynamite, which was more deadly than a gun and was easily concealed. But did these new elements require new laws? Adams's answer was that no new laws were needed because they would tend to be overbroad and censor protected expression and activity. The best solution was vigorous enforcement of existing criminal laws.

Christopher Tiedeman, a legal scholar who wrote one of the few treatises on constitutional law in the post-war years, agreed that breach of peace was a just cause for limiting the First Amendment, but took it one step further than Adams. Writing in the year of the Haymarket Riot, Tiedeman stated that whenever a publication incited people to commit crimes, the state was within its authority to shut it down.[29]

Tiedeman directly addressed publications that were designed to appeal to "dynamiters, socialists, nihilists and all other classes of discontents." The only effective remedy for such agitators was censorship so that the publications could be prevented, rather than punished afterwards. Such a censorship, according to Tiedeman, was constitutional because it would be carried out to promote the public welfare and would be sanctioned as an exercise of the police power of government.

This was an interesting argument from a scholar who, in the same writings, forcefully promoted the concept of laissez faire. He apparently was unable to see any similarity between the limitation of police power in economic matters and its limitation in matters of civil rights.

Tiedeman analogized to the concept in criminal libel that allowed arrests, peace bonds, and even suspension of publications because certain libels could lead to a breach of peace. Although criminal libel had almost disappeared from the courts by mid-century, the concept still lingered. If First Amendment rights can be restrained when a libeler threatens the peace of the community, so too, argued Tiedeman, can publications be restrained when their expression endangers the public safety, health, and morals of the community.

While "the newspapers of anarchists and nihilists cannot be subjected to censorship, or be absolutely suppressed, . . . they may very properly be punished, and without doubt the right to continue publication may be forfeited" if inflammatory appeals are made that urge people to commit crimes. The police are within their constitutional rights to enforce local regulations in order to protect the public against breaches of peace.

Despite this urging by two legal scholars, the radical labor press in America was free of censorship. With the exception of brief suspensions after the Haymarket Riot, even the most violent anarchist sheets were untouched by the law. Also, there are very few reported cases before the state courts in the last years of the nineteeth century involving municipal or state laws regulating public expression or assembly. In the few cases that did appear, the central issue was the state's power to protect the general welfare and not the protection of freedom of expression. As Justice Story has argued earlier, "is it not as plain that the right of government to punish the violators of [public rights and liberties] flows from the primary duty of self-preservation?"[30]

When the U.S. Supreme Court reviewed the *Spies* case, the decision was based upon the right of Illinois to use its police powers to protect the people and their property.[31] And in *Davis v. Massachusetts*, where a citizen was convicted for speaking in the Boston Commons without a permit, the Court used the concept of private property to justify denial, with barely a mention of the First Amendment right of speech or public assembly.[32]

Although it was not until after the assassination of President McKinley in 1901 that states and the federal Congress began the serious business of passing laws to suppress unpopular beliefs,[33] a new theory of freedom of expression was emerging in the last years of the nineteenth century as if in anticipation of more stressful times ahead.

James Bryce, an Englishman, wrote two years after the Haymarket executions: "So, America, in her swift onward progress, sees, looming on the horizon and now no longer distant, a time of mists and shadows, wherein dangers may lie concealed whose form and magnitude she can scarcely yet conjecture.... It will be a time of trial for democratic institutions."[34]

Bryce wondered whether the increased European immigration added to existing problems in America would prove so obstinate, that when the struggle grew harder "the masses will yield to the temptation to abuse their power and will seek violent... and useless remedies, for the evils which will afflict them." If such a crises occurred, "there may be pernicious experiments tried in legislation. There may be occasional outbreaks of violence. There may even be... a dislocation of the present frame of government. One thing, however, need not be apprehended.... There will not be anarchy." The habits of freedom will stand unimpaired and even be "confirmed and mellowed by longer use," predicted Bryce. "We may look forward to the future, not indeed without anxiety, when we mark the clouds that hang on the horizon, yet with a hope that is stronger than anxiety," concluded Bryce.

While Marx's forecast in 1865 of a workingman's revolution in America had not come to fruition, Bryce's prediction would. The assassination of President McKinley touched off a general witch hunt for anarchists, socialists, and communists which lasted through World War I. "Pernicious legislation" against anarchists and syndicalism was passed at state and federal levels, and with it came volumes of contemporary material on free speech and press.[35]

THE SPANISH-AMERICAN WAR

No study of freedom of press in nineteenth-century America can be complete without a look at the censorship activities that took place during the Spanish-American War of 1898. This was the second war that the United States had fought outside its borders. But during the Mexican War of 1845 there was little need for censorship of foreign dispatches because it took days if not weeks for the information to appear in American newspapers, too late for the information to be used to the injury of the army.

However, by 1898, sophisticated telegraphic communication existed throughout the world; ship-to-shore wireless was being used and transportation was much faster. A telegraph message from Washington to Santiago, Cuba, took only twenty minutes.[36] This increased capability brought about by modern technology made the adoption of some type of wartime censorship a must.

However, wartime censorship in the Spanish-American War was not as severe as it had been in the Civil War. In fact, censorship was complained about more because of the inconveniences it brought to reporters than because of any concern over keeping the American public informed of happenings.

Historians have offered a variety of theories about the seeds of the war, but most tend to agree that the yellow journalism of such newspapers as William Randolph Hearst's New York *Journal* and Joseph Pulitzer's New York *World* played a role, although minor, in precipitating the war.[37]

Cubans, in their effort to throw off the imperial yoke of the Spanish, rose in revolt in 1895. The Spanish answer was to place many Cubans in concentration camps and even to kill some of the rebel leaders. The American press began covering the insurrection from its earliest days. The stories tended to exaggerate the nature of the Spanish retaliation, daily reporting on new examples of atrocities and outrages perpetrated against innocent women and children.

On February 15, 1898, the U.S.S. *Maine* was blown up in the Havana harbor by a mine planted by unknown persons. President McKinley sent an ultimatum to Madrid demanding an immediate cessation to the fighting between Spanish and Cubans and a release of prisoners, including several American reporters. The Governor General of Cuba offered an armistice to the rebels, and the American minister to Spain believed that a peaceable solution could be worked out to provide Cubans the autonomy they demanded. But under pressure from Congress, McKinley accepted Congress's declaration of war in April 1898. Three months later, the Americans had defeated the Spanish. Only 289 Americans were killed; but ten times that many died of dysentery, yellow fever, malaria, or other diseases brought by tropical climate and unsanitary conditions.

Censorship of telegraphic dispatches in and out of Tampa, Florida; Key West; and New York began even before the declaration of war, when the Signal Corps took over the cable office in Key West and placed censors in the New York cable offices.[38] Newspapers complained about the censorship because it had cut off stories containing speculation and theories about future army and navy movements. The New York *Sun* correspondent wrote from Tampa, headquarters of the U.S. Expeditionary Force, that "all these writers had hitherto been untrammeled. They had been accustomed to wiring whatever they saw fit. Suddenly a man was thrust upon them with the power to 'kill' every word they wrote."[39]

The Signal Corps had orders to intercept cipher messages to Spain or the West Indies and also any messages "in plain text" which contained information about military operations contemplated or progressing. Brigadier General A. W. Greely, Chief Signal Officer, believed that telegraphic censorship served two purposes—to prevent damaging information from ending up in Spanish hands and to examine "the thousands of messages of unfriendly or neutral character" that passed through the telegraph offices. "From newspaper correspondents, blockade runners, Spanish agents, commercial messages, personal dispatches. etc., there was reaped a rich harvest of information."[40]

The duty of the telegraph censor in New York was not only to intercept outgoing messages, but to prevent information regarding projected movements of troops, vessels, and transports from reaching the press. In order to carry out this charge, it was necessary for at least two operators in every New York cable office to swear an oath that they would faithfully observe the orders of the military censor.[41]

When Lieutenant Grant Squires, former reporter for the New York *Tribune*, took over as New York telegraph censor, he exercised his job "with the least possible inconvenience to all legitimate commercial business, including press business," and when the messages did not conflict with censorship rules, "no delay or censorship was allowed to interfere with the free and prompt conduct of business."[42]

Although there was a telegraph censor in Tampa, the daily routine of censoring dispatches was left to the telegraph operators, working under orders of the censor. According to a reporter for the Chicago *Tribune*, if the telegraph operator did not like what he was sending, "he just cut it out to suit himself." When the story reached the next telegraph office in Jacksonville on its way to New York, another telegrapher could cut out whatever he felt was dangerous; "and by the time it reached the home office it was liable to be anything that the writer did not intend."[43]

This policy was later confirmed by Squires, who explained that "it was manifestly improper if a contraband message was stopped, delayed, or censored, to notify the sender or recipient of the standing or changed condition of his message." Since time was the most important element in the transmission of press dispatches, any delay was sure to cause friction between the cable companies and their newspaper clients. Therefore, censors were not allowed to give out any information as to the censored condition in which messages were sometimes delivered.[44]

In Tampa, when news reporters failed to heed censorship orders, the military censor threatened to revoke press passes to accompany the army into Cuba. At one point the censor required a copy of all papers to be filed daily for examination, in order to keep up with what the reporters in his charge were managing to get past the telegraph operators.[45]

In Key West, censorship was also tight. The Chicago *Tribune* reporter explained that "the censorship by the government on all dispatches from Key West has been made rigid." At the end of April, word was spread abroad that the Spanish had put to sail with a large fleet, heading for Cuba. When Admiral. W. T. Sampson, the officer in charge of the American fleet blockading Havana harbor, returned to Key West after word of the Spanish fleet had been circulated, the censorship of the press prevented for a few days the spread of speculation about Sampson's next mission. A correspondent for the Associated Press wrote:

Every newspaper man in Key West knew that the great battleships were steaming away from Havana in quest of Big Spanish game . . . but not a word would the censor permit to pass. . . . Everything that had the appearance of cipher—everything that was not absolutely plain and explainable—was stopped.[46]

Sampson was headed for Puerto Rico to engage the Spanish fleet.

When word finally came in May that troops in Tampa were ready to board transports for Cuba, telegraph censorship was again tightened. The New York *Tribune* reported that "simultaneously the most rigid censorship of press dispatches that has so far been undertaken by the government will be put into effect at Tampa and Key West tonight, and no messages relating to movements of troops or in any way speculating upon the expedition, will be permitted on the wire."[47]

The expedition was a success. Troops landed in Cuba in the last week of June and defeated the Spanish at San Juan and El Caney. Admiral Sampson's Atlantic Squadron finally caught up with the elusive Spanish fleet and defeated the Spanish navy as it steamed out of Santiago Bay.

Following the war, Brigadier Greely, in the annual report of the Secretary of War, tried to dispel the notion that the Signal Corps had exercised an extreme censorship over the press during the war.[48] The charge, he said, "is entirely unfounded." In fact, what he exercised "was a censorship of all matter which passed over such telegraph cables and land lines as were militarily occupied." That included all land lines in Florida, every cable system extending from the United States to any foreign country, and the French, English, and Cuban cables in the Caribbean. Most of those cables were only "constructively" seized, leaving their operation in the hands of their respective operators, but under the general supervision of the Signal Corps. Although the cable operators were for the most part cooperative and pledged themselves to the United States, it was still necessary for the Signal Corp to "fix the order of business and to decline such messages as were prejudicial to the military interests of the United States."

Lieutenant Squires, also wrote following the war that there was a general impression that the censorship was directed against the press to the exclusion of all other cable business. "As a matter of fact it was not directed against the press at all except incidentally." He admitted that "at times it fell with some severity upon the press, but at no time with anything like the degree of inconvenience it caused commercial interests."[49]

Despite telegraphic censorship, the Army could not prevent the press from printing rumors, exaggerations, speculations, and even hoaxes. Nor was it possible to keep reporters out of the war zone. Many of the major newspapers and wire services had their own boats that followed the navy and troop carriers. Reporters often hired boats to take them into Cuba so they could interview Cuban insurgents.

Reporters during the Spanish-American War even acted as spies, agents, and couriers for the Army and Navy. And despite the hardships of bad food, illness, unsanitary conditions, and censorship, the press managed to keep Americans informed at home. What censorship during the Spanish-American War did accomplish was again to fix in American minds that during war, some degree of censorship is necessary to safeguard military operations.

NOTES

1. Karl Marx and Frederick Engels, *The Civil War in the United States* (New York: International Publishers, 1974), pp. 273, 279-281.

2. Walter T. K. Nugent, *From Centennial to World War: American Society 1876-1917* (Indianapolis: Bobbs-Merrill Co., Inc., 1977), pp. 16-19.

3. Bingham Duncan, *Whitelaw Reid, Journalist, Politician, Diplomat* (Athens: University of Georgia Press, 1975), p. 61.

4. Chester McArthur Destler, *American Radicalism 1865–1901: Essays and Documents* (New York: Octagon Books, 1963), p. 3.

5. Lauren Kessler, *The Dissident Press: Alternative Journalism in American History* (Beverly Hills: Sage Publications, 1984), pp. 117-120.

6. See, Bernard K. Johnpoll, *The Impossible Dream: The Rise and Demise of the American Left* (Westport, Ct.: Greenwood Press, 1981).

7. U.S. v. Martin, 94 U.S. 200 (1877).

8. Henry David, *The History of the Haymarket Affair* (New York: Ferrar and Rinehart, Inc., 1936), pp. 164-169.

9. The story of the Haymarket Riot is taken from David, *The History of the Haymarket Affair*; Dyer D. Lum, *A Concise History of the Great Trial of the Chicago Anarchists in 1886* (Socialistic Publishing Co., 1887).

10. David, *The History of the Haymarket Affair*, pp. 189-92. Spies vowed that he had not written the word "Revenge!," that it had been added by a compositor without his knowledge; Lum, *A Concise History of the Great Trial*, pp. 96-97.

11. David, *The History of the Haymarket Affair*, pp. 209, 212.

12. Joseph Gary, "The Chicago Anarchists of 1886: The Crime, The Trial, The Punishment," 45 *The Century Magazine* 803, 812 (April 1893).

13. Gary, "The Chicago Anarchists of 1886," p. 836.

14. David, *History of the Haymarket Affair*, p. 390 19n.

15. In re Spies, 123 U.S. 131 (1887).

16. *New York Times*, May 7, 1886.

17. Ibid., May 8, 1886.

18. Ibid., May 7, 1886.

19. Ibid., May 12 and 28, 1886.

20. Ibid., May 29, 1886.

21. 32 *Albany Law Journal* 381 (May 15, 1886).

22. 36 *Albany Law Journal* 421 (1887).

23. David, *History of the Haymarket Affair*, p. 537.

24. Thomas Cooley, *A Treatise on the Constitutional Limitations Which Rest Upon the Legislative Power of the States of the American Union* 7th ed. (Boston: Little, Brown, and Co., 1903), pp. 642-43.

25. Joseph Story, *Commentaries on the Constitution of the United States* 5th ed., 2 vols. (Boston: Little, Brown & Co., 1891) 2: 641.

26. Thomas M. Cooley, *The General Principles of Constitutional Law in the United States of America* (Boston: Little, Brown & Co., 1898) pp. 302-305.

27. Cooley, *Treatise on the Constitutional Limitations*, p. 614.

28. Henry C. Adams, "Shall We Muzzle the Anarchists?" *Forum* July 1886, pp. 448-449.

29. Christopher Tiedeman, *A Treatise on the Limitations of Police Power in the United States* (St. Louis, 1886; reprint ed., New York: Da Capo Press, 1971), pp. 189-192.

30. Story, *Commentaries on the Constitution*, 2:642.

31. In re Spies, 123 U.S. 131 (1887).

32. 167 U.S. 43 (1897).

33. See, Margaret A. Blanchard, "Filling the Void: Speech and Press in State Courts Prior to *Gitlow*," in Bill Chamberlin and Charlene J. Brown, eds., *The First Amendment Reconsidered*, (New York: Longman Pub., 1982), pp. 14-59.

34. James Bryce, *American Commonwealth* (1908; reprint ed., New York: G. P. Putnam's Sons, 1959), pp. 594-95.

35. For an excellent study of the development of the First Amendment during the Progressive Period, see Linda Cobb-Reiley, "The Meaning of Freedom of Speech and the Press in the Progressive Era: Historical Roots of Modern First Amendment Theory," (Ph.D. Dissertation, University of Utah, 1986).

36. *Annual Reports of the War Department for the Fiscal Year Ended June 30, 1898*, House Doc. 2, 55th Cong., 3rd Sess., p. 967 (1899) [hereinafter referred to as *Report of the War Department*].

37. See, e.g, Philip Foner, *The Spanish Cuban American War and the Birth of American Imperialism* 2 vols. (New York: Monthly Review Press, 1972); C. J. Dierks, *A Leap to Arms* (New York: Lippincott, 1970); Edmund Traverso, *The Spanish American War: A Study in Policy Change* (Lexington, Ky.: D.C. Heath Pub., 1963).

38. *Report of the War Department*, p. 966.

39. New York *Sun*, May 2, 1898.

40. *Report of the War Department*, p. 893.

41. Ibid., p. 966.

42. Ibid., pp. 966-67.

43. Chicago *Tribune*, May 19, 1898.

44. *Report of the War Department*, p. 968.

45. Charles H. Brown, *The Correspondent's War* (New York: Charles Scribner's Sons, 1967), p. 228.

46. Ibid., p. 237.
47. New York *Tribune*, May 30, 1898.
48. *Report of the War Department*, pp. 891-95.
49. Ibid., p. 967.

Selected Bibliography

Author's Note: Literally hundreds of published materials, mostly dating to the nineteenth century, were used to compile this work. The reader needs only to scan the notes to grasp the variety of primary sources used—newspapers, pamphlets, sermons, diaries, books, letters, case reports, congressional and military reports, and treatises. In addition to the primary sources and collected works, the book is also informed by numerous secondary studies of the nineteenth century. Those secondary references which proved the most valuable are listed below.

BOOKS

Andrews, J. Cutler. *The North Reports the War*. Pittsburgh: University of Pittsburgh Press, 1985.
————. *The South Reports the War*. Princeton: Princeton University Press, 1970.
Bailyn, Bernard. *The Ideological Origins of the American Revolution*. Cambridge: The Belknap Press, 1967.
Berthoff, Rowland. *An Unsettled People: Social Order and Disorder in American History*. New York: Harper & Row, 1971.
Bloomfield, Maxwell. *American Lawyers in a Changing Society, 1776–1876*. Cambridge: Harvard University Press, 1976.
Bolgar, R. R., ed. *Classical Influence on Western Thought, AD 1650–1870*. Cambridge: Cambridge University Press, 1979.
Capers, Gerald M. *John C. Calhoun—Opportunist: A Reappraisal*. Gainesville, Fla.: University of Florida Press, 1960.
Carpenter, William Seal. *The Development of American Political Thought*. New York: Howard Fertig, 1968.
Chaffee, Zechariah, Jr. *Free Speech in the United States*. Cambridge, Mass.: Harvard University Press, 1964.
Colbourn, H. Trevor. *The Lamp of Experience*. Chapel Hill: University of North

Carolina, for the Institute for Early American History and Culture, Williamsburg, Va., 1965.

Cunningham, Noble E. Jr., ed. *Circular Letters of Congressmen to their Constituents 1789–1829.* 3 vols. Chapel Hill: University of North Carolina, for the Institute for Early American History and Culture, Williamsburg, Va., 1978.

Destler, Chester McArthur. *American Radicalism 1865–1901: Essays and Documents.* New York: Octagon Books, 1963.

Dillon, Merton L. *Elijah P. Lovejoy, Abolitionist Editor.* Urbana: University of Illinois Press, 1961.

Donald, David. *Lincoln Reconsidered: Essays on the Civil War Era.* New York: Alfrid A. Knopf, 1956.

Eaton, Clement. *A History of the Southern Confederacy.* New York: The MacMillan Co., 1954.

Foner, Eric. *Free Soil, Free Labor, Free Men: The Ideology of the Republican Party before the Civil War.* New York: Oxford University Press, 1970.

———. *Reconstruction: America's Unfinished Revolution.* New York: Harper & Row, 1988.

Foner, Philip. *The Spanish Cuban American War and the Birth of American Imperialism.* 2 vols., New York: Monthly Review Press, 1972.

Fowler, Dorothy. *Unmailable: Congress and the Post Office.* Athens: University of Georgia Press, 1977.

Freidel, Frank. *Union Pamphlets of the Civil War.* 2 vols. Cambridge: The Belknap Press, 1967.

Graham, Hugh Davis and Ted R. Gurr, eds. *The History of Violence in America: Historical and Comparative Perspectives.* New York: F. A. Praeger, 1969.

Harper, Robert S. *Lincoln and the Press.* New York: McGraw-Hill, 1951.

Hofstadter, Richard. *The Idea of a Party System: The Rise of Legitimate Opposition in the United States, 1780–1840.* Berkeley: University of California Press, 1969.

Horwitz, Morton J. *The Transformation of American Law, 1780–1860.* Cambridge: Harvard University Press, 1977.

Kessler, Lauren. *The Dissident Press: Alternative Journalism in American History.* Beverly Hills: Sage Publications, 1984.

Kling, Robert E. *The Government Printing Office.* New York: Praeger Publishing Co., 1970.

Lawhorne, Clifton O. *Defamation and Public Officials.* Carbondale: Southern Illinois University Press, 1971.

Levy, Leonard. *Emergence of a Free Press.* New York: Oxford University Press, 1985.

———. *Jefferson and Civil Liberties: The Darker Side.* Cambridge: The Belknap Press, 1963.

———. ed. *Freedom of the Press from Zenger to Jefferson: Early American Libertarian Theories.* Indianapolis: Bobbs-Merrill Co., 1960.

———. ed. *Blasphemy in Massachusetts.* New York: Da Capo Press, 1973.

Lofton, John. *The Press as Guardian of the First Amendment.* Columbia: University of South Carolina Press, 1980.

Medford, Martha. *Controversy Over the Use of the Mail for Distribution of Abolitionist Literature.* Thesis. Austin: University of Texas, 1940.

Mott, Frank Luther. *American Journalism*. New York: The Macmillan Co., 1950.
————. *Jefferson and the Press*. Baton Rouge: Louisiana State University Press, 1943.
Nye, Russel B. *Fettered Freedom: Civil Liberties and the Slavery Controversy*. Ann Arbor: Michigan State College Press, 1949.
Outland, Ethel R. *The "Effingham" Libels on Cooper*. Madison: University of Wisconsin Studies in Language/Literature, 1929.
Potter, David M. *The Impending Crises 1848–1861*. New York: Harper & Row, 1976.
Raper, Horace W. *William Holden, North Carolina's Enigma*. Chapel Hill: North Carolina University Press, 1985.
Ratner, Lorman. *Powder Keg: Northern Opposition to the Antislavery Movement, 1831–1840*. New York: Basic Books, Inc., 1968.
Riesman, David, et al. *The Lonely Crows: A Study of the Changing American Character*. New Haven: Yale University Press, 1950.
Richards, Leonard L. *"Gentlemen of Property and Standing: Anti-Abolition Mobs in Jacksonian America*. New York: Oxford University Press, 1970.
Robinson, William M. *Justice in Grey: A History of the Judicial System of the Confederate States of America*. New York: Russell & Russell, 1968.
Rowe, G. S. *Thomas McKean: The Shaping of an American Republicanism*. Boulder: Colorado Associated University Press, 1978.
Savage, W. S. *The Controversy over the Distribution of Abolitionist Literature, 1830–1860*. New York: Negro Universities Press, 1968.
Schlesinger, Arthur M. *Prelude to Independence*. New York: Alfred A. Knopf, 1958.
Sefton, James. *The United States Army and Reconstruction, 1865–1877*. Baton Rouge: Louisiana State University Press, 1967.
Suggs, Henry L., ed. *The Black Press of the South, 1865–1979*. Westport, Conn.: Greenwood Press, 1983.
Wiebe, Robert H. *The Opening of American Society*. New York: Alfred A. Knopf, 1984.
————. *The Segmented Society: An Introduction to the Meaning of America*. New York: Oxford University Press, 1975.
Wiecek, William M. *The Sources of Antislavery Constitutionalism in America, 1760–1848*. Ithaca: Cornell University Press, 1977.

JOURNAL ARTICLES

Baldasty, Gerald. "The Press and Politics in the Age of Jackson." 89 *Journalism Monographs* (August 1984).
Gilje, Paul A. "The Baltimore Riots of 1812 and the Breakdown of the Anglo-American Mob Tradition." 13 *Journal of Social History* 547 (Spring 1980).
Grimsted, David. "Rioting in Its Jacksonian Setting." 77 *American Historical Review* 361 (April 1972).
Hickey, Donald R. "The Darker Side of Democracy: The Baltimore Riots of 1812," 7 *Maryland Historian* 1 (1976).
Kielbowicz, Richard B. "Party Press Cohesiveness: Jacksonian Newspapers, 1832." 60 *Journalism Quarterly* 518 (Autumn 1983).

————. "The Press, Post Office, and Flow of News in the Early Republic." 3 *Journal of the Early Republic* 255 (Fall 1983).

Shallhope, Robert E. "Toward a Republican Synthesis: The Emergence of an Understanding of Republicanism in American Historiography." 29 *William and Mary Quarterly* 49 (3rd Ser. 1970).

Sloan, William David. "The Early Party Press: The Newspaper Role in American Politics, 1788–1812." 9 *Journalism History* 18 (Spring 1982).

Index

About the Author

DONNA LEE DICKERSON is Associate Professor and Chair in the Department of Mass Communications at the University of South Florida. She is the author of *Typestick of Texas History, Florida Media Law*, and co-author of *College Student Press Law*. She has also written several journal articles including "William Cowper Brann: 19th Century Press Critic," "Retraction Statutes and their Constitutional Implications," and "Fashioning a New Libel Defense: The Advent of Neutral Reportage."